D1479162

REVELATION
AND
CONVERGENCE

REVELATION
AND
CONVERGENCE

Flannery O'Connor
and the Catholic Intellectual
Tradition

Edited by Mark Bosco, SJ, and Brent Little

The Catholic University of America Press
Washington, DC

The paper used in this publication meets the minimum requirements of
American National Standards for Information Science—Permanence
of Paper for Printed Library Materials, ANSI Z39.48-1984.
∞

Cataloging-in-Publication Data available from the Library of Congress
ISBN 978-0-8132-2942-3

To Kimberly Rae Connor

CONTENTS

1   Introduction. O'Connor's Prayer Journal and the
    Life of Faith
    Mark Bosco, SJ

10 Chapter 1. Revelation in History: Displaced Persons,
    Léon Bloy, and Exegesis of the Commonplace
    Stephen Schloesser, SJ

51 Chapter 2. Breaking Bodies: O'Connor and the
    Aesthetics of Consecration
    Michael P. Murphy

78 Chapter 3. Mysterious Heart: Maritain, Mauriac,
    Chrétien, and O'Connor on the Fictional Knowledge
    of Others
    Stephen E. Lewis

99 Chapter 4. O'Connor's "Pied Beauty": Gerard Manley
    Hopkins and the Aesthetics of Difference
    Mark Bosco, SJ

118 Chapter 5. "The Baron Is in Milledgeville": Friedrich von Hügel's Influence on O'Connor

Michael Bruner

146 Chapter 6. The "All-Demanding Eyes": St. Augustine and the Restless Seeker

Andrew J. Garavel, SJ

166 Chapter 7. Mrs. May's Dark Night in O'Connor's "Greenleaf"

George Piggford, CSC

191 Chapter 8. O'Connor's Unfinished Novel: The Beginning of a Modern Saint's Life

Jessica Hooten Wilson

215 Bibliography

231 Contributors

235 Index

REVELATION
AND
CONVERGENCE

INTRODUCTION

O'Connor's Prayer Journal and the Life of Faith

Mark Bosco, SJ

Flannery O'Connor's fiction stands as a singular achievement of twentieth-century American literature, yet scholars and enthusiasts of her novels and short stories have been inevitably drawn to her posthumously published critical essays, *Mystery and Manners* (1969), and to her personal letters to friends and colleagues, *The Habit of Being* (1979). Reading these texts one gleans further insight into the extraordinary clarity of vision that inspired and focused O'Connor's talent. In *Mystery and Manners* one ap-

The editors and contributors wish to thank the Joan and Bill Hank Center for the Catholic Intellectual Heritage at Loyola University Chicago for its support in presenting and preparing the essays.

1

preciates the context of O'Connor's southern Catholic experience, allowing the reader to connect the dots between her erudite statements about the craft of fiction with the parable-like works that she created. The connection between her religious life and her creative life is made clear in *The Habit of Being*, letters filled with insight and humor of her struggle to bring a theological intelligence to bear on her understanding of herself as artist and friend. Readers are able to gain a knowledge of—and feeling for—the issues that came to shape her as a person of faith just as much as a person of remarkable talent. In a word, one is drawn to the authenticity of O'Connor's life story as much as to the authenticity of her stories.

One thus finds that O'Connor scholarship today traverses a broad range of disciplines; not only the literary critic but also the historian, the philosopher, and the theologian find in her life and work an extraordinary resource to understand twentieth-century American faith and culture. In 2011, Loyola University Chicago hosted an academic conference that brought together a diverse group of scholars interested specifically in the philosophical and theological influences that shaped O'Connor's imagination. During this conference, participants were privileged to hear the scholar and critic William Sessions read—for the first time—from the recently unearthed partial manuscript of O'Connor's diary, written intermittently between January 1946 and September 1947 while she attended graduate school at the University of Iowa. A personal acquaintance of O'Connor, and a frequent visitor to her home, Andalusia, Sessions found the diary while finishing a biography that he was commissioned to write by the Flannery O'Connor Trust. Published as *A Prayer Journal* in 2013, Sessions provides an introduction and context for this very early piece of writing that illustrates how well versed O'Connor was in the philosophy and theology of her time.

Only twenty-one years of age and away from home for the first time, O'Connor had been admitted to the newly established Iowa

Writer's Workshop. Over the course of the two years of the diary, O'Connor took classes with some of the most renowned authors and critics of her day: creative writing classes with the likes of Paul Engle, Robert Penn Warren, the poets Robert Lowell and Alan Tate, and courses on literary criticism, including one taught by Austin Warren, one of the founders of "New Criticism." Warren would have a great influence on O'Connor's own understanding of the craft and interpretation of fiction. In her diary, she recounts being introduced to the French Catholic literary revival of the early part of the twentieth century, especially the writer Léon Bloy, whose work had been newly translated into English while O'Connor was matriculating in Iowa.

An ordinary composition book contains her handwritten diary of prayers, twenty-seven pages in length. Sessions notes that many pages have been torn out. Although the intellectual air of her studies can be felt in the diary, O'Connor is rather more concerned with an intimate spiritual colloquy of prayers to God in her struggle to come to terms with her vocation as a writer. Readers glimpse not only the way the rituals and doctrines of Catholicism inform her prayer life but also the way that the Catholic literary heritage of the saints and spiritual writers shape and model her thoughts and prayers. In her desire to be honest and transparent before God, the reader senses the reverberations of Augustine in his *Confessions*, Ignatius of Loyola's colloquies in the *Spiritual Exercises*, Francis de Sales's *The Devout Life*, and Pascal's *Pensées*. That O'Connor is already theologically informed at this early moment of her career is evident. Always a realist, even in her dealings with the divine, this spiritual diary is a profound testament to the writer's intellectual life of faith. These prayers make clear that O'Connor understood her art to be a gift from God and that it was her greatest desire to make her art worthy of the Christian principles that had formed her.

Both readers and scholars alike have long recognized the influence of O'Connor's Catholic heritage upon her fiction. O'Connor notes it in her correspondence with Betty Hester ("A" in *The Habit of Being*): "I am a Catholic peculiarly possessed of the modern consciousness, that thing that Jung describes as unhistorical, solitary, and guilty."[1] Throughout her letters to Hester and to many others, the reader is taken on an articulate journey though Catholic thought and practice as O'Connor attempts to justify her Christian vision of reality. The correspondence, published fifteen years after O'Connor's death, opened a new door for O'Connor scholarship, as her letters showed such deep theological reading and reflection, whether about her own faith commitments to Catholicism or in discussing her often Protestant, Christ-haunted characters. John Desmond's *Risen Sons: Flannery O'Connor's Vision of History* (1987) was the first to offer a sustained reflection on the specifically Catholic metaphysical foundations of her art. Richard Gionnone's *Flannery O'Connor: Hermit Novelist* (2000) explored her fascination with the fourth-century desert fathers and their confrontation with worldly evil as archetypal models for her characters. Fr. George Kilcourse's *Flannery O'Connor's Religious Imagination* (2001) cites O'Connor's implicit dialogue with the works of twentieth-century Catholic intellectuals, Romano Guardini and William F. Lynch, in the development of her "Christic" or "analogical" imagination. And Susan Srigley's *Flannery O'Connor's Sacramental Art* (2004) and Christina Bieber Lake's *The Incarnational Art of Flannery O'Connor* (2005) build on the importance of the sacramental system of Catholic faith in understanding both aesthetic and ethical strategies in her work. All of these studies offer in broad strokes an artist fully engaged with her faith and the rich intellectual and artistic heritage of that faith tradition.

Yet reflecting on the writers O'Connor references and interprets in her early prayer journal, one quickly realizes that no single volume could trace some of the pivotal influences on O'Connor's religious imagination. The particular thinkers on whom O'Connor

---

1. Flannery O'Connor, *The Habit of Being: Letters of Flannery O'Connor*, ed. Sally Fitzgerald (New York: Farrar, Straus and Giroux, 1979), 90.

drew directly, or figures whose works help illuminate her artistic vision for readers today, emerge from her diary jottings and provide a place from which readers can better understand the writer, her context, and her ongoing popularity with both Catholic and non-Catholic readers. The essays in this collection focus on many of the names that O'Connor writes about in her prayer journal or in her many letters to friends and admirers—Léon Bloy, George Bernanos, Jacque Maritain, Gerard Manley Hopkins, and Friedrich von Hügel—while the final essays reveal O'Connor's intimacy with the saints as models and properties for her characters. Many of the Catholic thinkers central to O'Connor's creative development, such as Bloy or von Hügel, remain relatively obscure to contemporary readers. Other figures, such as Augustine of Hippo or St. John of the Cross, are certainly well known, but their connection to O'Connor's stories has received little attention. This volume, written by an array of scholars in theology, history, and literary studies, provides a much-needed hermeneutical lens that is often missing from contemporary criticism. With a recognition of O'Connor's multivalent and multidirectional absorption of her Catholic heritage, the reader deepens their appreciation of the rich Catholic textures embedded in O'Connor's life and work.

Our exploration into O'Connor's Catholic heritage begins with Stephen Schloesser's scholarly tour de force, "Revelation in History: Displaced Persons, Léon Bloy and the Exegesis of the Commonplace." O'Connor's reflections on Bloy's *Pilgrim of the Absolute*, the first translation of his work in English, abound in O'Connor's prayer diary. Bloy's fiery denunciations of bourgeois mediocrity and the deceptions of modern life touched a chord in O'Connor's own understanding of her vocation as an artist. Schloesser extends this scholarship by arguing that the impact of the French Catholic Left had a lasting impact on her imagination. Schloesser's argument stands as a corrective to the rather narrow assignation of religious conservatism that is often found in O'Connor studies. Furthermore, Schloesser recognizes how Bloy's "literary style, indelibly marked by rhetorical violence and vitriolic humor," resembles O'Connor's language and that his "privileging of suffering as redemption" responded to her own worldview. But it is Bloy's symbolist vision of history—the conviction that visible time and space are replete with symbols signifying an unseen cosmic drama—that provides a grounding for O'Connor's deeply historical sense that Schloesser explores in this essay.

In "Breaking Bodies: O'Connor and the Aesthetics of Consecration," Michael P. Murphy uses Bernanos to deconstruct theological dualisms in an attempt to reconstruct the unity of a sacramental and, thus, incarnational imagination. The spiritual principles that ground this unity paradoxically find expression in the painful journeys in broken bodies. A constant theme of the twentieth-century French Catholic Revival is the drama of theological kenosis as central to understanding human life. This conscious desire to empty oneself as a manifestation of love becomes a touchstone for O'Connor's Catholic literary modernism. Murphy argues that O'Connor is at once orthodox and experimental as she engages in the Manichaeism of twentieth-century life, seeing the broken bread of Eucharistic theology as a site for a convergence of the physical and the spiritual. "So what do we make of Flannery O'Connor among the French? It is Bouyer and Teilhard to be sure," Murphy asserts, "And it is Bernanos and St. Therese."

Questions about aesthetics and craftsmanship and about beauty and truth are also recorded in O'Connor's diary, as she was reading Jacques Maritain's neo-Thomistic theory of art, *Art and Scholasticism*, which was probably introduced to her during Allen Tate's spring 1947 seminar at the Iowa Writers Workshop. Tate and his wife, Caroline Gordon, converted to Catholicism under Maritain's personal influence in 1950. Stephen E. Lewis deepens this engagement in "Mysterious Heart: Maritain, Mauriac, Chrétien, and O'Connor on the Fictional Knowledge of Others." In his study, Lewis shows how O'Connor's fiction displays a critical engagement with the question of the fate of the "secrets of the heart" in modern fiction, as it was set out in a debate between Maritain and Mauriac, and as Chrétien subsequently extends the conversation to show how French theory can offer a fresh reading of O'Connor's work.

Crossing the channel to Great Britain, one discerns the broader expanse of O'Connor's theological and philosophical influences, including, as Mark Bosco demonstrates, other creative writers wrestling to make their art and their piety companions in their searches for meaning and beauty. O'Connor's letters collected in *The Habit of Being* document her absorption and judgment on much of the British Catholic Revival that was at its height while she was writing in her diary in Iowa. Bosco's "O'Connor's 'Pied Beauty': Gerard Manley Hopkins and the Aesthetics of Difference" picks up on the ongoing theme of dualisms that generated so much dialectical power for O'Connor's visionary creations and identifies Hopkins's poetry as offering a "philosophical and artistic platform" for the development of O'Connor's aesthetics of contrast and difference. By highlighting the role Hopkins played in the Catholic literary revival of the late nineteenth and early twentieth centuries, Bosco reveals important connections between two of the revival's greatest writers establishing "inscape" as a shared site of being that connects them to each other and to the Spirit they both sought to honor.

We can read Michael Bruner's essay, "'The Baron Is in Milledgeville': Friedrich von Hügel's Influence on O'Connor," as an extension of Hopkins's spiritual awareness turned mystical insight about physical nature. Bruner addresses the neglected importance of Friedrich von Hügel's bearing on O'Connor and makes claims that focus on two apparently contradictory truths: that Baron von Hügel—John Henry Newman's peer and author of some of the seminal books of the Catholic Intellectual Renaissance of the twentieth century—is ignored by most of O'Connor scholarship and that he was a major influence on O'Connor and her writing. Limiting his study to O'Connor's nonfiction (her reviews, essays, and letters) and drawing only general lines of influence from von Hügel, Bruner's careful research and intuitive critical lens demonstrate convincingly that O'Connor had compelling encounters with, and then fully adopts from, Baron von Hügel's writings. The central paradox of the incarnation, "long celebrated by the Church in the centrality of the cross," shapes both von Hügel's and O'Connor's understanding of art.

But O'Connor's absorption of her Catholic heritage extends beyond the nineteenth and early twentieth centuries, as can be observed in the pious urgency encountered in her prayer diary. Her devotional life included a broad range of influences and ideas that shaped the author's literary and religious principles. The writers gathered here illustrate the way that the Catholic literary heritage of the saints and spiritual writers shape and model her thoughts and prayers and eventually her fiction. Andrew J. Garavel explores the familiar trope of conversion in "The 'All-Demanding Eyes': St. Augustine and the Restless Seeker," but adds new insights when he reads O'Connor's fiction alongside Augustine's *Confessions*. Garavel identifies the theory of illumination set forth in Augustine's work as a guide for interpreting a character's conversion and validating O'Connor's commitment to a deeply sacramental imagination. O'Connor's story "Parker's Back" serves as the primary analogy for Garavel's study. He explains: "As a story of conversion, 'Parker's Back' has strong affiliations with Augustine's work, and while an appreciation of how *The Confessions* informs O'Connor's text does not entirely explain the story, it does, I believe, offer the reader a useful avenue to approach the mystery she sets out."

"Greenleaf" serves as the interpretative topic for George Piggford's essay, "Mrs. May's Dark Night in O'Connor's 'Greenleaf.'" Continuing the study of O'Connor among saints, Piggford makes a strong case for crediting a number of devout influences on this story—and by extension other works—including O'Connor's burgeoning friendship with Betty Hester, Evelyn Underhill's 1910 classic,

Mysticism, and St. John of the Cross. Piggford lauds O'Connor for making room for the possibility of redemption among her characters, despite her overriding conviction that Western culture was shrinking into a pervasive and terrifying dark night. As her mystic mentors showed her, the prospect of spiritual union with God remains, no matter how dark the world's night or how irredeemable the character.

"O'Connor's Unfinished Novel: The Beginning of a Modern Saint's Life" illustrates Jessica Hooten Wilson's extensive work in the O'Connor archives. The author reveals that in the more than three hundred pages of writing that compose the novel fragment "Why Do the Heathen Rage?," O'Connor is attempting to expand upon issues of social justice and race, yet she does this "by returning to pre-Reformation models." Rather than engage twentieth-century concerns and problems of her day unmoored from Christian tradition and spirituality, Hooten Wilson argues that O'Connor models the main character of the story on St. Jerome, as her way to remain faithful to a worldview that subordinates all earthly spheres of action to divine ends. Hooten Wilson expands our understanding of the unfinished novel by demonstrating that O'Connor sought to address a more theologically rich problem drawn from her reading of saints' lives: how does our contemplative life relate to our active life?

These essays, taken together, represent O'Connor's ongoing conversation with the Catholic theological and literary heritage. O'Connor's stories are redemptive acts because they depend on relationship: they send us, the readers, back to O'Connor's stories and beyond them to both the great chain of narrators and to each other, where we satisfy that "something in us, as storytellers and as listeners to stories, that demands the redemptive act, that demands that what falls at least be offered the chance to be restored."[2]

---

2. Flannery O'Connor, *Mystery and Manners: Occasional Prose*, ed. Sally and Robert Fitzgerald (New York: Farrar, Straus and Giroux, 1969), 48.

CHAPTER 1

 Revelation in History

*Displaced Persons, Léon Bloy, and Exegesis
of the Commonplace*

Stephen Schloesser, SJ

Anti-Semitism, a wholly modern thing, is the most horrible blow yet suffered by Our Lord in His ever continuous Passion, it is the bloodiest and
the most unforgivable because He receives it *upon His Mother's Face* and
at the hand of Christians.... The very abjectness of that Race is a divine
Sign, the very manifest sign of the constant lingering of the Holy Spirit
over these men so scorned by the world who are to appear in the Glory of
the Consoler at the end of ends.

—Léon Bloy, in *Pilgrim of the Absolute*,
ed. Raïssa Maritain (1947)

"Dear lady, I know your tender heart won't suffer you to turn the porrrrr man out. Think of the thousands of them, think of the ovens and the box-cars and the camps and the sick children and Christ our Lord."

"I'm a logical practical woman and there are no ovens here and no camps and no Christ Our Lord."

—Flannery O'Connor, "The Displaced
Person" (1955)

If other ages felt less, they saw more, even though they saw with the blind, prophetical, unsentimental eye of acceptance, which is to say, of faith. In the absence of this faith now, we govern by tenderness.... When tenderness is detached from the source of tenderness, its logical outcome is terror. It ends in forced labor camps and in the fumes of the gas chamber.

—Flannery O'Connor, "Introduction to
A Memoir of Mary Ann" (1961)[1]

Although it has been twenty-five years since Linda Schlafer investigated the seminal importance of Flannery O'Connor's encounter with the work of Léon Bloy (1846–1917), scholars have been slow to follow her lead.[2] Yet Bloy's literary style, indelibly marked by rhetorical violence and vitriolic humor, sounds much like character-

1. Léon Bloy, "The Mystery of Israel," in *Pilgrim of the Absolute*, ed. Raïssa Maritain, trans. John Coleman and Harry Lorin Binsse (New York: Pantheon, 1947), 245–273, at 268, 269; Flannery O'Connor, "The Displaced Person," in *The Complete Stories* (New York: Farrar, Straus and Giroux, 1971), 194–235, at 231; O'Connor, introduction to *A Memoir of Mary Ann*, in *Mystery and Manners: Occasional Prose*, coll. and ed. by Sally Fitzgerald and Robert Fitzgerald (New York: Farrar, Straus and Giroux, 1969), 213–228, at 227. For Bloy and R. Maritain location in O'Connor's library, see Arthur F. Kinney, *Flannery O'Connor's Library: Resources of Being* (Athens: The University of Georgia Press, 1985), #69. Hereafter, OCLIB.

2. Linda Schlafer, "The Habit of Becoming: Some French Influences on the Aesthetic of Flannery O'Connor" (PhD diss., Northern Illinois University, 1983), *Dissertation Abstracts International (DAI)* 45 (1984): 185A; cf. Schlafer, "Pilgrims of the Absolute: Léon Bloy and Flannery O'Connor," in *Realist of Distances: Flannery O'Connor Revisited*, ed. Karl-Heinz Westarp and Jan Nordby Gretlund (Aarhus [Denmark]: Aarhus University Press, 1987), 55–63. In R. Neil Scott's 2002 annotated reference guide to O'Connor criticism, only four entries (one of which is nonscholarly) are given for the subject "Bloy" under "Influence–Of other writers and artists on Flannery O'Connor." See Scott, *Flannery O'Connor: An Annotated Reference Guide to Criticism* (Milledgeville, Ga.: Timberlane Books, 2002), 1002, cf. 417.

izations of O'Connor's own "language of apocalypse" and "imagination of extremity."[3] Moreover, Bloy's privileging of "suffering"
as redemption apparently responded to O'Connor's felt need for
what Ralph Wood has called a "darker reading of human misery,
a more startling revelation of transcendent hope."[4] Perhaps most
important, Bloy's symbolist vision of history—the conviction that
visible time and space are replete with symbols signifying an
unseen cosmic drama (what Hans Urs von Balthasar might call
a *Theodramatik* or "Theo-Drama")—would seem to be the most
likely source for what John Desmond has identified as O'Connor's
own deeply historical sense.[5] For Bloy, the "exegetical" task of the
symbolist historian is to interpret appearances through the lens
of faith; only then are events of both world-historical significance
and the "commonplace" (*des lieux communs*) unveiled as "luminous and full of windows upon Mystery."[6] Annette Moran concludes that "O'Connor learned from Bloy to read the universe as if
it were a vast store of symbols."[7]

3. Frederick Asals, *Flannery O'Connor: The Imagination of Extremity* (Athens:
University of Georgia Press, 1982); and Edward Kessler, *Flannery O'Connor and the
Language of Apocalypse* (Princeton, N.J.: Princeton University Press, 1986).

4. Ralph C. Wood, "The Heterodoxy of Flannery O'Connor's Book Reviews,"
Flannery O'Connor Bulletin 5 (1976): 3–21, at 4; cf. Farrell O'Gorman, *Peculiar Cross-
roads: Flannery O'Connor, Walker Percy, and Catholic Vision in Postwar Southern Fiction*
(Baton Rouge: Louisiana State University Press, [2004] 2008), 77.

5. John F. Desmond, *Risen Sons: Flannery O'Connor's Vision of History* (Athens:
University of Georgia Press, 1987); Desmond, "Flannery O'Connor, Walker Percy,
and the Holocaust," in *At the Crossroads: Ethical and Religious Themes in the Writings of
Walker Percy* (Troy, N.Y.: Whitson Publishing Company, 1997), 94–101; cf. Ralph C.
Wood, "The Burden of Southern History and the Presence of Eternity within Time,"
in *Flannery O'Connor and the Christ-Haunted South* (Grand Rapids, Mich.: William B.
Eerdmans, 2004), 51–92. Hans Urs von Balthasar, *Theo-Drama: Theological Dramatic
Theory [Theodramatik]*, trans. Graham Harrison, 5 vols. (San Francisco: Ignatius
Press, 1988–1998).

6. Albert Béguin, *Léon Bloy: A Study in Impatience*, trans. Edith M. Riley (New
York: Sheed and Ward, 1947), 101; OCLIB #59; referencing Léon Bloy, *Exégèse des
lieux communs [Exegesis of Commonplaces]*, (Paris: Mercure de France, 1902); and
second series (Paris: Mercure de France, 1913).

7. Annette Moran, "The Church and the Fiction Writer: The Fiction of Flannery O'Connor and the Corpus Christi Mysticum Ecclesiology" (PhD diss., Graduate Theological Union, 1994), 121; cf. 123.

In addition to intertextual evidence, scholars have relied on small bits of information to substantiate Bloy's influence on O'Connor. She cites her reading of French Catholic Revivalist authors in four letters written between 1955 and 1957 and in 1963, and her preserved library contains two crucial works related to Bloy published in 1947.[8] However, William Sessions's recent discovery of O'Connor's spiritual journal from 1946 to 1947 pinpoints precisely the time at which she first discovered Bloy's work: May 1947.[9] This reading made a profound emotional impact on her as a beginning writer. She felt attracted to—and personally indicted by—Bloy's assault on religious "mediocrity," and she expressed her desire to embrace redemptive suffering in an extreme way.

But why Bloy's resurgence exactly three decades after his death? And why his sudden appearance in English translation in 1947? And why Iowa? Each successive examination of the multiple layers of these contingent historical circumstances reveals remarkable convergences. In the following pages, I disentangle the strands in an effort to make clearer their eventual coalescence:

First, I look closely at the chronology of French Catholic revivalist works published in English translation, revealing the exceptional character of 1947. Second, I examine Bloy in his historical context as a polemical writer in late-nineteenth- and early-twentieth-century France, especially in his symbolist role as a historical exegete of "The Jewish Question" and the Dreyfus Affair.

---

8. Flannery O'Connor to "A," August 28, 1955; O'Connor to Father John Mc-Cown, January 16, 1956; O'Connor to "A," April 20, 1957; O'Connor to Pierre Brodin, September 21, 1963; in O'Connor, *The Habit of Being: Letters of Flannery O'Connor*, ed. Sally Fitzgerald (New York: Farrar, Straus and Giroux, 1979), 97–99, 130, 216–217; and Pierre Brodin, *Présences contemporaines: écrivains américains d'aujourd'hui* (Paris: Nouvelles éditions Debresse, 1964), 206–207. For the French *renouveau catholique* (Catholic Revival), see Stephen Schloesser, *Jazz Age Catholicism: Mystic Modernism in Postwar Paris, 1919–1933* (Toronto: University of Toronto Press, 2005).

9. Flannery O'Connor, *A Prayer Journal*, ed. William A. Sessions (New York: Farrar, Straus and Giroux, 2013).

Third, an overview of Jacques and Raïssa Maritain—with respect to having had Bloy as their godfather in their Roman Catholic conversions; to their 1930s' efforts on "The Jewish Question"; and, in the 1940s, to the subsequent Holocaust—shows how Bloy's legacy was carried into circumstances whose horrors the 1890s could not have imagined.[10] Fourth, the postwar reemergence of Bloy during his birth centenary (1846–1946), his earlier symbolist-historical interpretation of "the Jews" now refashioned in light of the Holocaust, is seen as coinciding with O'Connor's first year in Iowa as a graduate student. This revisionist version of Bloy, now a foundation of postwar "left-wing Catholicism," is the one with which O'Connor collided.

Finally, O'Connor's encounter with Bloy's symbolist history overlapped with American debates between 1945 and 1952 over the postwar plight of the "Displaced Person," a distinctly mid-twentieth-century reiteration of the nineteenth century's "Wandering Jew."[11] Seen as an attempt at Bloy's symbolist method, O'Connor's "The Displaced Person" (1955) can be read as an "exegesis of the commonplace" within history's cosmic tragic sweep. In 1947, O'Connor had read a summary of the method: "[Bloy's] l'Exégèse des lieux communs ([Exegesis of Commonplaces] first series published in 1902, second series in 1913) is only superficially a humorous book; beneath the banalities of everyday life and the precepts of a bourgeois wisdom whose absurdity he lays bare, Bloy seeks to bring to the surface the secret knowledge and true mystery which, for his eyes, are to be found in *the language farthest removed from faith*."[12] This approach bridges two worlds, theologi-

10. In references following, "Maritain" refers to Jacques and "R. Maritain" to Raïssa.

11. Eugène Sue, *Le juif errant*, 10 vols. (Brussels: Meline, Cans et cie, 1844–1845). Sue's polemical work, both anti-Jesuit and anti-Catholic, became an instant international sensation and was immediately translated into several European languages including Danish, Dutch, English, German, Polish, and Spanish.

12. Béguin, *Study in Impatience*, 22; emphasis added; cf. "I Should Like to Show the Hidden Things of Language," in Bloy and R. Maritain, *Pilgrim of the Absolute*, 124–125.

cal and sociopolitical, often divorced in O'Connor criticism. Jon
Lance Bacon notes that "[t]he theological approach has deepened
our understanding of O'Connor, but it has also excluded her from
most analyses of American fiction that turn on social and political issues."[13] Just as the 1890s' Dreyfus Affair embodied the inseparability of the theological and sociopolitical for the symbolist Bloy, so, too, did the plight of "Displaced Persons" in the 1940s
and 1950s for O'Connor.

The Exceptionalism of 1947: Franco-American Catholic Literary Revivalism

Flannery O'Connor studied for her MFA at Iowa between the fall
of 1945 and the spring of 1947. Ten years later, she recounted that
period in a letter to "A": "When I went to Iowa ... I began to read
everything at once.... I read all the Catholic novelists, Mauriac,
Bernanos, Bloy, Greene, Waugh."[14] O'Connor was mistaken: for
the most part, the French writers had not yet been translated into
English. It is not a large fault: this informal recollection, jotted
down quickly from memory a decade after the fact, was hardly
intended for scholarly endnotes. Yet uncovering the exact chronology of those years reveals just how exceptional was the 1947
appearance of Léon Bloy—even in fragments—in English.

When Flannery O'Connor arrived at graduate school in Iowa
in the fall of 1945, what could she possibly have read of these
Catholic revivalists? The short answer is: not much. The transatlantic migration of translated works from France's "Jazz Age
Catholicism" seems to have begun in 1930 with the publication of Jacques Maritain's popular philosophical work, *Art and
Scholasticism.*[15] Although a decade later O'Connor would say that

13. Jon Lance Bacon, *Flannery O'Connor and Cold War Culture* (New York: Cambridge University Press, 1993), 5.
14. Flannery O'Connor to "A," August 28, 1955, *Habit of Being,* 97–99, at 98.
15. Jacques Maritain, *Art and Scholasticism: With Other Essays,* trans. J. F. Scan-

she had "cut [her] aesthetic teeth" on this work, she most likely had not been introduced to it until the Iowa visit of Allen Tate (a friend of Maritain) in April 1947 (recounted below).[16] In 1931, E. F. Carritt's *Philosophies of Beauty* appeared. A well-marked volume found in O'Connor's library, seemingly dating from at least her graduate school years, suggests that it was used as a textbook in Iowa. Underlining shows that she was introduced there to the writings of Henri Bergson (who had just died in 1941), a figure whose importance to French Catholic Revivalism cannot be overestimated.[17]

During the nine years between 1936 and 1945—that is, from the midst of the Great Depression until the end of the Second World War—five more books related to French Catholic revivalism were published: Karl Pfleger's *Wrestlers with Christ* (1936), Georges Bernanos's *Diary of a Country Priest* (1937), Léon Bloy's *The Woman Who Was Poor* (1939), Bernanos's *Star of Satan* (1940), and Wallace Fowlie's *The Spirit of France* (1944).[18] Pfleger's *Wrestlers with Christ*,

lan (New York: Charles Scribner's Sons, 1930), OCLIB #272, signed without date. For Maritain's book, see Schloesser, *Jazz Age Catholicism*, 151–162.

16. "I have sent you *Art and Scholasticism*. It's the book I cut my aesthetic teeth on, though I think even some of the things he [Maritain] says get soft at times." Flannery O'Connor to "A," April 20, 1957, *Habit of Being*, 216–217, at 216.

17. In Carritt's anthology, O'Connor read an excerpt from Henri Bergson's *Laughter* (1900): "The comic does not exist outside the pale of what is strictly human." Bergson's pragmatic theory of art as "a more direct vision of reality" accords with the fundamental action in O'Connor's stories: an event catalyzes a break with a character's habitual perception and constitutes a revelation. In her personal copy, O'Connor underlined Bergson's conclusion that "realism is in the work when idealism is in the soul, and that it is only through ideality that we can resume contact with reality ..." See Bergson excerpt in E. F. Carritt, *Philosophies of Beauty: From Socrates to Robert Bridges, Being the Sources of Aesthetic Theory* (New York: Oxford University Press, 1931), 204–209, at 207; emphasis original; in OCLIB #271. For possible influences of Bergson on O'Connor, see Sarah Gordon, "Seeking Beauty in Darkness: Flannery O'Connor and the French Catholic Renaissance," in *Flannery O'Connor's Radical Reality*, ed. Jan Nordby Gretlund and Karl-Heinz Westarp (Columbia: University of South Carolina Press, 2006), 68–84. For Bergson, see Schloesser, *Jazz Age Catholicism*, 61–64.

18. Karl Pfleger, *Wrestlers with Christ*, trans. E. I. Watkin (London: Sheed and Ward, 1936); Georges Bernanos, *The Diary of a Country Priest*, trans. Pamela Morris (New York: The Macmillan Company, 1937); Léon Bloy, *The Woman Who Was Poor, A*

translated from the German, was "the first book in English containing an account of Léon Bloy" along with a chapter on Charles
Péguy.[19] However, O'Connor's *Prayer Journal* indicates that she did
not discover Pfleger until September 1947.[20]

As will be shown, O'Connor read Bernanos's enormously popular *Diary of a Country Priest* in late 1946.[21] She might also have read
his *Star of Satan* (1940). Finally, O'Connor seems never to have
read Bloy's novel *The Woman Who Was Poor* (and no copy is found
in her library). Finally, after the war's conclusion, three translated
volumes appeared in 1946: Mauriac's *Woman of the Pharisees*, Bernanos's *Joy*, and Bergson's *Creative Mind*.[22] That O'Connor might
have read these during her 1945–1947 Iowa sojourn is conceivable.

This chronology underscores the importance of the spring of
1947, in which two books related to Bloy were published in English: Albert Béguin's *Léon Bloy: A Study in Impatience* and Raïssa
Maritain's collation of Bloy's writings titled *Pilgrim of the Absolute*.
O'Connor's library has copies of both these books: the Béguin
volume contains marginal notes, and Maritain's collation is dated "1947" on the front page. (Her library also contains a copy of
Mauriac's *Thérèse* published in translation that year.) Because few
books in O'Connor's library date from this period—understand-

---

Contemporary Novel of the French 'Eighties, trans. I. J. Collins (New York: Sheed and
Ward, 1939); Bernanos, The Star of Satan, trans. Pamela Morris (New York: Mac-
millan Co., 1940); and Wallace Fowlie, The Spirit of France. Studies in Modern French
Literature (London: Sheed and Ward, [1944] 1945), OCLIB #426.

19. Rayner Heppenstall, Léon Bloy (New Haven, Conn.: Yale University Press,
1954), 21; referencing Pfleger, Wrestlers with Christ (1936).

20. See entry of September 22, 1947: "Maybe the Lord had pity on me and sent
me wandering down the stacks to pick up Pfleger on Bloy & Péguy and some others." O'Connor, Prayer Journal, 35, facsimile 84–85, at 85.

21. Two later editions of Bernanos' Diary remain in O'Connor's library: 1957
(OCLIB #491, "Copy 2") and 1960 (OCLIB #490).

22. François Mauriac, Woman of the Pharisees (La pharisienne), trans. Gerard
Hopkins (New York: Henry Holt, 1946); Georges Bernanos, Joy, trans. Louise
Varèse (New York: Pantheon, 1946), OCLIB #492, signed; Henri Bergson, The Creative Mind: An Introduction to Metaphysics, trans. Mabelle L. Andison, Wisdom Library (New York: Philosophical Library, 1946); see OCLIB #9.

ably so, as she was a graduate student with limited finances—the presence of the two 1947 Bloy volumes is even more striking.[23]

Significantly, these volumes appeared during the spring semester in which O'Connor began working on *Wise Blood* in earnest (following its start during the preceding 1946 Thanksgiving break). O'Connor wrote drafts of four chapters, which received the Rinehart-Iowa Fiction Award in May 1947. After being granted her MFA from Iowa on June 1, she returned to Georgia and continued working on the novel. Hazel Motes, its country preacher protagonist, embodies the "Pilgrim of the Absolute." Mrs. Flood judges Motes's single-minded quest as being "like one of them gory stories, it's something that people have quit doing—like boiling in oil or being a saint or walling up cats." But Flood serves as a foil for Bloy: "*There is but one sadness . . . and that is for us* not to be SAINTS."[24]

The importance of 1947 is even more pronounced when compared to the four years following O'Connor's graduation. During the 1948–1951 period, only two French Catholic volumes seem to have appeared in translation: Mauriac's *Unknown Sea* (1948) and a reissue of Bernanos's *Diary of a Country Priest* (1937/1948).[25] In retrospect, the flood of French Catholic revivalist literature to the United States during the 1950s was a phenomenon of both the cold-war religious revival in America and the transatlantic alliances.[26] In 1952—the year in which O'Connor's *Wise Blood* was

23. Béguin, *Study in Impatience* (1947); Bloy and R. Maritain, *Pilgrim of the Absolute* (1947); François Mauriac, *Thérèse: A Portrait in Four Parts*, trans. Gerard Hopkins, foreword by Mauriac (New York: Henry Holt, 1947), OCLIB #574.

24. Flannery O'Connor, *Collected Works*, ed. Sally Fitzgerald (New York: Library of America, 1988), 127; Bloy, *La Femme pauvre* [*The Woman Who Was Poor*], excerpted in *Pilgrim of the Absolute*, ed. R. Maritain, 299–301, at 301; emphasis original.

25. François Mauriac, *The Unknown Sea*, trans. Gerard Hopkins (New York: Henry Holt, 1948), OCLIB #575; and Georges Bernanos, *The Diary of a Country Priest* (New York: Macmillan Co., [1937] 1948).

26. See "1946–1949: Turangalîla and Tanglewood: Cold War Holidays," in Stephen Schloesser, *Visions of Amen: The Early Life and Music of Olivier Messiaen* (Grand Rapids, Mich.: William B. Eerdmans Publishing Company, 2014), 477–482; and

published—François Mauriac won the Nobel Prize for literature, catalyzing further translations of his work.[27] Additionally, 1952 was also the year in which Jacques Maritain gave the first W. W. Mellon Lecture in the Fine Arts, published as *Creative Intuition*.[28] Emmanuel Mounier's definitive philosophical work, *Personalism*, appeared that same year. O'Connor's marginal notes in this book serve as a poignant commentary on her having been informed that summer that she had lupus. Next to Mounier's observation that "[l]ife is a struggle ... [to] overcome the fear of bodily evil," O'Connor wrote, "the violent bear it away."[29] Finally, 1952 was the year in which O'Connor seems to have discovered Max Picard and, either contemporaneously or as a result, Gabriel Marcel, the Catholic "existentialist" who wrote prefatory remarks for two of Picard's books.[30] In 1953, O'Connor acquired the two volumes of

---

Schloesser, "1939–1958: Perpetual *Peregrinus: Toute vue des choses qui n'est pas étrange est fausse*," in *Mystic Masque: Reality and Semblance in Georges Rouault, 1871–1958*, ed. Schloesser (Chestnut Hill, Mass.: McMullen Museum of Art; distributed by the University of Chicago Press, 2008), 341–356. Cf. Robert S. Ellwood, *The Fifties Spiritual Marketplace: American Religion in a Decade of Conflict* (New Brunswick, N.J.: Rutgers University Press, 1997); and Christopher Endy, *Cold War Holidays: American Tourism in France* (Chapel Hill: University of North Carolina Press, 2004).

27. François Mauriac, *The Loved and the Unloved*, trans. Gerard Hopkins, postscript by Mauriac (New York: Pellegrini and Cudahy, 1952), OCLIB #572; and *The Weakling [Le Sagouin] and The Enemy [Le Mal]*, trans. Gerard Hopkins (New York: Pellegrini and Cudahy, 1952), OCLIB #577.

28. Anthony Hecht, "Jacques Maritain 1882–1973: *Creative Intuition in Art and Poetry* 1952," in *The A.W. Mellon Lectures in the Fine Arts: Fifty Years*, ed. Judy Metro and Carol Eron (Washington, DC: National Gallery of Art, Center for Advanced Study in the Visual Arts, 2002), 29–30; Bernard Doering, "*Lacrymae rerum*: Creative Intuition of the Transapparent Reality," in Schloesser, *Mystic Masque*, 389–398; and Schloesser, "'Not behind but within': *sacramentum et res*," *Renascence* 58, no. 1 (Fall 2005): 17–39, esp. 23–24.

29. Emmanuel Mounier, *Personalism*, trans. Philip Mairet (New York: Grove Press, 1952), 49; for marginalia, see OCLIB #23.

30. Max Picard, *Hitler in Our Selves*, trans. Heinrich Hauser, introduction by Robert S. Hartman (Hinsdale, Ill.: Henry Regnery, 1947), OCLIB #253; *The Flight from God*, trans. Marianne Kuschnitzky and J. M. Cameron, note Gabriel Marcel, introduction by J. M. Cameron (Chicago: Henry Regnery, 1951), OCLIB #64, signed and dated 1952; and *The World of Silence*, trans. Stanley Godman, preface by Gabriel Marcel (Chicago: Henry Regnery, 1952), OCLIB #19, signed and dated 1952.

The Mystery of Being, Marcel's 1949–1950 Gifford Lectures.[31] Bergson's magisterial *Two Sources of Morality and Religion* appeared in translation the following year.[32]

The year 1955—during which O'Connor wrote "A" recalling having read Bernanos, Bloy, Greene, Mauriac, and Waugh in graduate school—serves as a useful cutoff point for a chronological survey. By this date, the French Catholic revivalist influence in America was in full swing.[33] The edition of Maritain's *Creative Intuition* found in O'Connor's library dates from this year.[34] Three publications by Mauriac, two novels and a volume of essays, appeared alongside the *Last Essays of Georges Bernanos*.[35] The Easter Sunday death (in April 1955) of the Jesuit paleontologist Pierre Teilhard de Chardin released his works from ecclesiastical censorship. Their publication, first in French, then in English, followed immediately, having an enormous impact not only on O'Connor (beginning in December 1959) but also on what was about to become the Second Vatican Council (1962–1965).[36] To be

31. Gabriel Marcel, *The Mystery of Being*, trans. G.S. Fraser, vol. 1, *Reflection and Mystery* (Chicago: Henry Regnery, [1950–1951]), OCLIB #6, signed and dated 1953; and *The Mystery of Being*, trans. René Hague, vol. 2, *Faith and Reality* (Chicago: Henry Regnery, [1950–1951]), OCLIB #7, signed and dated "June 1953."

32. Henri Bergson, *The Two Sources of Morality and Religion*, trans. R. Ashley Audra and Cloudesley Brereton with the assistance of W. Horsfall Carter (Garden City, N.Y.: Doubleday, Anchor A28, 1954), OCLIB #167.

33. O'Gorman, *Peculiar Crossroads*; and Paul Elie, *The Life You Save May Be Your Own: An American Pilgrimage* (New York: Farrar, Straus and Giroux, 2003).

34. Jacques Maritain, *Creative Intuition in Art and Poetry* (New York: Meridian M8, [1953] 1955), OCLIB #27.

35. François Mauriac, *Flesh and Blood* [*La chair et le sang*], trans. Gerard Hopkins (New York: Farrar, Straus, 1955), OCLIB #568; *The Lamb* [*L'agneau*], trans. Gerard Hopkins (New York: Farrar, Straus and Cudahy, 1955), OCLIB #570; and *Words of Faith* [*Paroles catholiques*], trans. Rev. Edward H. Flannery (New York: Philosophical Library, 1955), OCLIB #72; and Georges Bernanos, *The Last Essays of Georges Bernanos* (Chicago: Henry Regnery, 1955), OCLIB #433.

36. Stephen Schloesser, "Against Forgetting: Memory, History, Vatican II," in *Vatican II: Did Anything Happen?*, ed. David Schultenover (New York: Continuum, 2008), 92–152. For the date of O'Connor's first reading of Teilhard, see George A. Kilcourse Jr., *Flannery O'Connor's Religious Imagination: A World with Everything Off Balance* (Mahwah, N.J.: Paulist Press, 2001), 326n1; cf. Robert W. Gleason, SJ, *The*

sure, Mauriac's works continued to appear in translation up until the council's very eve.[37] Amid this voluminous transatlantic migration of French Catholic works from 1952 onwards, it is understandable that the two 1947 volumes of Bloy encountered just after the war would have faded somewhat from O'Connor's memory by the mid-1950s.

Sessions's discovery of O'Connor's 1946–1947 spiritual journal sheds new light on the fall of 1946, O'Connor's second year at Iowa. Thanksgiving Day fell on November 28, and over that holiday weekend break, O'Connor had begun writing her first novel, *Wise Blood*.[38] This momentous turn was the outcome of a profound change that had been some weeks in the making. Three weeks earlier, in her first dated journal entry (November 4), she wrote, "I have started on a new phase of my spiritual life—I trust. Tied up with it, is the throwing off of certain adolescent habits & habits of mind." At the end of the entry, she noted, "I have been reading Bernanos. It is so very wonderful. Will I ever know anything?"[39] The two possibilities for her reading in 1946 would have been *Diary of a Country Priest* (1937) or *Star of Satan* (1940). The protagonists in both novels are social outcasts, and although fools and failures in the eyes of the worldly wise, they are the true saints for those who can see beneath appearances. Although the country preacher Hazel Motes, the protagonist of *Wise Blood*, could have been modeled on either one of them, the more extreme character

World to Come (New York: Sheed and Ward, 1958), 164, OCLIB #157, signed and dated 1959.

37. François Mauriac, *Lines of Life* [*Destins*], trans. Gerard Hopkins (New York: Farrar, Straus and Cudahy, 1957), OCLIB #571; *Vipers' Tangle*, trans. Warre B. Wells (Garden City, N.Y.: Doubleday, Image D51, 1957), OCLIB #576; *Questions of Precedence* [*Préséances*], trans. Gerard Hopkins (New York: Farrar, Straus and Cudahy, 1959), OCLIB #573; *The Son of Man*, trans. Bernard Murchland (Cleveland, Ohio: World Publishing, 1960), OCLIB #124, O'Connor review in 1960; and *The Frontenacs* [*Le mystère Frontenac*], trans. Gerard Hopkins (New York: Farrar, Straus, 1961), OCLIB #569.

38. W. A. Sessions, introduction to *Prayer Journal*, vii–xii, at x.

39. Entry for November 4, 1946, in O'Connor, *Prayer Journal*, 20–21, 67–69.

was the one Bernanos wrote first: the *Star of Satan*'s Fr. Donissan.[40]

Because the prayer journal has several entries preceding the first dated one, judging whether they had been written over a period of weeks or perhaps only days is impossible. Moreover, the opening pages of the journal appear to have been lost. Whatever the time frame, O'Connor's use of the word "bourgeois" in her second (undated) entry suggests that she had been reading Bernanos as she began the journal. (Perhaps her encounter with *The Diary of a Country Priest* inspired her own diary of a country writer.) The term is unusual coming from an American, especially from someone raised in rural Georgia and now studying in 1940s rural Iowa: "If we could accurately map heaven some of our up-&-coming scientists would begin drawing blueprints for its improvement, and the bourgeois would sell guides 10¢ the copy to all over 65."[41]

However, the word *bourgeois* is a key word for Bernanos. About fifty pages into the *Diary*, the country priest recounts words spoken by his mentor, an aging curate: "Our democratic colleagues are very pleasant and full of zeal, but I find them just a little—how shall I put it?—a little *bourgeois*." Seventy pages later, the country priest muses: "No, I have not lost my faith. The expression 'to lose one's faith,' as one might a purse or a ring of keys, has always seemed to me rather foolish. It must be one of those sayings of *bourgeois* piety, a legacy of those wretched priests of the eighteenth century who talked so much." A hundred pages later the local landed gentry (good country people) are unmasked and revealed: "There's no longer any aristocracy, my friend, get that into your head.... The aristocrats of to-day are only shamefaced *bourgeois*."[42] In each case, the translator chose to italicize the

40. See "Georges Bernanos: Passionate Supernaturalism," in Schloesser, *Jazz Age Catholicism*, 249–281.

41. Undated entry, in O'Connor, *Prayer Journal*, 5–6, at 6; 48–50, at 50.

42. Bernanos, *Diary of a Country Priest* (1937), 51, 122, 187; emphasis original.

word *bourgeois*, perhaps to suggest that it did not translate well into American English or social class categories.

An even more significant textual clue occurs at the beginning of the dated entries. As noted, in the first (dated Monday, November 4), O'Connor ends by noting that she has "been reading Bernanos." In the next (dated Wednesday, November 6), she begins: "Mediocrity is a hard word to apply to oneself; yet I see myself so equal with it that it is impossible not to throw it at myself—realizing even as I do that I will be old & beaten before I accept it. . . . There must be some way for the naturally mediocre to escape it[.]"[43] Only two extremely brief dated entries follow this—O'Connor would have been occupied with semester's end and Christmas travel back to Georgia. She returned to the nagging concern on January 11, 1947, presumably after having returned to Iowa for the new year, new semester, and the composition of *Wise Blood*: "Maybe I'm mediocre. I'd rather be less. I'd rather be nothing. An imbecile. Yet this is wrong. Mediocrity, if that is my scourge, is something I'll have to submit to."[44]

Both the "mediocre" and "imbecile" are key words in Bernanos.[45] In *The Diary of a Country Priest*, "The mediocre priest is ugly . . . the bad priest is the mediocre one . . . a mediocre priest, alas, is nearly always sentimental." Yet that "golden mediocrity" has a salvific function: it might "weary humanity so profoundly" that holy poverty would soon "blossom forth in a new spring." So "[m]ediocrities are a trap set by the devil." Loathing them wastes both time and energy that should be spent in seeking Christ in unlikely places: "in the meantime we should shelter mediocrity, take it under our wing. Poor devils, they need some

43. Entry for November 6, 1946, in O'Connor, *Prayer Journal*, 22–23, at 22; facsimile 69–72, at 69.

44. Entry for January 11, 1947, in O'Connor, *Prayer Journal*, 26–27, at 27; facsimile 74–76, at 74.

45. See "Mediocrity and Scandal" and "The 'Imbecile,'" in Hans Urs von Balthasar, *Bernanos: An Ecclesial Existence*, trans. Erasmo Leiva-Merikakis (San Francisco: Ignatius Press, 1996), 340–357 and 358–368.

keeping warm!"[46] One scholar succinctly connects these Bernanos themes implicit in O'Connor's entries (beginning with the "bourgeois" who would sell blueprints for the improvement of heaven). Bernanos "deplored the materialistic determinism, sweetened by democratic illusion, that had come to be accepted as the norm rather than an abnormality. He saw the critical places in society filled by a new class of 'realist,' shrewd and aggressive in their mediocrity, men who exploited the instinctive morality of 'imbeciles' through an imposture which they justified as simple pragmatism."[47]

These themes and language were owed to Léon Bloy, who had died two decades before Bernanos's *Diary of a Country Priest*. One scholar has recently observed that "Bernanos's fulminations against his enemies can arguably be read in the light of Bloy's conclusion to his own *Exégèse des lieux communs* (*Exegesis of Commonplaces*), which, after excoriating all the axioms of bourgeois sensibility, concludes with this disarming appeal: 'You should think of this, poor imbecile, and in thinking of it, step back from being stupid and making the wretched suffer. For this is what we are, you and I, and nothing but this: great depths.'"[48] Jacques Maritain, deeply acquainted with both Bernanos and Bloy, appealed to the same language: "the mediocrity of a great number of Christians" frightened off those who imagined that "obedience to faith is incompatible with boldness of the intellect, or with the play and freedom of art and beauty." As a remedy, "Bloy, in crying

46. Bernanos, *Diary of a Country Priest* (1937), 74, 75, 94, 118.

47. Anthony Chapin, "Bernanos: Fundamentals Made Relevant" (review of Robert Speaight, *Georges Bernanos* [New York: Liveright, 1974]), *Cross Currents* 24, no. 1 (Spring 1974): 92–98, at 95–96. Compare "The Wisdom of the Bourgeois," in Bloy and R. Maritain, *Pilgrim of the Absolute*, 123–160.

48. Brian Sudlow, "Rethinking the Modernity of Bernanos: A Girardian Perspective," in *God's Mirror: Renewal and Engagement in French Catholic Intellectual Culture in the Mid-Twentieth Century*, ed. Katherine Davies and Toby Garfitt (New York: Fordham University Press, 2015), 162–85, at 167–68. "One of the words recurring with the greatest frequency in [Bloy's] *Disagreeable Tales* is 'imbecile'." Erik Butler, "Translator's Introduction: The Gospel of the Gutter," in Léon Bloy, *Disagreeable Tales*, trans. Butler (Cambridge, Mass.: Wakefield Press, 2015), vii–xii, at x.

out his disgust at all lukewarmness, in shouting on rooftops his thirst for the absolute, inspires these famished ones with a presentiment of the glory of God."[49]

That O'Connor should have moved from reading Bernanos to his progenitor Bloy is fitting. Journal entries made on May 30, 1947—two days preceding her award of the MFA from Iowa—and four months later on September 23—show that O'Connor was reading Bloy throughout the summer of 1947. The text also reveals what a monumental experience this was for her at the age of twenty-two—both devastating yet revealing—emotionally, intellectually, and spiritually. Understanding who Bloy was and why reading him prepared the way for "The Displaced Person" requires first situating him in his original context of fin de siècle France and the Dreyfus Affair. For it is here that seeds were planted for what eventually became the revisionist Bloy as represented after the Holocaust: a prophet of the catastrophe and a distant ancestor of postwar "leftist" Catholicism. For whether O'Connor was aware of it or not, the French Catholic writers to whom she turned in her early twenties—Bernanos, Maritain, Mauriac, Mounier, and Bloy himself—all represented this "left Catholicism."[50]

Léon Bloy: Symbolist Historian as Catholic Dreyfusard

The Dreyfus Affair altered the nature of Roman Catholicism in France unexpectedly, radically, and definitively. Beginning in 1890 with the arrest of a Jewish officer named Alfred Dreyfus on charges of espionage, it evolved into a political and cultural wa-

49. Jacques Maritain, introduction to Bloy and R. Maritain, *Pilgrim of the Absolute*, 7–23, at 17–18.

50. For historical perspective see Gerd-Rainer Horn and Emmanuel Gerard, eds., *Left Catholicism, 1943–1955: Catholics and Society in Western Europe at the Point of Liberation*, KADOC-studies, 25 (Leuven: Leuven University Press, 2001); Arthur Plaza, "From Christian Militants to Republican Renovators: The Third Ralliement of Catholics in Postwar France, 1944–1965" (PhD diss., New York University, 2008); and Joseph Anthony Amato, *Mounier and Maritain: A French Catholic Understanding of the Modern World* (Tuscaloosa: University of Alabama Press, 1975).

tershed that bitterly divided society's largest segments as well as intimate family dinner tables.[51] In the popular imagination, the affair polarized France into two incommensurable opposing blocs: the Dreyfusards on the left against the army—Republicans, anticlerical laicists, and (as they called themselves) "intellectuals"—and the anti-Dreyfusards on the right aligned with the army—monarchists, Catholic defenders of church-state unity, and (as they were portrayed) anti-intellectuals.[52] Left and right were portrayed monolithically as respectively philo- and anti-Semitic. In fact, significant segments of the Catholic population were virulently anti-Semitic. The flames of their hatred were most effectively fanned by the popular media resources of the Assumptionist religious order: its magazine *Le Pèlerin* (*The Pilgrim*), published at the shrine of Lourdes, and its daily newspaper, *La Croix* (*The Cross*).[53]

Throughout this affair and beyond, Léon Bloy did not play his role to type. This may account at least in part for the wide variety of his interpreters. For some he was an anti-Semite masquerading as a philo-Semite; for others he was (along with Charles Péguy) a paradox: an ultra-Catholic pro-Dreyfusard.[54] Understanding both

51. Schloesser, *Jazz Age Catholicism*, 49–82; cf. Michael Burns, *France and the Dreyfus Affair: A Documentary History* (Boston: Bedford/St. Martins, 1999). See also Piers Paul Read, *The Dreyfus Affair: The Scandal that Tore France in Two* (New York: Bloomsbury Press, 2012); Louis Begley, *Why the Dreyfus Affair Matters* (New Haven, Conn.; and London: Yale University Press, 2010); and Frederick Brown, *For the Soul of France: Culture Wars in the Age of Dreyfus* (New York: Alfred A. Knopf, 2010).

52. Ruth Harris, *The Man on Devil's Island: Alfred Dreyfus and the Affair that Divided France* (London: Allen Lane, 2010), xvi, 6, 8–9.

53. Ruth Harris, "The Assumptionists and the Dreyfus Affair," *Past and Present* 194, no. 1 (2007): 175–211; and Ruth Harris, *Lourdes: Body and Spirit in the Secular Age* (London: Allen Lane, 1999).

54. Brenna Moore, "Philosemitism under a Darkening Sky: Jews and Judaism in the French Catholic Revival (1900–1940)," *Catholic Historical Review* 99, no. 2 (2013): 262–297; cf. Moore, *Sacred Dread: Raïssa Maritain, the Allure of Suffering, and the French Catholic Revival (1905–1944)* (Notre Dame, Ind.: University of Notre Dame Press, 2012); and Robert Royal, ed., *Jacques Maritain and the Jews* (Mishawaka, Ind.: American Maritain Association; Notre Dame, Ind.: Distributed by University of Notre Dame Press, 1994).

Bloy's complex position, as well as the seemingly incommensurable critical estimations of his thought, requires situating his consideration of "The Jewish Question" within the larger framework of his symbolist theology and exegetical theory of history.

Bloy's historical approach was part of a complex fin de siècle association between Franco-Belgian Catholicism and the symbolists and decadents.[55] Bloy was one of the forerunners of the 1880s *renouveau catholique*, having first converted to Catholicism in 1869 (the year preceding the debacle of the Franco-Prussian War and Commune of 1870–1871) under the influence of Barbey d'Aurevilly. Symbolism had emerged in opposition to the dominant naturalist realism represented by Émile Zola. Bloy took symbolism, this vast movement uniting literature, painting, and music, and applied it to the study of history: "The visible is the footprint of the Invisible."[56] Bloy first cut his historian's teeth on the figure of Christopher Columbus. Pope Pius IX had been devoted to the cause of beatifying Columbus and inaugurated the proceedings; after his death in 1878, the continuation of this task fell to his successor, Pope Leo XIII.[57] In 1884, Bloy published his first symbolist-historical study with a preface supplied by d'Aurevilly: *The Revealer of the Globe: Christopher Columbus and His Future Beatification*.[58] In 1890, preempting by two years Pope Leo XIII's encyclical observing the Columbus quadricentennial (*Quarto Abeunte Saeculo*, July 16, 1892), Bloy published his own "encyclical" letter to the bishops of France, urging them to

55. For symbolism and Decadence, see Schloesser, *Jazz Age Catholicism*, 35–45.

56. Bloy, quoted as epigraph to chapter 3, "The Symbolism of History," in Béguin, *Study in Impatience*, 137. For realism, naturalism, and Zola, see Schloesser, *Jazz Age Catholicism*, 19–27.

57. Events surrounding the attempted beatification of Christopher Columbus are recounted in Alejo Carpentier's historical novel, *The Harp and the Shadow: A Novel*, trans. Thomas Christensen and Carol Christensen (San Francisco: Mercury House; St. Paul, Minn.: Distributed to the trade by Consortium Book Sales and Distribution, 1990).

58. For bibliography of Léon Bloy's publications here and following, see E. T. Dubois, *Portrait of Léon Bloy* (New York: Sheed and Ward, 1950), 119–121.

plead the cause of Columbus's beatification. Other historical topics later considered by Bloy included Marie Antoinette (1896),
Louis XVII (1900), Byzantium (1906), Mélanie Calvat (1912), Joan
of Arc (1915), the apparition at La Salette (1925), and, most important, *Napoleon's Soul* (1912). "History is like an immense liturgical text," Bloy wrote of Napoleon. "What is known as Genius
is simply the divine Will incarnate, if I may put it so, made visible and tangible in a human instrument brought to its highest
degree of force and precision, incapable, however, like a pair of
compasses, of going beyond its own greatest circumference."[59]

Bloy's theological exegesis of "The Jewish Question" and the
Dreyfus Affair depends on this broader symbolist-historical vision. In 1886, two years after publishing his first study of Columbus, Bloy had bitterly attacked Édouard Drumont's best-selling
anti-Semitic diatribe *La France juive* (*Jewish France*, 1886). Two
years after the beginning of the Dreyfus Affair, when Drumont
founded his anti-Semitic newspaper *La Libre Parole* (*Free Speech*;
popular among Catholics and especially the clergy), Bloy countered this and other anti-Semitic Catholic campaigns with the
book that would largely define his legacy: *Salvation from the Jews*
(1892).[60] Like its author, this work has been widely interpreted
from diametrically opposed positions. The reason is that his
symbolist-historical framework portrays "the Jews"—an essential-
ized transhistorical category—as the privileged means by which
the world will be saved precisely because they are the most abject of all earth's suffering people.[61] In Bloy's theological frame-

59. Léon Bloy quoted in Heppenstall, *Léon Bloy*, 32.
60. Léon Bloy, *Le Salut par les juifs* [*Salvation from the Jews*] (Paris: A. Demay,
1892).
61. One scholar observes that "[a]rguably, philosemites and antisemites have
both tended to essentialize the Jewish object of their admiration or antipathy, with
occasional, sometimes troubling overlap between two seemingly disparate modern
phenomena." Richard Francis Crane, "'Heart-Rending Ambivalence': Jacques Maritain and the Complexity of Postwar Catholic Philosemitism," *Studies in Christian-
Jewish Relations* 6, no. 1 (2011): 1–16, at 3, http://ejournals.bc.edu/ojs/index.php/scjr/
article/view/1820/1698. Cf. Martine Sevegrand, *Israël vu par les catholiques français:*

work (shared by many other fin de siècle Catholics), salvation is inextricably bound up with "vicarious suffering" and "mystical substitution."[62]

Indeed, Bloy's position on "suffering"—a position that would have great appeal for Flannery O'Connor—was extreme: not merely a *privileged* path to redemption but, in fact, the *exclusive* path. "I have meditated long and often on suffering," Bloy wrote during the decade preceding the Dreyfus Affair. "I am now convinced that nothing else is supernatural in this world. All the rest is human."[63] Suffering was a sure road to redemption: "Every time we recommence the sacrifice of Calvary, we start the Redemption; our sufferings always redeem someone or something." We ought never to refuse suffering, he argued, because "*We are made for that and for that alone*." As Bloy applied this broad theology of suffering to the specific historical case of "the Jews," he drew a symbolist conclusion: "the Jews" were "the *Race* out of which the Redemption comes forth [*Salus ex Judaeis*] *which carries visibly, like Jesus himself, the sins of the World* ... the race of Israel, which is to say of the Holy Spirit, whose exodus will be the marvelous wonder of Abjection."[64]

Bloy most famously (or infamously) applied this vision to the particular case of Alfred Dreyfus. In 1898, the naturalist Zola had published his legendary open letter to the president of the Third

1945–1994 (Paris: Éditions Karthala, 2014); and Sarah Hammerschlag, *The Figural Jew: Politics and Identity in Postwar French Thought* (Chicago: University of Chicago Press, 2010).

62. Schloesser, *Jazz Age Catholicism*, 44. For a recent overview, see Robert Ziegler, "The Palimpsest of Suffering: Léon Bloy's *Le Désespéré*," *Neophilologus* 97, no. 4 (October 2013): 653–662.

63. Bloy in Béguin, *Study in Impatience*, 25.

64. Schloesser, *Jazz Age Catholicism*, 67–70; emphasis original. Bloy quotes Jesus's words (Jn 4:22) from the Latin Vulgate: *Salus ex Judaeis* = "Salvation is from the Jews." His capitalization of "Abjection" refers to the Suffering Servant described by the prophet Isaiah as read in the Good Friday Catholic liturgy: "Despised, and the most abject of men, a man of sorrows, and acquainted with infirmity." (Is 53:3 Douay-Rheims) See the chapter "The Mystery of Israel. Salvation is of the Jews," in Bloy and R. Maritain, *Pilgrim of the Absolute*, 245–273.

Republic titled "J'Accuse!" Two years later, the symbolist Bloy published his riposte titled *Je m'accuse* (*I Accuse Myself*, 1900) in which he deployed his exegetical method.[65] For Bloy, Dreyfus was the fin de siècle's Jewish scapegoat: one visible historical incarnation—in one particular place and time—of the invisible, eternal drama of Christ, unjustly judged, and suffering agony to the end of time. Thus, for Bloy, the Dreyfus Affair was only "an illusion"—the "*human and hideous appearance of a DIVINE COURT CASE for which the moment has not yet come to be revealed in the light.*"[66] It was a particular application of Bloy's broader exegetical approach to historical events as symbols unveiling the revelation of God: "'While men toss and turn in the visions of sleep, God, alone capable of action, really does something. *He writes his own Revelation in the appearance of the events of this world*, and that is why what is called history is so utterly incomprehensible.' The word has been uttered: *Revelation.*"[67]

1935 to 1945: Bloy's Godchildren—Exegeting the Passion of Israel

Bloy served as godfather at the baptisms of numerous converts to Catholicism. Among his most well-known godchildren were Jacques and Raïssa (née Oumançoff) Maritain. Jacques had grown up in a freethinking Protestant family; Raïssa was a Jewish Russian emigrée whose parents escaped with her to Paris after a czarist pogrom. In February 1906, Jacques gave Bloy the money to finance republication costs of a new edition of *Salvation from the Jews*.[68] This 1906 edition was dedicated to the Jewish Raïssa, whom Bloy deeply loved. Just as the book appeared, Raïssa, sickly

65. Léon Bloy, *Je m'accuse. Vignettes et culs-de-lampe de Léon Bloy* [*Vignettes and Cul-de-lampes of Léon Bloy*] (Paris: Édition de "La Maison d'art," 1900).

66. Schloesser, *Jazz Age Catholicism*, 69; emphasis original.

67. Béguin quoting Bloy in "Symbolism of History," *Study in Impatience*, 137–192, at 143; emphasis original.

68. Léon Bloy, *Le salut par les Juifs*, rev. ed. (Paris: J. Victorion, 1906).

throughout her life, suffered a life-threatening illness. This traumatic event seems to have intensified the couple's religious quest. Four months later, Jacques and Raïssa were baptized as Catholics; Bloy stood in as their godfather.[69]

Three decades later (and forty-odd years after the Dreyfus Affair), the trauma of the Great Depression led to yet another rightwing anti-Semitic wave in Europe. The most infamous case was the electoral victory of the Nazis in Germany in 1933; their rise to power was soon followed by the Nuremberg Laws passed in 1935, laws forbidding an "interracial" marriage such as Jacques and Raïssa's. But there was also an anti-Semitic revival in France as right-wing factions grew in numbers and power.[70]

Beginning in 1935, both Jacques and Raïssa followed their late godfather's lead and worked in earnest to counteract this new wave.[71] Raïssa published her article titled "The History of Abraham: Sanctity in the State of Nature" while Jacques's preface appeared in Erik Petersen's landmark *The Mystery of Jews and Gentiles in the Church.*[72] In 1937, Jacques's essay "Impossible Antisemitism" appeared in a collection titled *The Jews*; it was expanded and reprinted the following year in his book *Questions of Conscience.*[73] In 1938, the year of September's Munich Appease-

69. Schloesser, *Jazz Age Catholicism*, 56–79.

70. William Brustein, *Roots of Hate: Anti-Semitism in Europe Before the Holocaust* (New York: Cambridge University Press, 2003); Vicki Caron, "The Antisemitic Revival in France in the 1930s: The Socioeconomic Dimension Reconsidered," *The Journal of Modern History* 70, no. 1 (March 1998): 24–73; and Paul J. Kingston, *Anti-Semitism in France during the 1930s: Organisations, Personalities, and Propaganda* (Hull, UK: University of Hull Press, 1983).

71. Richard Crane, *Passion of Israel: Jacques Maritain, Catholic Conscience, and the Holocaust* (Scranton, Pa.: University of Scranton Press, 2010); and Jean-Luc Barré, *Jacques and Raïssa Maritain. Beggars for Heaven*, trans. Bernard E. Doering (Notre Dame, Ind.: University of Notre Dame Press, 2005), 341–385.

72. Raïssa Maritain, *Histoire d'Abraham ou La sainteté dans l'état de nature* (Fribourg: Fragnière Frères, 1935); Jacques Maritain, preface to Erik Petersen, *Le Mystère des Juifs et des Gentils dans l'église: suivi d'un essai sur l'Apocalypse*, trans. Ernest Kamnitzer, Pierre Corps, and Georges Massoulard (Paris: Desclée de Brouwer, 1935).

73. Jacques Maritain, "L'Impossible antisémitisme," in *Les Juifs*, Paul Clau-

ment and November's Kristallnacht, Jacques gave an address published immediately thereafter as *The Jews among the Nations.*[74] As the war clouds of 1939 approached, the Maritains saw the handwriting on the wall and, like many other French intellectuals, exiled themselves to New York City.[75]

In New York, Jacques became associated with the École Libre des Hautes Études at the New School for Social Research, founded by refugees and supported by Belgian and French Resistance resources.[76] Another vital refugee institution was Éditions de la Maison française, a publishing venture housed in the Rockefeller Center. Its print list featured the collection titled "La Voix de France" (Voice of France). In the late summer of 1941, a year after France's catastrophic "strange defeat" by the Germans (and just four months before Pearl Harbor), *Time* magazine put Charles de Gaulle on its cover and featured a story on the Éditions de la Maison française.[77]

That same year, both of the Maritains published volumes (in French) with the exiled Maison française. Raïssa's *Les Grandes amitiés* (*Great Friendships: Memories*, 1941), her first of two volumes of remembrances of great French figures, included mem-

del et al. (Paris: Plon, 1937); and "L'Impossible antisémitisme," in *Questions de conscience* (Paris: Desclée de Brouwer et Cie, 1938).

74. Jacques Maritain, *Les Juifs parmi les nations* (Paris: Les Éditions du Cerf, 1938); cf. *A Christian Looks at the Jewish Question* (New York: Longmans, Green, 1939).

75. Jeffrey Mehlman, *Émigré New York: French Intellectuals in Wartime Manhattan, 1940–1944* (Baltimore: Johns Hopkins University Press, 2000.). The self-exile to New York was fortuitous since Raïssa, like the Maritains' friend Max Jacob, would undoubtedly have been deported to the death camps. See Schloesser, *Jazz Age Catholicism*, 207–208.

76. Aristide Zolberg and Agnès Callamard, "The École Libre at the New School, 1941–1946," *Social Research* 65, no. 4 (Winter 1998): 921–951.

77. Marc Bloch, *Strange Defeat: A Statement of Evidence Written in 1940*, tr. Gerard Hopkins (New York: Octagon Books, 1968); orig. *L'étrange défaite: témoignage écrit en 1940* (Paris: Société des éd. Franc-tireur, 1940). "Books: Languages in Exile," *Time*, August 4, 1941, http://www.time.com/time/magazine/article/0,9171,884430,00 .html, accessed January 15, 2016. For cover, see http://www.time.com/time/covers/ 0,16641,19410804,00.html, accessed February 18, 2016.

ories of the philosopher Henri Bergson, who died that year. She also engaged in a series of exchanges in the Catholic periodical *Commonweal* regarding him.[78] Jacques published French, English, and German editions of *Through the Disaster*, as well as a work on *The Thought of Saint Paul* in both French and English editions.[79] Maritain presented Paul's theology of Christianity as a branch grafted on to the Jewish tree, a descendent of Judaism to which Christianity owed its very life and sustenance. Meanwhile, as world events escalated beyond the worst predictions, tragedy struck the commonplace domestic world of Flannery O'Connor. Her father, Edward, died of lupus in February, devastating his daughter as she approached her sixteenth birthday. Ten months later, following the Japanese attack on Pearl Harbor, America entered the war.

In 1942, those who were paying attention already knew what was happening to European Jewry. Jacques himself "estimated that by the end of 1942, one to two million Jews had already perished, with five or six million still menaced with death in German-occupied Europe."[80] His mounting horror catalyzed a remarkable output in writing and broadcast messages, includ-

78. Raïssa Maritain, *Les grandes amitiés: souvenirs*, Collection "Voix de France" (New York: Éditions de la Maison française, 1941); R. Maritain, "Henri Bergson," *The Commonweal* 33, no. 13 (1941): 317–319; cf. *We Have Been Friends Together, Memoirs*, trans. Julie Kernan (New York and Toronto: Longmans, Green and Co., 1942). After Bergson's death (January 4, 1941), Raïssa entered into a public discussion partly involving the question of whether Bergson had been secretly baptized before he died. (Although Bergson had long been interested in Catholicism and was central to Catholic Revivalism, he did not do so out of Jewish solidarity.) Raïssa's *Grandes amitiés* was thus published as the work of a patriot in exile, an evocation of France's cultural and intellectual heritage, by a Resistance publishing house in exile, in the series "The Voice of France."

79. Jacques Maritain, *À travers le désastre* ..., Collection "Voix de France" (New York: Éditions de la Maison française, 1941); *Durch die Katastrophe: à travers le désastre* (New York: Éditions de la Maison française, 1941); *France, My Country, through the Disaster* (New York: Longmans, Green, 1941); *La pensée de Saint Paul: textes choisis et présentés* (New York: Éditions de la Maison française, 1941); *The Living Thoughts of Saint Paul*, trans. Harry Lorin Binsse (New York: Longmans, Green and Co., 1941).

80. Crane, *Passion of Israel*, 86.

ing a prolific amount of writing and editorial work for the Maison française where he assumed editorship of a series titled "Civilization." Under these auspices he published his own landmark work, *The Rights of Man and Natural Law* (1942), a creative hybridization of two seemingly incompatible discourses: Enlightenment "rights" and Catholic "natural law."[81] In 1943, Jacques wrote the preface to the French translation (from German) of John Oesterreicher's *Racism–Antisemitism–Antichristianity*, a documentary collection also published by the Maison française.[82] In an article titled "World Trial" (1943), Jacques followed the lead of his long-deceased godfather, Bloy, who had exegeted the Dreyfus Affair as a "Divine Court Case." So, too, Jacques now argued that the Holocaust was a historical moment in the perennial "passion of Israel ... taking on more and more distinctly the form of the Cross."[83]

Meanwhile, across the Atlantic, a similar Resistance publishing effort was being led by Albert Béguin in Switzerland. Béguin believed that the Swiss position of neutrality in the war ethically demanded that its citizens nevertheless do what they could on behalf of Occupied France. He founded the *Cahiers du Rhône* (*Notebooks of the Rhône*) series dedicated to emphasizing and celebrating France's cultural heritage.[84] Béguin also published two

81. Jacques Maritain, *Les droits de l'homme et la loi naturelle*, Collection "Civilisation" (New York: Éditions de la Maison française, 1942); *The Rights of Man and Natural Law*, trans. Doris C. Anson (New York: Scribner, 1943). Maritain's book "took what would be a fateful step for postwar intellectual history as a whole, making the claim that a revival of natural law implies a broad set of pre-political human rights." Samuel Moyn, "Personalism, Community, and the Origins of Human Rights," in *Human Rights in the Twentieth Century*, ed. Stefan-Ludwig Hoffmann (New York: Cambridge University Press, 2010), 85–106, at 94.

82. Jacques Maritain, preface to John M. Oesterreicher, *Racisme, antisémitisme, antichristianisme: documents et critique* (New York: Éditions de la Maison française, 1943). For Oesterreicher, see John Connelly, *From Enemy to Brother: The Revolution in Catholic Teaching on the Jews, 1933–1965* (Cambridge, Mass.: Harvard University Press, 2012); and Michael Phayer, *The Catholic Church and the Holocaust, 1930–1965* (Bloomington: Indiana University Press, 2000).

83. Jacques Maritain, "World Trial: Its Meaning for the Future," *Contemporary Jewish Record* 6 (August 1943): 339–347; see Crane, *Passion of Israel*, 91; cf. 74.

84. France's Rhône region, named after the river originating in the Swiss

wartime works on Bloy with an eye to revisionism. The first was a collection of Bloy's writings, *Choix de textes*, published in 1943. This was the model for Raïssa's English-language collection, *Pilgrim of the Absolute*, published in 1947, which was O'Connor's introduction to him in Iowa.[85] The second was an interpretative study of Bloy (*The Impatient*) published in 1944—the year of the D-Day landings and the liberation of France—underscoring Bloy's exegesis of the Jews and their salvific role in history. In 1947, this book appeared in English translation simultaneously with Maritain's collation, providing O'Connor with a broader background to Bloy's life and thought.[86]

But for now, O'Connor (aged seventeen to twenty) spent the war years (September 1942–June 1945) at the Georgia State College for Women. There she read, as she would later say, not much of anything. That was about to change.

1946 to 1947: The Bloy Centenary and "Displaced Persons"

In a timely coincidence, the 1946 centenary of Bloy's birth became inextricably linked with the immediate post-Holocaust era. In August 1944, Paris had been liberated. In May 1945, Germany surrendered, and the war in Europe was over. That August, Japan would also surrender in the wake of two atomic bombs. In this

---

Alps and flowing through Lyon on its way to the Mediterranean Sea, lies in southeastern France. In Vichy France, Lyon was a center of Christian anti-Nazi resistance; see Renée Bédarida and François Bédarida, *Témoignage chrétien, 1941–1944: les armes de l'esprit* (Paris: Éditions ouvrières, 1977). For Béguin's project, see Olivier Cariguel, *Les cahiers du Rhône dans la guerre, 1941–1945: la résistance du "Glaive de l'Esprit"* (Fribourg: Université de Fribourg, 1999); and Françoise Frey-Béguin, *Les Cahiers du Rhône: "refuge de la pensée libre"* (La Chaux-de-Fonds: Éd. de la Baconnière, 1993).

85. Albert Béguin, ed., *Léon Bloy. Choix de textes et introduction par Albert Béguin* (Fribourg: Éditions de la Librairie de l'Université, 1943); cf. Bloy and R. Maritain, *Pilgrim of the Absolute* (1947).

86. Albert Béguin, *Léon Bloy, l'impatient* (Fribourg: Egloff, 1944); translated as Béguin, *Léon Bloy: A Study in Impatience* (1947).

postfascist context, Bloy's centenary publications reinterpreted him as a prophet whose seemingly paradoxical position in the fin de siècle as a Catholic Dreyfusard had prefigured postwar left Catholicism.

Béguin's wartime literary resistance efforts easily flowed into this postwar epoch, publishing a "Centennial Edition" (1946) collection of homages to Bloy for his centenary. These included a reprint of Jacques' essay "Ungrateful Beggar" and Raïssa's "Memories" of Bloy, excerpted from her 1941 book *Les Grandes amitiés* (*Great Friendships*), published by New York's Maison française.[87] In 1947, Stanislas Fumet published a revised edition of his prewar *Mission of Léon Bloy*, and Joseph Bollery published the first volume of what would become a large study of Bloy.[88] In short, Bloy's disciples on both sides of the Atlantic used the 1946 centenary as an occasion to both recover and revise his legacy in light of the recent catastrophe.

Meanwhile, Jacques was participating in major postwar projects: the creation of the United Nations in 1945 and the writing of the Universal Declaration on Human Rights, soon to be passed in 1948.[89] His wartime writings, including most especially his book on *Human Rights and Natural Law*, first published in French and then in English, had catapulted him into international prominence as "the premier postwar philosopher of human rights."[90] His postwar influence was such that one American complained in spring 1948 that speeches promoting the (Pan-)American Dec-

87. Léon Bloy, *Léon Bloy. Édition du centenaire augmenté de textes inédits*, ed. Albert Béguin, Les Cahiers du Rhône, no. 11 (Neuchâtel: Éditions de la Baconnière, 1946).

88. Stanislas Fumet, *Mission de Léon Bloy*, rev. ed. (Bruges: Desclée de Brouwer, [1935] 1947); and Joseph Bollery, *Léon Bloy. Essai de biographie*, 3 vols. (Paris: A. Michel, 1947–1954).

89. Barré, *Jacques and Raïssa Maritain*, 386–398.

90. Moyn, "Personalism, Community, and the Origins of Human Rights," 87; cf. Moyn, *The Last Utopia: Human Rights in History* (Cambridge, Mass.: Belknap Press of Harvard University Press, 2010), 54, 64–65, 67, 76, 252n16; and Moyn, *Christian Human Rights* (Philadelphia: University of Pennsylvania Press, 2015).

laration of the Rights and Duties of Man "were laced with Roman Catholic social philosophy, and it seemed at times that the chief protagonists in the conference room were the Roman Catholics and the communists, with the latter a poor second."[91]

The new language of "human rights" was immediately tested by a massive postwar humanitarian crisis: the "Displaced Person."[92] As early as July 1945—just two months after Victory in Europe Day—*Life* magazine had featured a heart-breaking spread on the plight of millions of "displaced persons" (DPs) in Europe titled "DPs. Millions of 'Displaced Persons' Stream across Europe to their Homes."[93] Very likely, O'Connor would have pored over this issue in the summer heat of her Georgia home. Having just graduated from the women's college, she was about to move to Iowa in a matter of weeks. Perhaps, given her age (she was twenty), the vivid photographs of young Danish German couples being forcibly broken up might have made an impact. There was also the gruesome image of the "DP" playing soccer in his Buchenwald concentration camp shirt—the only shirt he owned. And

91. John Humphrey quoted in Moyn, *Last Utopia*, 66. For postwar linkages of Catholicism and communism circa 1947–1948, see Bacon, *Flannery O'Connor and Cold War Culture*, 73–76.

92. Mark Wyman, *DPs: Europe's Displaced Persons, 1945–1951* (Ithaca, N.Y.: Cornell University Press, 1998); Haim Genizi, *America's Fair Share: The Admission and Resettlement of Displaced Persons, 1945–1952* (Detroit, Mich.: Wayne State University Press, 1993). Recent studies include Gerard Daniel Cohen, *In War's Wake: Europe's Displaced Persons in the Postwar Order* (Oxford: Oxford University Press, 2012); Anna Marta Holian, *Between National Socialism and Soviet Communism: Displaced Persons in Postwar Germany* (Ann Arbor: University of Michigan Press, 2011); Jessica Reinisch and Elizabeth White, *The Disentanglement of Populations: Migration, Expulsion and Displacement in Post-War Europe, 1944–49* (New York: Palgrave Macmillan, 2011); Ben Shephard, *The Long Road Home: The Aftermath of the Second World War* (New York: Alfred A. Knopf, 2011); and Tara Zahra, *The Lost Children: Reconstructing Europe's Families after World War II* (Cambridge, Mass.: Harvard University Press, 2011).

93. "DPs. Millions of 'Displaced Persons' Stream across Europe to their Homes," *Life* 19, no. 5 (July 30, 1945): 13–19. Instead of *stream*, the table of contents used the verb *swarm*. Cf. Bacon, *Flannery O'Connor and Cold War Culture*, 79–82; Leonard M. Olschner, "Annotations on History and Society in Flannery O'Connor's 'The Displaced Person,'" *Flannery O'Connor Bulletin* 16 (1987): 62–78.

the heart-wrenching portrait of seven Poles, the only survivors of what had been three families, living in a single room.

That September, as O'Connor entered the Iowa Writers' Workshop, President Harry S. Truman wrote General Dwight D. Eisenhower about the plight of the DPs. At Christmastime, the president followed up Eisenhower's report with a directive aimed at dealing with this humanitarian disaster. Congress, however, dragged its feet on enacting any legislation. Truman's political position worsened after the 1946 midterm elections handed Congress over to the Republicans. Two months later, in the first-ever televised State of the Union address, Truman requested a Displaced Persons Act. In July 1947, he repeated that request; and repeated it again six months later in the State of the Union address of January 1948.[94] Along with Truman's proposed national health insurance and other stalled Fair Deal initiatives, the crisis of DPs became a highly visible struggle between Congress and a White House represented by its opponents as "followers of the Moscow party line."[95] It would have been difficult to miss.

As this national drama unfolded, O'Connor spent her two years in Iowa. During the week of April 21, 1947, Allen Tate visited the Iowa campus.[96] Both Tate and his wife, Caroline Gordon, were acquaintances of the Maritains from Jacques's teaching days at

94. All of Truman's documents relating to Displaced Persons have been archived online at the American Presidency Project (americanpresidency.org), established in 1999 by John T. Woolley and Gerhard Peters at the University of California, Santa Barbara: http://www.presidency.ucsb.edu/index.php, accessed February 18, 2016. See documents dated September 29, 1945; December 22, 1945; January 6, 1947; July 7, 1947; and January 7, 1948.

95. The "Moscow" characterization had been made by the American Medical Association in opposition to Truman's 1945 proposal for national health insurance. See Monte M. Poen, "National Health Insurance," in *The Harry S. Truman Encyclopedia*, ed. Richard S. Kirkendall (Boston: G. K. Hall and Co., 1989), 251; and http://www.trumanlibrary.org/anniversaries/healthprogram.htm, accessed February 18, 2016. Cf. also Kenneth Weisbrode, *The Year of Indecision, 1946: A Tour through the Crucible of Harry Truman's America* (New York: Viking, 2016).

96. For date of Tate's visit, see Brad Gooch, *Flannery: A Life of Flannery O'Connor* (New York: Little, Brown and Co., 2009), 137; cf. O'Gorman, *Peculiar Crossroads*, 85.

Princeton (1941–1942). Gordon was about to convert to Catholicism in December of that year; Tate's conversion followed three years later.[97] On May 30, five weeks after Tate's visit to Iowa, O'Connor recorded in her spiritual diary: "Bloy has come my way."[98]

1947: Postwar Left Catholicism

Although it had been one thing to read Bloy in his own fin de siècle French context, it was quite another to read him in 1947 postwar post-Holocaust America. Who was the Bloy read by O'Connor at age twenty-two? He was the prophetic voice constructed by his disciples, the Resistance publisher, Béguin, and the Jewish exile, Raïssa. In their hands, Bloy became the prophetic foe of antisemitism, the historical symbolist who penetrated beneath surface appearances and discerned the hidden significance of suffering Jews in modernity.

Bloy also became an icon for what one 1948 book review appearing in *Jewish Social Studies* designated postwar "left-wing Catholicism." Connecting three books appearing in 1947, all of them concerned with "the Jewish question," this reviewer wrote,

Antisemitism Bloy branded as "the most horrible injury our Lord has received in his Passion, which is still going on; it is the most outrageous and unforgivable buffet, for he receives it *on the Face of his Mother* and from Christian hands." ... The thought of [Charles] Péguy and Bloy is not only important for understanding the social Catholic movement represented today by the [Mouvement Républicain Populaire] in France; it is also the foundation upon which is built the current attitude

97. For Tate, Gordon and the Maritains, see O'Gorman, *Peculiar Crossroads*, 51–102, esp. 66–67; Thomas F. Haddox, "Contextualizing Flannery O'Connor: Allen Tate, Caroline Gordon, and the Catholic Turn in Southern Literature," *Southern Quarterly: A Journal of the Arts in the South* 38, no. 1 (1999): 173–190; Paul Giles, *American Catholic Arts and Fictions: Culture, Ideology, Aesthetics* (New York: Cambridge University Press, 1992), 191–209; and Ross Labrie, *The Catholic Imagination in American Literature* (Columbia: University of Missouri Press, 1997), 32–71.

98. Entry for May 30, 1947, in O'Connor, *Prayer Journal*, 33–34, at 33; facsimile 83–84, at 83.

towards Jews found in left-wing Catholicism and represented today most notably in the thought of Jacques Maritain.[99]

In her encounter with Béguin's Bloy, O'Connor met first and foremost the apostle of suffering.[100] Béguin's first chapter is devoted to suffering because it is at the center of Bloy's worldview. O'Connor underlined these words of Bloy:

> Through our understanding or our feelings we can never keep pace with the present. That is why sufferings are generally less painful than they may seem; for we bear them by degrees, almost unawares. *Do you know why Jesus Christ has suffered so much?* I will try to give you a transcendent idea of it in a few words. *It is because in his soul, all his lifetime, the present, the past and the future were absolutely one and the same.* This is strikingly true of the Agony in the Garden. But that thought is an abyss.[101]

Given O'Connor's fondness for the trope of "revelation," Bloy's linkage must have struck her: *"A heart without affliction is like a world without revelation; it sees God only in the faint gleam of twilight."*[102]

However, if Bloy's vision had only been about suffering, it would have given O'Connor no transcendent framework with which to write her own stories of revelation and transfiguration. Béguin's other three chapters provided O'Connor with a foundation on which to build her own symbolist vision of history. The second chapter—"Poverty, Money and the People of Israel"—unfolds Bloy's theory about Jewish "abjection" and its salvific role in history. The third—"The Symbolism of History, and the Soul of Napoleon"—lays

---

99. Koppel S. Pinson, review of Bernard Lazare, *Job's Dungheap* (New York: Schocken Books, 1947); Daniel Halévy, *Péguy and Les Cahiers de la Quinzaine* (New York: Longman's Green and Co., 1947); and Albert Béguin, *Léon Bloy*, trans. Edith M. Riley (New York: Sheed and Ward, 1947); in *Jewish Social Studies* 10, no. 2 (April 1948): 194–196, at 196. For context, see Horn and Gerard, *Left Catholicism, 1943–1955.*

100. Compare Bloy's influence on Raïssa Maritain; in Moore, *Sacred Dread*; Moore, "Feminized Suffering in Modern French Catholicism: Raïssa Maritain (1883–1960) and Léon Bloy (1846–1917)," *Spiritus: A Journal of Christian Spirituality* 9, no. 1 (2009): 46–68.

101. Béguin, *Study in Impatience*, 56.

102. Bloy quoted in Béguin, *Study in Impatience*, 39; emphasis in original.

out Bloy's exegetical theory: events in the visible world point beyond earthly appearances to invisible cosmic dramas, whether in great world-historical events and figures (like Columbus and Napoleon) or in the "commonplaces" (*des lieux communs*) of everyday life. Finally, the fourth—"A Prophet of Our Catastrophe, and His Impatience"—reinterprets the fin de siècle polemicist in light of the Holocaust. Read in the aftermath of a Second World War, Bloy's symbolist-historical exegesis of *Napoleon's Soul* (published on the eve of the First World War) seemed prescient: "For Napoleon and for the infinite multitude of lesser men the fact remains that *we are, all of us, symbols of the Invisible* and that we cannot lift a finger or massacre two million men without meaning something which is inscrutable until made manifest by the Beatific Vision."[103]

Set next to Béguin's collection, Raïssa's collation of Bloy's writings—*Pilgrim of the Absolute*—is a very different composition. At the end of her life O'Connor told an interviewer that she had never read Bloy's fiction, "only some essays."[104] It is possible that her memory failed her at this time. But that she hadn't realized what she had been reading in the Maritain collation is also likely. And if so, this is a testimony to Raïssa's editorial deftness and subtlety in assembling the volume.

103. Bloy quoted in Béguin, *Study in Impatience*, 156; emphasis original.
104. O'Connor in letter to Brodin, *Présences contemporaines*, 206–207. In 1987, Linda Schlafer recalled O'Connor's letter to Pierre Brodin (in September 1963) stating "that she had 'never read any of Bloy's fiction' (which she didn't think she would have liked) 'only some essays.'" However, Schlafer then mentions four instances from *The Woman Who Was Poor*, "which at least suggest O'Connor's acquaintance with it." In conclusion, she wonders whether O'Connor had forgotten in 1963 that she had read Bloy's novel or whether "it should simply make us cautious in pressing the causality of any literary predecessor on the grounds of material resemblance." In 2006, Sarah Gordon followed these textual clues and concluded that "O'Connor read and absorbed Bloy in graduate school, especially *La femme pauvre* [*The Woman Who Was Poor*]." The puzzle is solved by seeing that, although O'Connor never read the novel in its complete form, she read excerpts of it in Raïssa's 1947 collation. Schlafer, "Pilgrims of the Absolute," 61–62; Gordon, "Seeking Beauty," 79; cf. O'Connor to Brodin, in Brodin, *Présences contemporaines*. For excerpts from *La Femme pauvre* [*The Women Who was Poor*], see Bloy and R. Maritain, *Pilgrim of the Absolute*, 161–164, 167–174, 207–213, 299–301, 305–312.

Raïssa had been confronted with a basic problem. The published work for which Bloy had been most notorious in France largely consisted of his diaries.[105] They were thoroughly topical and would not have appeal to—indeed, they would not have been comprehensible to—an audience unfamiliar with turn-of-the-century French culture wars. Raïssa's daunting editorial task had been to take a voluminous body of work, excerpt brief passages from various genres—diaries, historical essays, novels, correspondence—and largely abstract them from their highly specific and time-bound contexts. Raïssa then assembled this mash-up into what eventually looked like a seamless flow of prose essays arranged by topics. This surface appearance would have been even more pronounced for the reader who did not read French and hence could not decipher the original sources in Bloy provided by Raïssa at the back of the book.[106]

As a result, the Bloy whom the twenty-two-year-old O'Connor began reading in the late spring of 1947 was indeed the author in his own words. However, it was Bloy filtered through the exacting editorial hand of Raïssa (née Oumançoff) Maritain: the Jewish Raïssa who had fled Russian pogroms as a child, converted to Catholicism under the influence of her godfather Bloy, exiled herself to New York during the Holocaust, and was now introducing her godfather, the fin de siècle Catholic Dreyfusard, to an American English-speaking audience grappling with postwar humanitarian crises. If there are pages in O'Connor that sound as though they come from Bloy's novels, that is because she had, in fact, read them—although as fragments excerpted by Raïssa and collated with nonfiction bits from diaries, letters, and essays.

On May 30, 1947, recently turned twenty-two, O'Connor recorded Bloy's devastating impact: "He is an iceberg hurled at me to break up my Titanic and I hope my Titanic will be smashed."

105. For the list of Bloy's diary publications, see Béguin, *Study in Impatience*, 23; full citations in Dubois, *Portrait of Léon Bloy*, 120–121.

106. Bloy and R. Maritain, "Sources," *Pilgrim of the Absolute*, 353–358.

Her imagery is not original; she was paraphrasing Bloy as found in Raïssa's edited *Pilgrim of the Absolute*: "I am an ocean of contempt," Bloy had written, "and I was the one who hurled the block of ice which burst the sides of the *Titanic*."[107] Just as in reading Bernanos the previous fall, O'Connor here again felt personally indicted by Bloy's fulminations against "mediocrity": "I am also mediocre of the spirit," she wrote, "but there is hope." She also appropriated Bloy's theory of vicarious suffering and mystical substitution: "What about these dead people I am living with? What about them? We who live will have to pay for their deaths. Being dead what can they do. It is for them, I presume, that the saints died."[108]

Soon after writing this entry, O'Connor graduated from Iowa and returned to Georgia for the summer, where she continued working on *Wise Blood*. In September she returned to Iowa for a semester of postgraduate studies including a seminar on "European Literature." Her next diary entry was made on Monday, September 22: "9/22 and Bloy again. It should be a great instigator of humility in me that I am so lukewarm as to need Bloy always to send me into serious thought—and even then it is not sustained very long." She noted that she had been impelled to wander into the library stacks to find Karl Pfleger's 1936 *Wrestlers with Christ*, the translated study including chapters devoted to "Bloy, the Pilgrim of the Absolute" and "[Charles] Péguy, the Good Sinner." Again Bloy's recurrent theme of "mediocrity": "Too weak to pray for suffering[,] . . . I don't want to be doomed to mediocrity in my feeling for Christ."[109]

The following day, Tuesday, September 23, O'Connor used a somewhat horrifying image, especially in light of her even-

107. Entry for May 30, 1947, in O'Connor, *Prayer Journal*, 33–34, at 33; facsimile 69–70, at 69; paraphrasing Bloy, in Bloy and R. Maritain, *Pilgrim of the Absolute*, 64.

108. Entry for May 30, 1947, in O'Connor, *Prayer Journal*, 33–34, at 33; facsimile 69–70, at 69.

109. Entry for September 22, 1947, in O'Connor, *Prayer Journal*, 35; facsimile 84–85; referencing Pfleger, *Wrestlers with Christ* (1936).

tual suffering and death from lupus. Implicitly evoking the protagonist who dies from stomach cancer in Bernanos's *Diary of a
Country Priest*, O'Connor prayed that she might receive the grace
of thinking about and wanting Christ all the time, "to have the
want driving in me, to have it like a cancer in me. It would kill
me like a cancer and that would be the Fulfillment."[110] A day later,
Wednesday, September 24, O'Connor expressed thanks for the gift
of "Catholicity" calling it God's "provision for all mediocre souls—
a tool for us." Her reference to "Bloy's statue"—that is, the figure
of Our Lady of La Salette ("She Who Weeps")—exemplifies having
read a fragment from Bloy's *Woman Who Was Poor* without, perhaps,
having known the source.[111] O'Connor reinterpreted the statue's
meaning in her own nascent incarnational terms: "[H]ow to call it?
God on earth? God as nearly as we can get to Him on earth."[112]

Finally, on Thursday, September 25, O'Connor prayed that she
might become a "mystic" without delay: "Oh Lord, I am saying, at
present I am a cheese, make me a mystic, immediately. But then
God can do that—make a mystic out of cheese.... But I would like
to be a mystic and immediately."[113] This self-image also derived

---

110. Entry for September 23, 1947, in O'Connor, *Prayer Journal*, 36; facsimile
86–87, at 86.

111. Béguin quotes the lines from *La Femme pauvre* [*The Poor Woman*] in which
Bloy recalls the first time he saw the statue at the shrine of La Salette: "What shall I
tell you? When I reached the top and saw the Mother sitting on a stone and weeping
into her hands ... I fell down at the foot of the enclosure and poured forth tears and
sobs, asking mercy of Her who was called *Omnipotentia supplex* [all-powerful inter-
cessor]." Béguin then glosses the "transfiguration" that began to take place in Bloy
following this "revelation of La Salette": "Bloy entered more fully into the experience that suffering brings nearness to God. La Salette by inspiring him with the
conviction that God suffers, and with adoration for this God who weeps, filled him
with that most profound understanding granted only to the importunity of love."
Béguin, *Study in Impatience*, 53–55.

112. Entry for September 24, 1947, in O'Connor, *Prayer Journal*, 37; facsimile
88–89, at 88.

113. Entry for September 25, 1947, in O'Connor, *Prayer Journal*, 38–39, at 38;
facsimile, 89–91, at 89. The notion of the "mystic poet" would have been rein-
forced by Wallace Fowlie's chapters on Charles Baudelaire, Paul Claudel, and "The
Poet and the Mystic," in *The Spirit of France. Studies in Modern French Literature* (Lon-

from Bloy via Béguin: after he had "passed through an agonising ordeal," Bloy had been set "more firmly in the path of mysticism." Indeed, Bloy viewed himself in this way: "I have become a kind of mystic poet, immured in the sempiternal contemplation of invisible harmonies, ravaged by all the furies of desire for God, and consumed body and soul by all the famines of earth and heaven."[114]

O'Connor's prayer journal concluded the following day: Friday, September 26, 1947. "My thoughts are so far away from God," she wrote. "He might as well not have made me. . . . There is nothing left to say of me."[115] Although O'Connor might not have had anything left to say of herself, she would soon go on to write her own "mystical" exegesis of the world-historical "Displaced Person," a figure constantly in the news of the late 1940s and early 1950s. Béguin's reading of Bloy informed her method: his "studies in symbolical exegesis" had taught him

the multiple significance of words and the allusive value of symbols. Looking below the surface, he set out to discover what each thing typified and what place it occupied in the plan of God; to fit it into the endless success of analogies which forms the secret fabric of the created world and extends mysteriously into the invisible. . . .

Thus, painfully tracing through a thousand forms "the history of the Three Persons of the Trinity," . . . Bloy makes us aware that everything is incomprehensible and forces us to marvel.[116]

In 1947—the era of DPs and the state of Israel—Bloy's vision could be seen more clearly as prophetic:

------

don: Sheed and Ward, [1944] 1945), OCLIB #426. In 1947 during her postgraduate semester that fall, O'Connor took a seminar on "European Literature." Compare Fowlie's other work published that year, a study of Charles Péguy, Georges Rouault, and Jacques Maritain, with a note on Max Jacob, the Maritains' friend who had died three years earlier in the Drancy internment camp: *Jacob's Night: The Religious Renascence in France* (New York: Sheed and Ward, 1947).

114. Béguin, *Study in Impatience*, 16; quoting Bloy at 4–5.

115. Entry for September 26, 1947, in O'Connor, *Prayer Journal*, 40; facsimile 91–92.

116. Béguin, *Study in Impatience*, 10.

[T]he exegeses of history and of the state of humanity, sustained by Bloy's inward knowledge, are becoming clear to us in the light of events. We can no longer remain blind to his wonderful views on Suffering, Poverty, the scandal of money, the destiny of the people of Israel, history as an instrument of Providence, the amazing figure of Napoleon, or the war of the nations.[117]

DPs: Symbolist Exegesis of the Commonplace

In December 1953, O'Connor gave a live reading of a first draft of "The Displaced Person" to friends. The most immediate inspiration for the story seems to have come from a group of Polish immigrants, "displaced persons," arriving in Andalusia to work the farm earlier that August. However, as seen above, the subject had made its way into the popular press as early as the July 30, 1945, issue of *Life* magazine; and into the news media as President Truman made "displaced persons" one of his postwar legislative priorities between 1945 and 1952.

Here again, 1947 stands out as exceptional. During this summer, in which O'Connor was first reading Bloy, the ship named Exodus set sail with displaced Jews headed for Palestine. The voyage provoked an international outcry when the British intercepted the vessel, blocked it from proceeding to Palestine, and returned its passengers to internment camps.[118] The more lasting effect of this incident was the creation of the state of Israel the next May and its immediate de facto recognition by the Truman administration. Congress passed the Displaced Persons Act one month later, its hand having been forced by this turn of events. The president signed it reluctantly accompanied by a strong critique. It was

---

117. Béguin, *Study in Impatience*, 11.

118. Aviva Halamish, *The Exodus Affair: Holocaust Survivors and the Struggle for Palestine*, trans. Ora Cummings (Syracuse, N.Y.: Syracuse University Press, 1998). For contemporaneous account, see Ruth Gruber, *Destination Palestine, The Story of the Haganah Ship, Exodus 1947* (New York: Current Books, 1948); cf. Gruber, *Exodus 1947: The Ship that Launched a Nation* (New York: Times Books, 1999).

insufficient, he said; moreover, it discriminated against Jews and Catholics.[119]

DPs had now become a "Catholic" cause as well as a humanitarian one. The Jesuits' *America* magazine underscored the point in July by publishing a small but dense volume co-written by Fr. William J. Gibbons, SJ: *Refugees Are People. The Plight of Europe's Displaced Persons* (1947). It included a "Statement on Displaced Persons" that had been adopted three months earlier by the National Catholic Rural Life Conference at their meeting in Des Moines, Iowa. The statement reasoned that "[s]ince many of the displaced persons are rural people, it is highly desirablbe [sic] that they be directed to the land and away from our congested cities."[120] The conference had taken place in Iowa on April 16, 1947, the week preceding Allen Tate's visit.

However, Congress's reluctant attitude fundamentally changed after 1949. In the last week of August that year, the Soviet Union exploded its first atomic bomb; a month later, Mao Zedong proclaimed the establishment of the People's Republic of China, prompting mutual American accusations of "Who lost China?" In this new geopolitical context, DPs were no longer refugees from world war; rather, they were now cold-war escapees from communist totalitarianism seeking asylum. Congress's 1950 amendment of the 1948 Displaced Persons Act took this new state of affairs into account, as did President Truman when he signed it enthusiastically. "H.R. 4567 corrects the discriminations inherent in

119. See documents related to Displaced Persons dated January 6, 1947; July 7, 1947; January 7, 1948; June 25, 1948; and October 4, 1948, at *The American Presidency Project*, accessed February 24, 2016, http://www.presidency.ucsb.edu/index.php. See also Allis Radosh and Ronald Radosh, *A Safe Haven: Harry S. Truman and the Founding of Israel* (New York: Harper, 2009); Michael J. Devine, Robert P. Watson, and Robert J. Wolz, *Israel and the Legacy of Harry S. Truman* (Kirksville, Mo.: Truman State University Press, 2008); and Michael T. Benson, *Harry S. Truman and the Founding of Israel* (Westport, Conn.: Praeger, 1997).

120. Walter Dushnyck and William J. Gibbons, SJ, *Refugees Are People. The Plight of Europe's Displaced Persons* (New York: The America Press, [July] 1947). For statement of National Catholic Rural Life Conference see Appendix 4, 74–77, at 76.

the previous act," he stated. "Now, the postwar victims of totalitarianism will be on an equal footing with earlier victims of Nazi aggression."[121]

One of these "postwar victims" is the Polish Catholic Mr. Guizac, who ends up on Mrs. McIntyre's farm in O'Connor's "Displaced Person." As the story opens, Mrs. Shortley recalls "a newsreel she had seen once of a small room piled high with bodies of dead naked people all in a heap . . . ," their legs sticking out where their arms should be.[122] The contorted image returns at the end of the story when Mr. Guizac is pinned cruciform beneath the tractor: "She could not see his face, only his feet and legs and trunk sticking out." It is evoked yet again after his spine is crushed: "Mr. Guizac's body was covered with the bent bodies of his wife and two children and by a black one"—Fr. Flynn in cassock administering extreme unction in Latin—"which hung over him, murmuring words she didn't understand."[123] As O'Connor morphs the Guizac family's heaped bodies with newsreel images of earlier victims of Nazi aggression, this refugee from world-historical Soviet totalitarianism—and now commonplace target of petty rural jealousy—is the naturalist type par excellence in Zola's bestiary: a victim of the "human, all too human" savagery haunting history.[124]

However, in the antinaturalist type of symbolist-historical

121. See documents related to Displaced Persons dated June 16, 1950 (two documents); March 24, 1952; April 14, 1952; August 9, 1952, at *The American Presidency Project*, accessed February 24, 2016, http://www.presidency.ucsb.edu/index.php. For contemporaneous works, see Frank L. Auerbach, *The Admission and Resettlement of Displaced Persons in the United States*, rev. ed. (New York: Common Council for American Unity, 1950); and George Minton and Stuart Portner, *New Americans Under the Displaced Persons Act*, Displaced Persons Commission Research Series, report no. 1 (n.p., [1952?]).

122. O'Connor, "The Displaced Person," 196. References to the Holocaust are found in three O'Connor stories: "The Displaced Person" (1954), "A Circle of Fire" (1954), and "Revelation" (1964). See Rachel Carroll, "Foreign Bodies: History and Trauma in Flannery O'Connor's 'The Displaced Person,'" *Textual Practice* 14, no. 1 (2000): 97–114.

123. O'Connor, "The Displaced Person," 234.

124. Friedrich Wilhelm Nietzsche, *Human, All Too Human: A Book for Free Spirits* [1878], trans. R. J. Hollingdale (New York: Cambridge University Press, 1986).

imagination embodied by Bloy—most especially in his exegeses of the commonplace (*exégèses des lieux communs*)—this DP both sacramentally embodies and yet points beyond himself to a vast invisible cosmic drama. Like Colonel Dreyfus, Mr. Guizac is the visible symbol of "an invisible DIVINE COURT CASE." Like the archetypal "Wandering Jew" with no homeland to which he can return, the "Displaced Person" is among the most abject of the earth.[125] Paradoxically, at least in the imaginations of Bloy and his Maritain godchildren, this abjection and hence vicarious suffering makes Mr. Guizac a privileged—perhaps even necessary—means of revelation, transfiguration, and redemption.

O'Connor embraced this symbolist-historical method in her own exegesis of the commonplace—a moment in which the everyday "co-penetrates" the world-historical and time the eternal.[126] Mrs. McIntyre, although blind to the dramatic irony, gets it half-right: "As far as I'm concerned," she says to Fr. Flynn, "Christ was just another D.P."[127] However, she cannot follow the incarnational logic to its other side and see that the D.P.—Mr. Guizac—is just another Christ, the visible temporal footprint pointing beyond himself to the co-penetrating invisible, eternal drama.

This fuller revelation and transfiguration is unveiled only for the mystic eyes of Fr. Flynn. He stares at the peacocks and stands "transfixed, his jaw slack." "Mrs. McIntyre wondered where she had ever seen such an idiotic old man. 'Christ will come like that!,' he said . . . 'The Transfiguration,' he murmured. . . . She had

125. This nineteenth-century trope gained new life in the postwar. One New York film critic wrote in 1949 that "[t]he classical concept of the wandering Jew is given a contemporary twist in the new Italian picture that opened yesterday at the Little Cine Met, 'The Wandering Jew' covers in a few brief kaleidoscopic scenes 2,000 years of Jewish persecutions, starting with the Roman sacking of Jerusalem down through the ages to the atrocities committed in the name of nazism." T. M. P., "L'Ebreo Errante (1947). Italian Picture at Little Cine Met," *The New York Times* (March 11, 1949); reviewing Goffredo Alessandrini, *The Wandering Jew* [*L'Ebreo Errante*], screenplay by Alessandrini and Flaminio Bollini (after the novel by Eugène Sue) (Rome: Cinematografica Distributori Indipendenti, 1948).

126. For "compénétration," see Schloesser, *Jazz Age Catholicism*, 270–271.

127. O'Connor, "The Displaced Person," 229.

no idea what he was talking about. 'Mr. Guizac didn't have to come here in the first place,' she said, giving him a hard look.... The cock lowered his tail and began to pick grass. 'He didn't have to come in the first place,' she repeated, emphasizing each word.... The old man smiled absently. 'He came to redeem us,' he said."[128]

128. O'Connor, "The Displaced Person," 226.

CHAPTER 2

Breaking Bodies

O'Connor and the Aesthetics of Consecration

Michael P. Murphy

George Bernanos, the great French writer (or "scribbler," as he called himself) of the twentieth-century French Catholic literary revival, wrote in the "Sermon from an Agnostic on the Feast of St. Therese of Lisieux" episode from his 1938 work *The Great Cemeteries under the Moon* the following: "Because you do not live your faith, your faith has ceased to be a living thing. It has become abstract—bodiless. Perhaps we shall find that the disincarnation of the Word of God is the real cause of all our misfortune."[1] This propensity—the tendency to idealize experience and "disincar-

1. Georges Bernanos, *The Heroic Face of Innocence: Three Stories* (New York: Eerdmans, 1998), 36.

nate" theological phenomena from it—is no less a steady feature of twenty-first-century Western culture than when Bernanos wrote it or when Flannery O'Connor might have read it in the middle of the twentieth century. It has taken various forms in history: in the Manicheanism embraced (and then rejected) by St. Augustine, in premodern heresies such as Catharism, and in the many other gnostic religious revivals that have followed since. Its more modern form was well described as the "Angelic Imagination" by O'Connor's friend, Allen Tate, who tracked its dualistic roots to the Cartesian split between mind and matter three hundred years earlier. Both Tate and O'Connor recognized the core logic of Bernanos's critique and saw through to its theological heart. The stark division between linguistic sign (*signum*) and reality (*res*) continues to challenge our ability to detect, affirm, and inhabit, finally, a physical ground for transcendent, nonphysical concepts such as mind, imagination, revelation, and belief—phenomena that most often indicate, inform, and communicate theological mystery.

But Bernanos's agnostic puts it best for our purposes: the Catholic faith is an incarnational and sacramental faith. It means next to nothing without the flesh and blood embodiment of the *Logos*, the living Word of God. O'Connor, an avid reader of Bernanos, was likewise moved by this orienting premise.[2] Because she was an artist, it fired her theological imagination, and she responded by drawing literary scenarios where complex phenomena and characters were set free to collide, their many internal

2. Bernanos's *Last Essays* were part of O'Connor's library, but her reading and integration of his work transcends the borders of this single text. Bernanos had a special resonance from O'Connor's formative days: "I have been reading Bernanos. It is so very wonderful." This entry (from November 4, 1946), likely in response to *The Diary of a Country Priest*, was her first dated entry in her recently released *A Prayer Journal* (2013). Ted Spivey also explores O'Connor's intertextual relationship with Bernanos in *Flannery O'Connor: The Woman, the Thinker, the Visionary* (Macon, Ga.: Mercer University Press, 1995), as does Paul Wilkes in "Through a Glass Darkly: The Worlds of Flannery O'Connor and George Bernanos," *Church* 6 (Fall 1990): 5–12.

and external tensions sharpened in the light and immediacy of this expansive vision. Like Bernanos and other French thinkers who reacted against the gnostic vacuum of Cartesianism (all the way back to Pascal), O'Connor never hesitated to name the source of such tensions: original sin and the "fallen-ness" of human nature—the postlapsarian "existential dualism that keeps our broken world from insight into a transcendent order of Being."[3]

In a variety of narrative admixtures, O'Connor explores how the Edenic rupture impedes intimacy with the divine and alienates human unity—all while consciously writing for an audience that lacks this conventional theological starting point. But, as importantly, her tales also contemplate the mysterious logic of divine grace that explodes on the scene under these precise conditions, even in "territory held largely by the devil."[4] That O'Connor tracks such gracious eruptions in her fiction under the light of a colder-seeming Christology, one totally devoid of sentimentality, is well known: "This notion that grace is healing omits the fact that before it heals, it cuts with the sword Christ said He came to bring."[5] But what is often overlooked is how human fallenness is divinely encompassed and consecrated in her fiction as if in a liturgical space—a literary sacramentality, like liturgy itself, which is both precise in its care and cosmic in its scope.

The task of this chapter, then, is to observe how expertly and credibly O'Connor renders such mystery in her prose to amplify the tripartite connection among incarnational, sacramental, and liturgical expressions. To this end, I first establish the structural ground for O'Connor's sacramental vision by placing it in

3. Albert Gelpi, *American Poetry after Modernism: The Power of the Word* (New York: Cambridge University Press, 2015), 51. O'Connor wrote of her collection *A Good Man Is Hard to Find* in a 1954 letter to Fitzgerald: "Here are nine stories about original sin, with my compliments"; see Flannery O'Connor, *The Habit of Being: Letters of Flannery O'Connor*, ed. Sally Fitzgerald (New York: Farrar, Straus and Giroux, 1979), 74.

4. Flannery O'Connor, *Mystery and Manners: Occasional Prose*, ed. Sally and Robert Fitzgerald (New York: Farrar, Straus and Giroux, 1969), 118.

5. O'Connor, *The Habit of Being*, 354.

orienting conversation with key French Catholics with whom O'Connor shares important theological affinities. Next, I expand this perspective by delving deeper into the dynamics of liturgical theology, particularly using the French theologian Louis Bouyer. Finally, I conclude by presenting distillations of liturgically charged moments in several of O'Connor's short stories. The objective throughout is to explore how O'Connor's sacramental imagination is not just embedded in a vague or general definition of sacramentality but is also shaped by the movements of the liturgy as she would have seen them described by Bouyer. In this way, I observe one important line in the genealogy of O'Connor's theological aesthetic—a vision that not only builds on the mystery of liturgy and the aesthetic spirit of French Catholicism but one that has also emerged as radically distinct and occupies a singular space in late modern literature.

As liturgy both recapitulates and performs a grace-in-brokenness (and is premised on participation and action, both God's and ours), close attention to its claims on dynamic unity become central in any aesthetics of consecration. Liturgical consecration amplifies a moment in history and is located precisely in the broken body of Christ. For this reason, astute attention to the liturgical quality of O'Connor's fiction discloses a vision that is both realist and unconventional—a vision that navigates the mystery of what is unseen and opens to a more textured, transcendent, and expansive cosmology. To acknowledge the liturgical shape of O'Connor's fiction, moreover—where circles are drawn around the sacred and then exploded to reveal a unique power—is also to reveal the paradox that resides at the dramatic heart of her theological aesthetics, an insight required for any comprehensive reading of O'Connor and the narrative *telos* that informs her literary imagination.[6]

6. To propose the indivisible nature of incarnation, sacrament, and liturgy is also to participate in an analogical theory of art where integrity and dynamism are held together. Taking the transcendental integrity among the true, the good, and

French Connections: Writing a Catholic Imagination

In addition to Bernanos, O'Connor was also an avid reader of other French writers, particularly those of the early-twentieth-century Catholic literary revival.[7] The members of this cohort were hyperattentive to the "iceberg" of original sin, but they were also orators of the mercy implicit in any theology of Incarnation. In her recently released *A Prayer Journal*, O'Connor meditates about "the age of The Fall" and how it affects her abilities as a developing writer who seeks to write fiction "worthy of what I ought to be." In this case, it is not Bernanos but Léon Bloy who teaches her about refining her art—particularly in regards to characterization: "These modern 'Christs' pictured on war posters & in poems—'every man is Jesus; every woman Mary' [—] would have made Bloy retch. The rest of us have lost the power to vomit."[8] As readers, this hits close to home and, like O'Connor, who truly loves her characters, we are moved to compassion. In an age of spiritual marketplaces and theological imprecision, we identify

the beautiful as a starting point (and using Pseudo-Dionysius, Jacques Maritain, and Hans Urs von Balthasar to support such a reading), I read O'Connor this way in chapter 3 of *A Theology of Criticism: Balthasar, Postmodernism, and the Catholic Imagination* (New York: Oxford University Press, 2008). The liturgical dynamic implicit therein, while inchoate, is unique in that it hopes to "activate" and connect a sacramentality that fewer critics take as foundational (or, if they do, it's a more "static" and nominal sacramentality) in O'Connor's fiction to disclose its dynamic theological quality.

    7. It is well recorded in *The Habit of Being* and elsewhere how O'Connor loved the French Catholic literary aesthetic and was formed significantly by it. As O'Connor reports in *The Habit of Being*, "I read all the Catholic novelists, Mauriac, Bernanos, Bloy, Greene, Waugh" (98). In addition, O'Connor also read Charles Péguy, Paul Claudel, Julien Green, Simone Weil, and Andre Malreaux. There are also French philosophical influences; Gabriel Marcel's theological existentialism and the French neo-Thomism of Jacques Maritain and Etienne Gilson are of such importance that they require another space for adequate comment. Of course, it goes without saying that the focus on the French in these pages in no way diminishes O'Connor's other influences.

    8. Flannery O'Connor, *A Prayer Journal* (New York: Farrar, Straus and Giroux, 2013), 35.

intimately with the pathos of her characters and recognize our-selves so clearly in them.

Perhaps this is why O'Connor "reaches back" and focuses, time and again, on the Thomistic algebra that undergirds her theological imagination: the proposition that grace builds on na-ture. As O'Connor wrote to the novelist Cecil Dawkins, "All hu-man nature vigorously resists grace because grace changes us and change is painful."[9] This insight implies tensions with precise contextual factors, which, for O'Connor, become Southern set-tings where God is ever hard at the work of graciously consecrat-ing creation even if, as she observed, it takes the form of "beat-ing matter until we find the spirit in it."[10] O'Connor, moreover, is ever-fixed on distilling the splendor of this integrative mys-tery—on drawing an aesthetic of consecration—especially at the very moments when her characters are breaking open and falling apart. As an artist with realist concerns, this is what is entailed in navigating complicated existential distances and faithfully representing *things-as-they-are*, especially important because the moments O'Connor depicts, rife with conflict and tension, also become the very seat of spiritual transformation, even if (and especially because) they present credible settings for what she called "crisis theology."[11]

In 1958, O'Connor illustrated the crisis explicitly in two letters. As "modern people," she wrote, we live in a "society where religion is bred out of us" and so believe that "man is ultimately perfectible," not by God's grace, "but by his own efforts" as a matter of course.[12]

---

9. O'Connor, *The Habit of Being*, 307.

10. O'Connor returns to this theme time and again and the phrasing is per-haps the best example of her so called "hillbilly Thomism." In a book review of Teilhard de Chardin's *The Phenomenon of Man*, she puts it more conventionally: "His is a scientific expression of what the poet attempts to do: penetrate matter until the spirit is revealed in it." See Flannery O'Connor, *The Presence of Grace, and Other Book Reviews of Flannery O'Connor*, comp. Leo Zuber, ed. Carter W. Martin (Athens: University of Georgia Press, 1983, 2008), 130.

11. O'Connor, *The Habit of Being*, 306.

12. O'Connor, *The Habit of Being*, 300, 302.

Moreover, the observation illuminates several ways that one of the most prophetic voices of the mid-twentieth-century Catholic literary revival has penetrated to an even deeper register of relevance in the "post-Christian" age. Even amid those who would dismiss the theological heart of her art as archaic, idiosyncratic, or untenable, O'Connor remains a vital interlocutor with contemporary discourses that explore how theology intersects with literature and the various modes of interpretation that engage such discourses. In this way, O'Connor becomes, for a twenty-first-century theology of art, an artist who we are only just beginning to understand—and one who is speaking to a new generation in constructive ways.

As O'Connor recognizes, the paradoxical mystery of the Incarnation of God addresses human experience most comprehensively and respects its vast complexity. *Ressourcement* theologian Henri de Lubac, also cautioning against the late modern disincarnation of God, follows this line to its logical conclusion: "Without God, without this personal and transcendent God in the world, this Spirit and Father God, who reveals himself first to Abraham, to Moses and to the prophets and who is made definitively manifest in Jesus, this God of the conscience and of reason who has scattered everywhere signs of his presence but who uncovers his whole face and compels attention with a necessary firmness only within the Christian faith, without this God the human problem, even in the structures of the earthly city, finds no solution."[13] O'Connor was an ardent reader of de Lubac, and the passage alludes to the central paradox of Christianity—that is, the condescension of God in Christ who, as William Lynch posits, "moved down into all the realities of man to get to His Father."[14] O'Connor makes strategic use of this axial paradox, and it becomes the central element that orients her fiction of "Christian Realism."[15]

13. Henri de Lubac, *Theology in History* (San Francisco: Ignatius Press, 1996), 452.

14. William Lynch, SJ, *Christ and Apollo: The Dimensions of the Literary Imagination* (Lanham, Md.: Sheed and Ward, 1960), 28.

15. The importance of "Christian Realism" as a self-conscious genre cannot

But paradox, as a sign of sacramental action, is also much more than a mere device—a crucial fact revealed by the liturgical and consecratory movement of her prose. As O'Connor observed in her 1957 review of de Lubac's *Further Paradoxes,* paradox "exists in reality before it exists in thought" and that, in their roots, "paradoxes are based on the experience of all thinking Christians."[16] In this way, we observe how O'Connor builds an aesthetic that is based not only on a normative metaphysics but one that is also so firmly constituent and historically rooted in Christian theology as well. As de Lubac posits, paradox is more than an ephemeral "thought form." Rather, he viewed paradox as fundamental for any authentic Christian theology: "Remember, after all, that the Gospel is full of paradoxes, that man himself is a living paradox, and that, according to the Fathers of the Church, the Incarnation is the supreme paradox."[17] Opposing narrative expressions (the kind we find in O'Connor's literary landscapes), perceived properly in terms of paradox, are understood neither to contradict one another nor to fuse into each other dialectically. Instead, together they point beyond themselves to the phenomenon that lies both "beneath" and "above" them. Paradox thus interpreted "does not sin against logic but is its most profound expression."[18] For O'Connor, the transcendent heart of paradox becomes more

---

be emphasized enough. O'Connor qualifies its position in a 1955 letter to Betty Hester: "I believe too that there is only one Reality and that that is the end of it, but the term, 'Christian Realism,' has become necessary for me, perhaps in a purely academic way, because I find myself in a world where everybody has his compartment, puts you in yours, shuts the door and departs. One of the awful things about writing when you are a Christian is that for you the ultimate reality is the Incarnation, the present reality is the Incarnation, and nobody believes in the Incarnation; that is, nobody in your audience. My audience are the people who think God is dead. At least these are the people I am conscious of writing for"; O'Connor, *The Habit of Being,* 92.

16. O'Connor, *The Presence of Grace,* 59.

17. Henri de Lubac, *Paradoxes of Faith,* trans. Paule Simon et al. (San Francisco: Ignatius Press, 1987), 8.

18. David L. Schindler, from the preface to Henri de Lubac's *Discovery of God* (New York: Eerdman's, 1960, 1996), x.

than a literary device: it becomes a revelatory sign of God's presence in the world.

To glean the logic of de Lubac's insights, then, is to paraphrase a principle of sacramentality that undergirds O'Connor's literary imagination: what is always and everywhere true must be brought to our attention and be embraced (or rejected) in some concrete experience at some particular time and place.[19] We need a place to hang our hats, as it were, a place where transcendent concepts are grounded in all of their attendant complication. An aesthetic of sacramentality, the kind so deftly practiced by O'Connor, animates de Lubac's insights and calls the human actor to vigilant attention. Such an aesthetic, moreover—one that explodes generatively from the mystery of the Incarnation and one that pays proper attention to history—is again becoming attractive and persuasive to thinkers of all stripes.[20]

O'Connor wrote about the relationship between literary art and theology in the context of the mid-twentieth century, an era she saw as afflicted spiritually by what she called, famously, "Christ Hauntedness."[21] O'Connor addressed this issue in a 1962

19. This version of the "Sacramental Principle" is a paraphrase of Michael Himes's famous formulation.

20. This interest is seen for instance in the writings of Milton scholar Regina Schwartz, no Orthodox Catholic, who comments, "We are still haunted by the Eucharist, haunted not only by its promise of divinity but also by its promise of justice"; see Regina Mara Schwartz, *Sacramental Poetics at the Dawn of Secularism: When God Left the World* (Stanford, Calif.: Stanford University Press, 2008), 15. Schwartz, however, does not make the move to embrace the Incarnation in a religious sense. The real presence that haunts "nonreligious" liturgy is located in the literature she studies and in the empty space left by cultural relics.

21. In one of O'Connor's many prophetic moments, she wrote the following in her 1963 essay "The Catholic Novelist in the Protestant South": "it is safe to say that while the South is hardly Christ-centered it is most certainly Christ-haunted. It is interesting that as belief in the divinity of Christ decreases, there seems to be a preoccupation with Christ figures in our fiction. What is pushed to the back of the mind makes its way forward somehow. Ghosts can be very fierce and instructive"; O'Connor, *Collected Works*, 841. It may be that—in the terrain of twenty-first-century literary criticism—we are not only "Christ-Haunted" but also haunted by the remnants of sacramental and liturgical imaginations as well. Again, see Schwartz's *Sacramental Poetics*.

letter to poet Alfred Corn: "One of the effects of modern liberal Protestantism has been gradually to turn religion into poetry and therapy, to make truth vaguer and vaguer and more and more relative, to banish intellectual distinctions, to depend on feeling instead of thought, and gradually to come to believe that God has no power, that he cannot communicate with us, cannot reveal himself to us, indeed has not done so and that religion is our own sweet invention."[22] O'Connor's strong critique of those "for whom the supernatural has become an embarrassment and for whom religion has become a department of sociology or culture or personality development" becomes an even more apt description of much thought today.[23] Many seek to reduce O'Connor's sacramental aesthetic to the cultural or the political or the psychological, as is found in some contemporary critical writing on the subject.[24]

For O'Connor, however, sacramentality is not a cultural or aesthetic novelty, but an epistemology—a way of knowing par excellence and a way of seeing the world. To this end, many critics with religious sensibilities have done well to locate and illuminate the mystery of the Incarnation of God that explains and undergirds O'Connor's sacramental imagination.[25] The best of these critics

22. O'Connor, The Habit of Being, 479.

23. Flannery O'Connor, Collected Works, ed. Sally Fitzgerald (New York: Library of America, 1988), 859.

24. For instance, see Katherine Prown, Revising Flannery O'Connor: Southern Literary Culture and the Problem of Female Authorship (Charlottesville: University Press of Virginia, 2001) and Sarah Gordon, Flannery O'Connor: The Obedient Imagination (Athens: University of Georgia Press, 2003). Both of these texts are original studies that expand the scope of O'Connor criticism, but they are also at times too dismissive of O'Connor's theological vision and often confuse theology with psychology or conflate it with the by-products of gender politics.

25. There are several excellent texts to cite in this regard dating back to second wave of O'Connor criticism in the 1980s—written by Marion Montgomery, Richard Giannone, Frederick Asals, and others. More recent scholarship indicates both amplification of and increased theological precision with the topic, and O'Connor's sacramental imagination is explored in innovative and constructive ways by Susan Srigley in Flannery O'Connor's Sacramental Art (Notre Dame, Ind.: University of Notre Dame Press, 2004); Christina Bieber Lake in William Kirkland's The Incarnational Art of Flannery O'Connor (Macon, Ga.: Mercer University

approach her work as she did—as an aesthetic of Christian realism. O'Connor wrote in a letter to Betty Hester in 1955 that there
is only "one Reality,"[26] and her fiction points to and participates
in the transcendent mystery, not of "what" is true, but of the Who
that is True, a markedly different kind of "turning to the subject"
than the kind that appears in most late modern critical discourse.
O'Connor's fiction moves from the *concretum* of her southern subjects (and subject matter) to the *concretum universal* of the Incarnate God, which is to say her sacramental imagination begins
from the ground up.

But O'Connor's structural aesthetic can also be described as
more than merely "sacramental." As introduced earlier, it is also
Eucharistic and liturgical. In this sense, her fiction often performs a kind of "Mass on the World," to employ a concept developed by French theologian and scientist Teilhard de Chardin—a
cosmic happening of spiritual gravitas that explodes from a local scene. Teilhard, whose work O'Connor respected so much that
it figures significantly in much of her writing (both fiction and
nonfiction), wrote in his posthumously published *Hymn of the
Universe*:

This restless multitude, confused or orderly, the immensity of which
terrifies us; this ocean of humanity whose slow, monotonous wave-
flows trouble the hearts even of those whose faith is most firm: it is to
this deep that I thus desire all the fibres of my being should respond. All
the things in the world to which this day will bring increase; all those
that will diminish; all those too that will die: all of them, Lord, I try to
gather into my arms, so as to hold them out to you in offering. This is the
material of my sacrifice; the only material you desire.[27]

Press, 2005); and Farrell O'Gorman in *A Peculiar Crossroads: Flannery O'Connor,
Walker Percy, and Catholic Vision in Postwar Southern Fiction* (Baton Rouge: Louisiana
State University Press, 2008).

26. O'Connor, *The Habit of Being*, 92.

27. Teilhard de Chardin, *Hymn of the Universe* (New York: Harper and Row,
1961), 20. There is prolific praise of Teilhard's singular mind in O'Connor's let-

Readers of O'Connor may immediately associate Teilhard's prayer with the startling vision that Ruby Turpin receives in "Revelation" (1964). The hierarchical lineup of souls marching to heaven, however, is not the kind of Christian convergence that Ruby expects or hopes to see on Judgment Day. Allusions to Teilhard's notion of *Christogenesis* and convergence theology are in play, and we witness more profoundly the textual resources O'Connor utilizes in developing the structure of her aesthetics of consecration.[28] The censer swings and the bells ring, as it were, at the Hallelujah point at which Ruby begins to realize that she is not the center of the universe but a mere swimmer in Teilhard's "ocean of humanity." The resolution of Ruby's crisis is to learn, suddenly and abruptly, that God loves her—loves us—not for what we do, but, as the psalmist reminds us, just for our very selves—because we belong to God and God calls us by name.[29]

Teilhard's convergence theology was attractive to O'Connor precisely because it is liturgically charged and recognizes the central need to "circumscribe," a concept I develop more fully in short order. As Teilhard muses in The *Phenomenon of Man* (1955),

---

ters—twenty entries alone where he appears in *The Habit of Being*. O'Connor referred to him as "the most important non-fiction writer" whose "direction is to face it [i.e. the modern scientific age] toward Christ"; de Chardin, *The Habit of Being*, 570, 388. O'Connor was so saturated in Teilhard's thought that it not only inspired the title to her famous short story, but it also informs her integral vision. Sally Fitzgerald notes in the introduction to Part II of *The Habit of Being* that O'Connor's acceptance of her illness even in Teilhardian terms, that of "passive diminishment." Teilhard's "Mass on the World," furthermore, contains many of the same concepts articulated in his *The Phenomenon of Man* (a book O'Connor reviewed in 1960) and *The Divine Milieu* (a book O'Connor reviewed in 1961).

28. Teilhard's *Christogenesis* is a main component of his convergence theory, which O'Connor employs explicitly in "Everything That Rises Must Converge" but elsewhere as well. This energy moves his notion of an evolutionary cosmological vision. The "Phenomenon of Man" that Teilhard describes is a meditation of human life in Christ who, as both "Point Alpha" and "Point Omega" encompasses all creation and who draw persons to himself to "Christify" the universe.

29. Cf. Psalms 139:14–15: "You created my inmost self, knit me together in my mother's womb. For so many marvels I thank you; a wonder am I, and all your works are wonders. You knew me through and through, my being held no secrets from you, when I was being formed in secret, textured in the depths of the earth."

"[h]owever narrowly the heart of an atom may be circumscribed, its realm is co-extensive, at least potentially, with that of every other atom. This strange property we will come across again, even in the human molecule."[30] To play with ideas of contextual narrowness and the biological precision of the circumscribed "human molecule"—and then to situate such phenomena onto the larger cosmological stage—discloses again the holistic scope and power of the sacramental imagination. It is noteworthy to add that O'Connor also recognized in de Lubac's *Further Paradoxes* Teilhardian strains of convergence: "the higher life rises, the richer, more interior it becomes, the more ground paradox gains," an observation that threads-in seamlessly with her developing aesthetics of consecration of which "the mystical life is its triumph."[31]

Such advents of gracious catastrophes like Ruby's are the precise "moments of grace" that thrust O'Connor's characters into new spiritual realities and are staples of O'Connor's theological aesthetic. However, to explore O'Connor's liturgical aesthetics more deeply—and to amplify the consecratory moments that are woven through so many of her pieces—it is imperative to look at another imaginative French theologian, Fr. Louis Bouyer of the Oratory.

Tending to Riven Things: Writing a Liturgical Consciousness

O'Connor read Bouyer, wrote reviews of at least three of his books, and recommended his work to her friends and correspondents. By 1960 she viewed Bouyer as "one of the most interesting theologians writing today," a thinker who was making "choice contributions to Catholic intellectual life."[32] Bouyer has a large

30. Teilhard de Chardin, *The Phenomenon of Man*, trans. Bernard Wall (New York: Harper Perennial, 1959, 1976), 41.
31. O'Connor, *The Presence of Grace*, 59.
32. O'Connor, *The Presence of Grace*, 101, 72.

scope and corpus of work and wrote about things as disparate as feminine spirituality, mysticism, and the dynamic relationship between Protestant and Catholic theologies. His approach is one that also reveals him, like de Lubac, as a member of the *ressource-ment* school, the "new" theology that returned focus to patristic sources (and much more) to retrieve the beauty of theology and to rescue it from both formulaic Scholasticism and Enlightenment abstraction. But Bouyer's most enduring scholarship was in the field of liturgical theology. Through books like *Liturgical Piety* (1954), *Christian Initiation* (1958), and *Eucharist: Theology and Spirituality of the Eucharistic Prayer* (1968), we observe specific ways that Bouyer's liturgical theology influenced not only O'Connor but also the development of a liturgical practice that would later result from Vatican II.

Bouyer's book, *Eucharist,* as one example, is an expansive, meticulously stitched study of "The Sacrament"—one that builds on his previous work and one that makes superb use of a host of historical resources.[33] According to Bouyer, the Liturgy of the Eucharist, which is ceaseless and derives from the Jewish benediction of *berakah*, is rooted in the one moment where Jesus prayed "over the bread and cup as a consecration of his body broken and his blood shed, in order to reconcile his own body."[34] The great hope—and the great work—of the Eucharist is that, by faithful participation, we all might be consecrated and that our lives be continually deepened by God "in whom we live, move, and have our being."[35] In his work, Bouyer, a Lutheran convert, counsels not only active, prayed participation as a hallmark of liturgy but also as an orientation that sees divine action outside the cir-

33. O'Connor praised Bouyer's *Christian Initiation* in a 1960 book review and owned several of his books including *The Spirit and Forms of Protestantism* (1956).

34. Louis Bouyer, *Eucharist: Theology and Spirituality of the Eucharistic Prayer*, trans. Charles Quinn (Notre Dame, Ind.: University of Notre Dame Press, 1968), 464. It is interesting to note that, given the high liturgical language of the most recent edition of the Roman Missal, Bouyer uses "cup" instead of "chalice."

35. Cf. Acts 17:28.

cumscribed confines of ritual. Liturgical participation, because it is historically rooted, is also fully open to the unseen scope of mystery of God's presence in sacramentality, a passionate and relational receptivity "in which all of our being surrenders to the Father's will revealed in his Word."[36] The center of this in liturgy is the great poetry of the Eucharistic prayer that culminates in liturgical consecration and, as Bouyer exclaims, "[s]tands out like a meteorite"—a continuing flashpoint that reveals the sacramentality of creation itself—and that we, as creatures, are the *imago Dei* and are therefore called to intimate participation in divine life. For Bouyer, along with many late modern theologians, the fruits of participation nourished by the Eucharist engender and culminate in conversion, in the very "communion" advertised and promised by the sacrament: a turning toward one another as persons-in-relationship in total concert as we all turn together, liturgically, "as one in *the* One."[37]

The mysteries that exist in formal liturgy abound, and it is striking to slow things down and make an account of what is really happening, especially in regards to Eucharist and consecration. Moreover, it is precisely in the liturgy of the Eucharist that we locate the narrative structure that constitutes O'Connor's aesthetics of consecration. In the interest of illuminating liturgical integrity, one could illustrate how movements in many of O'Connor's narratives correspond with the components that constitute not only the mass in full figure (i.e., the liturgies of both "Word" and "Eucharist") but also the multiple elements of the Eucharistic prayer itself (*thanksgiving, acclamation, oblation*, etc.).

36. Bouyer, *Eucharist*, 469. Clearly we are well into the inner mechanics of faith, but we cannot put too fine a point on it. As O'Connor wrote in 1959, "[w]hat people don't realize is how much religion costs. They think faith is a big electric blanket, when of course it is the cross. It is much harder to believe than not to believe"; O'Connor, *The Habit of Being*, 354.

37. Bouyer, *Eucharist*, 471. I note here that *conversion* finds its root in the Latin *convertere*, which means "to turn around"—another play on the implicit, structural quality of circles.

However, the main focus here is in tracking particular instances of *epiclesis* (invocation) and *anamnesis* (remembrance) in select moments of O'Connor's work—specific movements that encircle, amplify, and then institute the liturgical moment of consecration.

These moments overflow in O'Connor's fiction and are essential to track, distill, and juxtapose against one another. They are elements, rife with analogical power, that transmute her settings into circumscribed zones of transformation. More precisely, as cornerstones of sacramental theology, *anamnesis* and *epiclesis* are the specific phenomenological invocations that signal transcendent action.[38] I will show, in short order, how O'Connor integrates this metaphysical dynamic into her fiction. But it is interesting to note that Bouyer proceeds along this line, that to consecrate, in effect, is to *circumscribe*; it is to draw a giant circle around a specific moment in time that, in turn, both derives from and pushes out concentrically to the eternal.

To be sure, both O'Connor and Bouyer spend significant amounts of space contemplating the incarnational foundation of the Eucharist. For O'Connor, her famous quip "Well, if it's a symbol, to hell with it" is always interesting to quote because the cosmological stakes of the mystery are so decisively and humorously captured in her utterance. But what is perhaps more telling is what O'Connor writes in the next sentence of her 1955 letter to Betty Hester as she attempts to make deeper sense of this Eucharistic insight: "I realize now that this is all I will ever be able to

38. In section 1106 of the *Catechism of the Catholic Church*, a very fine point is put on this concept. An insight from St. John Damascene is then added to expand it: "Together with the anamnesis, the epiclesis is at the heart of each sacramental celebration, most especially of the Eucharist: 'You ask how the bread becomes the Body of Christ, and the wine ... the Blood of Christ I shall tell you: the Holy Spirit comes upon them and accomplishes what surpasses every word and thought.... Let it be enough for you to understand that it is by the Holy Spirit, just as it was of the Holy Virgin and by the Holy Spirit that the Lord, through and in himself, took flesh.'" *Catechism of the Catholic Church*, 2nd ed. (Vatican: Libreria Editrice Vaticana, 2000), http://www.vatican.va/archive/ccc_css/archive/catechism/p2s1c1a1.htm.

say about it, outside of a story, except that it is the center of existence for me; all the rest of life is expendable."[39] Likewise, for his part, Bouyer is fixed on the indispensable mystery. Is Eucharist truly circumscribed? Is it set apart and localized, bound, tamed, and corralled into a monstrance or tabernacle? Can there be Eucharistic moments outside of liturgy? What limits do we place on the Body of Christ? Although Bouyer has fairly conventional commitments about validly ordained ministers consecrating the Eucharist, he also knows a vital tradition in the church, one that embraces and conveys a blend of humility and liberation: when he as a priest consecrates, in the tradition of the apostolic *anaphoras*, he is consecrating "[i]nsofar as he can"—insofar as he is able, for, "the consecrator of all of these eucharists is always Christ alone, the Word made flesh."[40] This provision is also central in any Catholic theology of art and serves as a resource in mystery from which O'Connor continually draws.

Mass on the World I: Burning Our Virtues Clean

Still, that O'Connor, as an orthodox Catholic, did not seek to supplant formal liturgy and sacrament to be liturgical and sacramental in her art is well known. Her chief contribution to literature is a narrative practice that is a theological aesthetic—one in which her literary art is called upon to communicate, among many other things, the performative power of liturgy in its evocation of mystery. In O'Connor, the circle expands, and the mystery that is usually circumscribed within the mass, or confined in the chapel monstrance, is vastly enlarged and creatively reconfigured. The physical architecture of O'Connor's aesthetics of consecration, moreover, is described well by a living and nurturing geometry. Lines and circles (but mostly circles) become the elements that signal and bear the literary freight of transformative moments.

39. O'Connor, *The Habit of Being*, 124.
40. Bouyer, *Eucharist*, 3, 467.

Circularity figures prominently in so many stories: woods and clearings, suns and moons, eyes and circular eyeglasses. Hats, hearts, and circles drawn in the red Georgia soil.

To create a circumscribed zone in her short story "Revelation," O'Connor makes excellent use of echo, the audible and resonant circularity of uttered speech. Late in the story, the *epiclesis* initiated and secured ("What do you send me a message like that for?"), Ruby is nudged closer to the consecratory moment. Her interior tally of why she is better than the "trash," "niggers," and snuff-spitting-good-for-nothings[41] serves as the upside-down *anamnesis*, a remembrance not of the Paschal sacrifice of God but of her own deeds, the deeds of a self-satisfied narcissist who lacks the faculty of authentic empathy. Ruby's anger increases, and the space becomes circumscribed by the sound waves of her vocalized complaints as they bounce violently off the landscape: "'Go on,' she yelled, 'call me a hog! Call me a hog again. From hell. Call me a wart hog from hell. Put that bottom rail on top. There'll still be a top and a bottom!' A garbled echo returned to her. A final surge of fury shook her, and she roared, 'Who do you think you are?'"[42]

By no means a rhetorical question, her query transcends the setting and creates a dialogical moment that carries "over the pasture and across the highway and the cotton field and returned to her clearly like an answer from beyond the wood,"[43] the courtesy of a divine reply that asks, in no uncertain terms, "Who do you think you are, [Ruby]?" The work of the sacramental echo chamber is completed, and there can be no language in the consecratory moment, only silence: "She opened her mouth but no sound came out of it." Ruby finds the truth of things in this moment of revelation—that she is both a sinner and saved, that she is both a bottom rail and a top, and that she is both hog and human—para-

41. O'Connor, *Collected Works*, 652.
42. O'Connor, *Collected Works*, 653
43. O'Connor, *Collected Works*, 653.

doxes that carry the cargo of divine mystery. God encircles Ruby at the moment when she fully identifies with her doppelgänger, the old sow, who has settled in the corner of the pig parlor. The sow, resigned and humble, is "grunting softly" and blessing, as it were, the childless Ruby; all the other hogs encircle the sow and "pant with the secret life" that irradiates and enfolds the space in a glow of red light. All is encompassed by the great silence of the Word "for five or six minutes" until the silence gives way to Ruby's famous vision—the "vast swinging bridge extending upward from the earth through a field of living fire," where people like her and her husband Claud get their virtues burned clean while the "freaks" dance and proceed before them through the pearly gates.[44] The message, finding its mark, is then enriched by the theological naturalism of a consecrated music: "invisible cricket choruses" striking up the "Hallelujah" that encircles the setting in a reoriented sonic loop and complete the vision. Incantations of gratitude—prayers offered over Ruby's exposed brokenness— "sung upward into the starry field" from the gloaming of the day.[45]

Mass on the World II: A Square in the Circle

Her earlier story "A Good Man Is Hard to Find" (1955) is a parody of circumscription, but the consecration entailed by it is as powerfully credible as the "hieratic" sounds and visions that O'Connor draws in "Revelation." Moreover, the physical act of drawing is uniquely important to the tale and can be viewed as another central texture of O'Connor's art. O'Connor was also a gifted visual artist who loved to draw and paint, and her aesthetics of consecration relies on baroque-seeming depictions because, famously, "[t]he novelist with Christian concerns will find in modern life distortions which are repugnant to him. . . . When you can assume that your audience holds the same beliefs you do,

44. O'Connor, *Collected Works*, 653–654.
45. O'Connor, *Collected Works*, 654.

you can relax a little and use more normal ways of talking to it; when you have to assume that it does not, then you have to make your vision apparent by shock—to the hard of hearing you shout, and for the almost blind you draw large and startling figures."[46]

In the story, O'Connor draws a large and startling consecration presided over by a kind of antipriest, "the Misfit." This parody of liturgical consecration, however, is no black mass; rather, it becomes an expression of O'Connor's larger concern, one that depicts the world as off-kilter and nihilistic because "a distorted image of Christ is better than no image at all."[47] The *epiclesis* in "A Good Man Is Hard to Find" is performed by the Misfit when he draws a circle in the ground (like Jesus) but with "the butt of his gun" (unlike Jesus).[48] He then speaks inverted words of liturgical *anamnesis*: "'Jesus was the only One that ever raised the dead,' The Misfit continued, 'and He shouldn't have done it. He thown everything off balance. If He did what He said, then it's nothing for you to do but thow away everything and follow Him, and if He didn't, then it's nothing for you to do but enjoy the few minutes you got left the best way you can—by killing somebody or burning down his house or doing some other meanness to him. No pleasure but meanness,' he said and his voice had become almost a snarl."[49] The snarl reveals the implicit acknowledgment that there is a crisis of faith, to put it mildly: "'I wasn't there so I can't say He didn't,' The Misfit said. 'I wisht I had of been there,' he said, hitting the ground with his fist."[50] The admission also serves a double effect proper to sacramental art. First, it is an implicit acknowledgment that the Misfit has closed himself off to the inner harmonies that engender spiritual fitness; second, it discloses that, in his gnawing memory, he knows the stakes of

---

46. O'Connor, *Collected Works*, 805.

47. Flannery O'Connor, "The Catholic Novelist in the Protestant South," in *Collected Works*, ed. Sally Fitzgerald (New York: Library of America, 1988), 859.

48. O'Connor, *Collected Works*, 148.

49. O'Connor, *Collected Works*, 152.

50. O'Connor, *Collected Works*, 152.

the death of God but that the void it creates is too much to admit to, let alone bear. The second end of the proposition, the Misfit's hardened rage at God's perceived abandonment and his mounting incredulity at the empty space left behind, encapsulates O'Connor's concept of "Christ Hauntedness" mentioned earlier and serves as a choice literary example of the kind of postmodern spiritual wound alluded to in the first part of this chapter.

In any case, O'Connor's Misfit is an exemplary late modern subject in that, by his own volition, he is closed to grace and prefers his own devices. The result is not the psychic woundedness of anxiety or depression, as in most late modern cases, but unbridled anger that leads to serial violence: "'It ain't right I wasn't there because if I had of been there I would of known. Listen lady,' he said in a high voice, 'if I had of been there I would of known and I wouldn't be like I am now.'" The grandmother, who through this encounter sees (and feels) the truth for the first time in years, reaches out to enfold this lost lamb in a loving embrace. She speaks, in some newly found tongue: "Why your one of my babies, you're one of my own children."[51] But this circle is not the kind the Misfit wants, and he immediately recoils from her touch, punctuating his fury and his rejection of a love offered by shooting a dark trinity of bullets into the grandmother's transformed heart.

In a fallen world and from his own brokenness, the Misfit knows "it's no real pleasure in life." But this state also reveals a subtle transformation wrought by the liturgical dynamic implicit in the story's structure, one that both decisively moves the narrative and at the same time reveals the presence of grace cracking the Misfit's protective shell. Before the grandmother's gesture of love, there was for the Misfit "no pleasure but meanness"; at the end of the story, he decides that "it's no real pleasure in life."[52] The subtle shift in grammar indicates a germ of grace taking hold, and the reader too recognizes full well that, while the grandmother

51. O'Connor, *Collected Works*, 152.
52. O'Connor, *Collected Works*, 152–153.

experiences the gracious phenomenon of authentic, redemptive love, for the Misfit, the plot is only beginning to thicken.

Mass on the World III: The Circle in the Circle

The most sustained example of consecration-in-circularity occurs in "Greenleaf" (1956), and the short story is propelled by so many circles in their various forms, sizes, and guises that one begins to lose count. Mrs. May is pursued by a scrub bull (masquerading as a Song of Songs–type lover stag) from the very beginning, and the "gentleman" creature draws the circle tighter around her as the narrative unfolds. Mr. and Mrs. Greenleaf, on the other hand, are consecrated in de facto priestly roles. Mrs. Greenleaf is ever trying to encircle the earth in her apostolate of prayer, "a huge human mound, her legs and arms spread out as if she were trying to wrap them around the earth."[53] Mr. Greenleaf, with a face "shaped like a rough chalice," has a deeper sense of the liturgy unfolding around him, embodying it—the kind of man who walks "on the perimeter of some invisible circle, and if you wanted to look him in the face, you had to get in front of him."[54] He encircles the scrub bull throughout the story because he is singularly aware of its feral, mysterious power.

Silent moments of *epiclesis* prepare Mrs. May, quite literally, for *compunction* and the unique violence that catalyzes her transformative encounter. She drives to her outdoor altar, a place circumscribed for her at "the center of the pasture."[55] She sits on her bumper and closes her eyes, "the red-hot sun" shining and the "white light" forcing her eyes shut so she can begin to remember why she is "so tired." The *anamnesis* is invoked by Mrs. May with signature pride: "she was tired because she had been working continuously for fifteen years" while the shiftless Greenleafs

53. O'Connor, *Collected Works*, 507.
54. O'Connor, *Collected Works*, 503.
55. O'Connor, *Collected Works*, 522.

were "loitering" with their useless marathons of prayer. The scene is now set for an unimaginable consecration, the bull approaching with a "gay almost rocking gait as if he were overjoyed to find her again."[56] He bounds on Mrs. May—fixed and unswerving—in a "violent black streak." Distances are suddenly transmuted and laid flat; the "green arena encircled almost entirely by woods" is imbued with the atmosphere of dramatic tension. Implacable, the bull embraces her, "like a wild tormented lover," and bores in, one horn piercing her heart and the other closing her in the circle of an "unbreakable grip." The last thing she sees is Mr. Greenleaf approaching "on the outside of some invisible circle" before he shoots four bullets into the sacramentally charged animal. The last vision imparted to the reader, on the other hand, accesses the heart of the Eucharist, foreshadowed almost playfully (and, again, with full attention on the notion of "compunction" that drives the story) in the first movement of the narrative by Mrs. Greenleaf's prayerful invocation: "Oh, Jesus, stab me in the heart." Mrs. May's punctured heart elicits a kind of a postcommunion insight, uttered intimately from a would-be altar of God: "she seemed, when Mr. Greenleaf reached her, to be bent over whispering some last discovery into the animal's ear"[57] that might well have been "Oh Jesus, stab us in the heart so that, from our brokenness, we may offer you our pride. Amen."[58]

In the Eucharistic liturgy, after the sacrament is consecrated it is also broken to be shared. O'Connor amplifies this aspect of the liturgical drama in two later stories in ways that show both theological maturity and ironic humor. In her literary characterizations of two very different protagonists possessed of a similar problem—Julian in "Everything That Rises Must Converge" (1965) and O. E. Parker in "Parker's Back" (1965)—we observe

56. O'Connor, *Collected Works*, 523.
57. O'Connor, *Collected Works*, 522–524.
58. Perhaps the discovery is, in the spirit of St. Therese of Lisieux, "Only God is sufficient."

other variations of an aesthetic of consecration. Julian, an ineffectual intellectual, wants to write but sells typewriters instead; O. E., aimless and angry, likes to be written on (tattooed, that is, and therefore, the story has become a favorite of a new generation of inked-up readers), but he has yet to get true sense of the depths that images entail, especially the *imago Dei*, on which, unbeknownst to him, he is already physically and spiritually inscribed. Both are assailed by fear, pride, and alienation and only begin to recollect themselves when broken open by crisis. The spiritual tonic that follows, not surprisingly, is a slow cure and generates from the process of dying-to-self so that, paradoxically, the self (i.e., the person) may be restored. By naming—and being called by name—each protagonist begins the hardscrabble process of spiritual reorientation. Julian cries "Momma, Momma," speaking properly to his mother for the first time in years, restoring right relationship just as she strokes-out on the sidewalk, "postponing from moment to moment his entry into the world of guilt and sorrow."[59] O. E., in response to his rightfully spooked bride, speaks, finally, his own name: "Obadiah Elihue"—recalling his baptism, reclaiming a regal name, and acknowledging, in some small way, the vocation that befits such a moniker. He leans against a tree, the gnostic wedge having been beaten out of him by his broom-wielding wife, and cries "like a baby."[60] Such suffering cracks the tablet open and helps to recover the intimacies—hard and soft—proper to authentic relationality and the humanity of Christian realism.

Mercy Street: A Liturgical Consummation of Fiction

To be encircled. To be broken open. To be written upon. O'Connor gives readers a sacramental aesthetics that recapitulates and extends the liturgical mystery of Bouyer's great insight: the conse-

59. O'Connor, *Collected Works*, 500.
60. O'Connor, *Collected Works*, 675.

crator of all of these Eucharists is always Christ alone, the Word
made flesh for, as Jesus prayed, "I consecrate myself for them, so
that they also may be consecrated in truth ... so that they may all
be one, as you, Father, are in me and I in you, that they also may
be in us."[61]

Under this light, we think again with Bernanos's agnostic
about the unique power of incarnational presence and sacramental awareness, about how God writes consecration on all of creation and encompasses it in a liturgical reality. In a rare setting
in which an explicitly Catholic practice plays a role, O'Connor
provides a most illustrative literary text:

> The child knelt down between her mother and the nun and they were
> well into the "Tantum Ergo" before her ugly thoughts stopped and she
> began to realize that she was in the presence of God. Hep me not to be
> so mean, she began mechanically. Hep me not to give her so much sass.
> Hep me not to talk like I do. Her mind began to get quiet and then empty
> but when the priest raised the monstrance with the Host shining ivory-
> colored in the center of it, she was thinking of the tent at the fair that
> had the freak in it. The freak was saying, "I don't dispute hit. This is the
> way He wanted me to be."[62]

This episode in "A Temple of the Holy Ghost" (1954) is the only
space in her fiction where O'Connor sets action not only in a
Catholic ritual but also in the circumscribed space of Eucharistic mystery. This carries weight; it also carries with it another
important inscription of the *imago Dei*, this time on a proud and
sassy little girl, perhaps a Ruby Turpin or a Mrs. May in training:
"[T]he big nun swooped down on her mischievously and nearly
smothered her in the black habit, mashing the side of her face
into the crucifix hitched onto her belt and then holding her off
and looking at her with her little periwinkle eyes."[63] The body of
Christ writes on the soul in the same moment that the image of

61. John 17:19, 21.
62. O'Connor, *Collected Works*, 208–209.
63. O'Connor, *Collected Works*, 209.

Christ is impressed on the soft cheek of the child. It smarts and stings, of course, precisely because it is an inscription that lasts.

O'Connor's wide exploration of the aesthetics of consecration pulsates with authenticity precisely because it artistically circumscribes and remains faithful to the inner vitality of both the cosmic event and the liturgical act from which the aesthetic vision derives and draws life. O'Connor's literary imagination is truly Eucharistic because it stares unflinchingly at the scope of what can be experienced—the delight of being incarnated, the complexity of sacramental awareness, the audacity of paschal trial, and the pathos of suffering—and finds within it the unity of its liturgical heart. O'Connor, time and again, enacts a pastoral approach, shepherding her readers into the full circumscription of transformative concern. What's more is that, in her call to expose our more pedestrian notions of faith and belief, O'Connor also addresses the legitimate doubt that attends any age, postmodern or otherwise—an exercise that makes a refreshing space for one to "dwell" (i.e., live authentically and unsentimentally in the rich mystery of life). "Faith comes and goes," wrote O'Connor in 1961. "[I]t rises and falls like the tides of an invisible ocean. If it is presumptuous to think that faith will stay with you forever, it is just as presumptuous to think that unbelief will."[64]

So what do we make of Flannery O'Connor's aesthetics of consecration? It is Teilhard and Bouyer to be sure. And it is DeLubac who, along with O'Connor, reminds us that without a vision of "charity" that transcends (and the fully inhabited liturgical imagination that grounds such a vision), "the human problem, even in the structures of the earthly city, find[s] no solution."[65] And it is Bernanos and St. Therese. "Grace is everywhere" says Bernanos's country priest as he dies—in loving homage to St. Therese of Lisieux, who said the same thing. The Grace of God, finally, encom-

---

64. O'Connor, *The Habit of Being*, 452.
65. De Lubac, *Theology in History*, 453.

passes all. The rest of us are doing the good work of consecration, insofar as we are able.

> For it was fitting that he,
> for whom and through whom all things exist . . .
> He who consecrates and those who are being consecrated
> all have one origin.
> Therefore, he is not ashamed to call them "brothers."[66]

66. Hebrews 2:10–11.

CHAPTER 3

Mysterious Heart

Maritain, Mauriac, Chrétien, and O'Connor
on the Fictional Knowledge of Others

Stephen E. Lewis

In his 1925 book *Trois réformateurs* (*Three Reformers: Luther, Descartes, Rousseau*), in the section devoted to Jean-Jacques Rousseau, Jacques Maritain denounced the modern fiction writer's "shameless" claim to provide the reader with knowledge of the secret and innermost interiority of a human being's "heart," in the biblical sense of the term. Such knowledge of another's heart, writes Maritain, is "hidden from the angels, and open only to the priestly knowledge [*la science sacerdotale*] of Christ." Maritain continues: "A Freud to-day attempts to violate [these secrets] by psychological tricks. Christ looked into the eyes of the adulterous woman and pierced to the very depths; He alone could do so without stain. Every novelist reads shamelessly in those poor eyes, and leads his reader to the show."[1] The Catholic novelist François Mauriac acknowledged the "serious [*grave*]" and "most unsettling [*rien de plus troublant*]" import of Maritain's point, and felt compelled to grapple with it and respond, ultimately doing so in his 1928 book *Le Roman* (*The Novel*).[2] There, Mauriac agrees that the contemporary novelist is bent on violating the secrets of the human heart, but, he claims, the work of the best modern novelists—he mentions his own fiction, as well as that of Gide, Joyce, Colette, Morand, and de Lacretelle but singles out Dostoevsky and Proust—proves that "in violating what is most secret in the human being, we will advance in our knowledge of him further even than the geniuses who preceded us"; the best sort of modern novelist, writes Mauriac, "dare[s] to read the expression in the poorest eyes, because nothing makes us indignant, nothing disgusts us that is human."[3]

Contemporary philosopher Jean-Louis Chrétien registers this debate in his 2009 study of the rendering of consciousness in the modern novel, titled *Conscience et roman, I: La conscience au grand jour* (*Consciousness and the Novel, Vol. I: Consciousness in the Light of Day*), and notes that one of its most interesting aspects is that it opposes two fervent Christians and two possibilities or styles of Christian engagement with narrative art.[4]

1. Jacques Maritain, *Three Reformers: Luther, Descartes, Rousseau*, [no translator indicated] (London: Sheed and Ward, 1928, 1947), 119 (modified). For the original French, see Jacques Maritain, *Trois réformateurs* (Paris: Plon-Nourrit et cie, 1925), 170; cf. Jacques et Raïssa Maritain, *Oeuvres complètes*, vol. 3 (Fribourg [Switzerland] and Paris: Editions Universitaires Fribourg/Editions Saint-Paul, 1984), 551–552.

2. François Mauriac, *Oeuvres romanesques et théâtrales complètes*, ed. Jacques Petit, vol. 2 (Paris: Gallimard, Bibliothèque de la Pléiade, 1979), 757–758. Subsequent citations of this book are signaled by the abbreviation ORTCII. Translations are my own unless otherwise indicated.

3. Mauriac, ORTCII, 757, 761.

4. Jean-Louis Chrétien, *Conscience et roman, I: La conscience au grand jour* (Paris: Editions de Minuit, 2009), 16–18. The second volume of Chrétien's study is titled *Conscience et roman, II: La conscience à mi-voix* (Paris: Editions de Minuit, 2011). For

In what follows, I wish to show how Flannery O'Connor's fiction displays a critical engagement with the question of the fate of the "secrets of the heart" in modern fiction, as it was set out in this debate between Maritain and Mauriac and as it has been subsequently deepened by Chrétien.[5] Narration, and in particular the relationship of the narrator to the often violent humiliation of O'Connor's fictional characters, has, of course, been a major concern in several excellent scholarly studies of O'Connor's fiction.[6] But I want to suggest that an approach to O'Connor's fiction like the one undertaken here—one that focuses on the question of the fate of the "secrets of the heart"—holds some significant benefits, precisely because it is clearly grounded in a Catholic Christian discussion of narrative art that was alive and interest-

---

further background on the Maritain–Mauriac debate, see Philippe van den Heede, *Réalisme et vérité dans la littérature. Réponses catholiques: Léopold Levaux et Jacques Maritain* (Fribourg [Switzerland]: Academic Press Fribourg, 2006), 196–203.

5. A note on the use of the adjective *modern* in this essay: the adjective's meaning differs somewhat among the three French authors concerned, and in my use in this chapter, I follow Chrétien's usage. For Maritain and Mauriac, *modern* means "post-Balzacian" fiction, including Mauriac's own, with special reference to Proust as well as Dostoevsky. Chrétien's study, which is guided throughout by his attention to various forms of *cardiognosie* (see my discussion and note 17 of this chapter), focuses in volume I principally, but not exclusively, on the various forms of interior monologue found in Stendhal, Balzac, Hugo, Woolf, Faulkner, and Beckett whereas in volume II he directs his attention to the techniques of narration, especially free indirect style (*style indirect libre*), as developed and perfected by Flaubert and James. Thus, when reference is made in this essay to "modern fiction," the reader should understand that we are talking about a wide range of literary efforts and techniques undertaken to represent human consciousness in fiction that probably first takes decisive form in Stendhal's *Le Rouge et le noir* (1830). The suggestion here is that Chrétien's focus, as developed in part out of the debate sketched between Maritain and Mauriac but also in dialogue with many other sources, is a valuable tool for analyzing what is at stake in the fictional representation of human consciousness—in O'Connor, certainly, but also in the work of virtually any fiction writer of the last two hundred years.

6. Provocative discussions of O'Connor's narration are to be found especially in Robert H. Brinkmeyer Jr., *The Art and Vision of Flannery O'Connor* (Baton Rouge: Louisiana State University Press, 1989); Donald E. Hardy, *Narrating Knowledge in Flannery O'Connor's Fiction* (Columbia: University of South Carolina Press, 2003); and Christina Bieber Lake, *The Incarnational Art of Flannery O'Connor* (Macon, Ga.: Mercer University Press, 2005).

ing to O'Connor herself. Thus, its pertinence to the fiction does
not need to be established in an overly speculative fashion. Indeed, O'Connor's reading, on one hand, and her interactions with
her friend and reader Caroline Gordon, on the other, show that
O'Connor herself absorbed what was at stake in the Maritain–
Mauriac debate in both direct and indirect ways.

In terms of direct knowledge, we can confidently conclude
that, although O'Connor may not have read Maritain's *Three Reformers* and could not have read Mauriac's *Le Roman* (which, as far
as I have been able to determine, has never been translated into
English), she did read Mauriac's book *God and Mammon*, published in French two years after his *Le Roman*, and first published
in English translation in 1936, as well as Maritain's *Art and Scholasticism*, originally published in French in 1920, second edition
1927, with an American translation of the second edition in 1930.
Mauriac's *God and Mammon* continues the debate with Maritain
about the secrets of the heart by shifting it toward the question of
"the novelist's responsibility" with regard to the literary depic-
tion of evil. In *God and Mammon*, Mauriac quotes a sentence from
Maritain's second edition of *Art and Scholasticism* that sets up the
question in the following terms:

"The essential point," [Maritain] says, "is not to know whether a novelist may or may not portray a given aspect of evil. The essential point is
to know at what altitude he is when he makes this portrayal and whether
his art and his soul are pure enough and strong enough to make it without conniving at it. The more the modern novel plunges into human
misery, the more are superhuman virtues demanded from the novelist." . . . As far as the novel is concerned, Jacques Maritain has stopped at
the old naturalistic ideas. It is a condition of art that the novelist should
connive at the subject of his creation, in spite of Maritain's warning, for
the real novelist is not an observer, but a creator of fictitious life. It is
not his function to observe life, but to create it. He brings living people
into the word; he does not observe them from some lofty vantage point.
He even confuses and, in a way, loses his own personality in the subject

of this creation. He is one with his creation, and his identification with it is pushed so far that he actually becomes his creation.[7]

For Mauriac, modern fiction requires the novelist to risk great intimacy with his or her characters, but to do so does not inevitably involve overstepping or violating a boundary and falling into damnation, as Maritain seems to imply in *Art et scolastique* and quite bluntly states in *Trois réformateurs*. At the conclusion of this particular chapter of *God and Mammon*, Mauriac returns to Maritain's argument, countering that "the saints advance in the double knowledge of God and of their own hearts," and as a consequence, they come to know their own wretchedness and "naturally" begin to humble themselves.[8] Thus, the "superhuman virtues" that Maritain invoked as necessary to the modern novelist who delves into the representation of sin often become God's gift to him, if he is receptive: "There is no doubt that our books have a deep resemblance to ourselves, and we can quite rightly be judged and condemned by them.... People of my calibre complicate the 'drama of the Catholic novelist.' The humblest priest would tell me, like Maritain: 'Be pure, become pure, and your work too will have a reflection in heaven. Begin by purifying the source and those who drink of the water cannot be sick.' And I give the last word to the priest."[9] Several of O'Connor's letters

7. François Mauriac, *God and Mammon* [no translator indicated] (London: Sheed and Ward, 1946), 56, 57; ORTCII, 815, 816. The passage that Mauriac quotes from Maritain's *Art et scolastique* only appears in Maritain's book starting with the second edition of 1927, from which the English translation owned by O'Connor was made (the third and definitive French edition was published in 1935 and the first in 1920); see *Art et scolastique* (Paris: Art catholique, 1920, 1947), 233–234, n163. In O'Connor's copy of the English translation, the passage is located in note 154: Jacques Maritain, *Art and Scholasticism: With Other Essays*, trans. J. F. Scanlan (New York: Charles Scribner's Sons, 1930), 224–225. (The book is listed as part of O'Connor's library in Arthur F. Kinney, *Flannery O'Connor's Library: Resources of Being* [Athens: The University of Georgia Press, 1985], 93.) See also Jacques and Raïssa Maritain, *Oeuvres complètes*, vol. 1 (Fribourg [Switzerland] and Paris: Editions Universitaires Fribourg/Editions Saint-Paul, 1982), 786.

8. Mauriac, *God and Mammon*, 61, trans. modified; ORTC II, 818.

9. Mauriac, *God and Mammon*, 63; ORTCII, 820.

make clear that *God and Mammon*'s discussion of the "novelist's responsibility" and, with it, the underlying question of the availability of the "secrets of the heart" to narration, contributed profoundly to O'Connor's own thinking about the ultimate meaning and significance of fiction writing—especially indicative of this is her letter of March 10, 1956, to Eileen Hall.[10]

Indirect evidence suggesting the pertinence for O'Connor of the question of the "secrets of the heart" can be found in her discussions about narration with Caroline Gordon. As Gordon's writings on narration as well as certain of her letters to O'Connor make clear, she always taught that the writer's decision about how to narrate a fiction necessarily involves questions of authority and truth. Like her mentor Gordon, O'Connor finds the aesthetics of narration to be closely bound with ultimate questions of artistic truth and the author's loyalty to reality.[11]

In moving forward, then, I propose to deepen our thinking about the issues raised by the Maritain–Mauriac debate about fictional access to the secrets of the heart with the help of Jean-

10. Flannery O'Connor, *The Habit of Being: Letters of Flannery O'Connor*, ed. Sally Fitzgerald (New York: Farrar, Straus and Giroux, 1979), 143–144. Other references to this discussion outlined above from Mauriac's *God and Mammon* occur at 213 and 360.

11. Caroline Gordon, *How to Read a Novel* (New York: The Viking Press, 1953, 1957, 1964). On narrative authority, see, for example, chapter 5, "The Center of Vision," 72–95; on loyalty to reality, chapter 11, "The Novelist and His World," 192–219. Brad Gooch, *Flannery: A Life of Flannery O'Connor* (New York: Little, Brown and Company, 2009), 253–255, discusses Caroline Gordon's correspondence with O'Connor having to do with narrative revisions to several of the stories O'Connor would include in her 1955 collection *A Good Man is Hard to Find, and Other Stories*. Benjamin B. Alexander has kindly shared with me a copy of one of these letters (undated but written some time in 1954 or early 1955, and drawn from the Sally Fitzgerald papers, Robert Woodruff Library, Emory University, Atlanta, Georgia), in which Caroline Gordon comments on a draft of O'Connor's story "The Artificial Nigger." Regarding a sentence describing Mr. Head, taken from what would become the third paragraph in the final version of the story, she urges O'Connor: "We don't want [Mr. Head] or his vocabulary or even his thought here. We want to see him, at the beginning of this story, as God sees him." Thus the issue of narrative "omniscience," in a form relative to the Maritain–Mauriac debate, is clearly at the center of their conversation.

Louis Chrétien, thereby drawing from and carrying forward Christian thinking about subjectivity and the ethics surrounding its representation in and alteration through narrative art; in this way, we shall carry on cultural work in a manner very much in keeping with O'Connor's own manner of working.

To give a further sense of what is at stake in the Maritain–Mauriac debate, I next highlight certain features of Chrétien's argument. Then I look at how this background helps us to make sense of central dramatic aspects of the stories "Good Country People" and "The Artificial Nigger" and of a scene central to the novel *The Violent Bear It Away*. Indeed, it becomes clear as we allow this perspective to shape our reading that the fate of the "the heart" constitutes the central dramatic focus of much of O'Connor's fiction.

In *Conscience et roman, tome I: La conscience au grand jour (Consciousness and the Novel, Vol. 1: Consciousness in Broad Daylight)*, Jean-Louis Chrétien claims that the new level of intimacy with the heart's secrets found in modern fiction (generally speaking, fiction since the mid-nineteenth century) became possible only as a result of a complex relationship that developed over time between, on one hand, narrative practice—the fictional techniques that produce in the reader the experience of feeling "as if" he or she *is* a character—and, on the other, the biblical understanding of what it is to be a human creature of God, that is, a created being endowed with what the Bible calls "the heart."

How does the biblical "heart" enter in here? In the Bible, the heart is the seat of human intelligence and volition, and its depths and contours are known by God alone, and never by man, unless God chooses to give him such knowledge.[12] Indeed, in the

12. Biblical passages that evoke the heart as "the depths of one's being, where the person decides for or against God" (*Catechism of the Catholic Church*, no. 368), include Deuteronomy 29:3; Psalms 44:20–21; Psalms 7:9; Psalms 25:2; Jeremiah 11:20, 17:9–10, 31:33; Isaiah 29:13; Ezekiel 36:26; Matthew 6:21; Mark 7:19, 21; and Mark 12:30=Matthew 22:37=Luke 10:27=Deuteronomy 6:4; Luke 8:15; Romans 5:5; 1 Corinthians 14:25; Acts 1:24; and Acts 15:8.

Bible a human being cannot even know the depths of her own heart—St. Augustine, among others, witnesses eloquently and often to this biblical anthropological insight.[13]

Yet, in modern fiction, it is precisely this secret consciousness, this "heart," to which the reader is given fictional access. The access is typically given not only to the consciousness and perceptions of a character as these appear to the character him- or herself; frequently, often through irony, access is given to the thoughts, feelings, and desires that the character is unable or unwilling to acknowledge (readers of O'Connor's fiction recognize this experience). Thus, the reader is frequently put into the position of judging the "heart" of the character, something that is, biblically speaking, the prerogative of God alone.[14] As Chrétien puts it, "[t]he interiority explored by the modern novel thus has a theological and biblical origin. The biblical 'heart' is its condition of possibility (accounting, of course, for the deepening that the 'heart' underwent in the course of many centuries)."[15]

For most readers, the experience of feeling as if one is inside, or holding a commanding grasp of, the consciousness of each of a host of characters present in the world that a fiction offers is one of the primary pleasures gained in reading a modern novel or short story. We are so used to this level of fictional intimacy with another's consciousness that it may be useful to take stock for a moment of just how radical modern narratives are in this regard and, thus, how radical our reading experience has become. Chré-

---

13. Recall, for instance, *Confessions* X.v.7, where the saint writes, "[Y]et is there something of man which 'the spirit of man which is in him' itself knows not.... I will confess also what I know not concerning myself." See St. Augustine, *Confessions*, trans. Henry Chadwick (Oxford: Oxford World's Classics, 1992, 2008), 182 (translation modified). Chrétien, *Conscience et roman I*, 26–27, offers several examples from various texts of St. Augustine; see also Jean-Luc Marion's incisive discussion of the central place of human unknowability to the self in St. Augustine's thought: Jean-Luc Marion, *Negative Certainties*, trans. Stephen E. Lewis (Chicago: University of Chicago Press, 2015), especially 15–21.

14. Chrétien, *Conscience et roman I*, 35, 37.

15. Chrétien, *Conscience et roman I*, 23.

tien writes that, after a certain point in the eighteenth century, the novel

will no longer content itself with lifting the roof from houses, nor with seeing through the walls of the most secret bedrooms, but ... will instead lift the roof from the house of the soul, and see directly [into ...] our most secret intentions, just as it will hear the silent murmurings of consciousness. Every secret will be revealed, the inviolable will be violated; it is, in the etymological sense of the term, the apocalypse of the novel. There corresponds to this new novel—that of the last two centuries—a new reader.... The experience of books—the experience that these books strive to give us ... changes its object: it becomes the experience of the inexpressible, the experience, in fiction, of that which, in principle and for essential reasons, we cannot experience in reality, observing from within another consciousness than our own, without anything escaping us. By giving us access to that which has no direct access, to that into which it is the only path, fiction rises to the fullness of its essence.[16]

How should we judge the ultimate value of this "apocalyptic" readerly experience of intimacy, what Chrétien terms "cardiognosy,"[17] and that he affirms as superior to the less-precise term "omniscience"? The respective positions of Maritain and Mauriac are variations on what had become, by the time they were writing, traditional arguments: at the beginning of the phenomenon of fictional cardio-gnosy (in the eighteenth century), supporters suggested that people who are deprived of this readerly experience are at a disadvantage in life when they encounter other people who have been exposed to it; the latter are sophisticated and able to manipulate people and situations to their advantage while those who do not read novels are naïve and easily taken advantage of.[18] François Mauriac does not speak of manipulation, but he certainly sees life advantages resulting from the fictional experi-

16. Chrétien, *Conscience et roman I*, 13.
17. After the New Testament Greek *kardiognôstès*—see, for example, Acts 1:24.
18. Chrétien, *Conscience et roman I*, 7–8.

ence of cardio-gnosy. In contrast, among the most eloquent and earliest of the critics of fictional intimacy is Mme. de Staël who, in the late eighteenth century, in her book *De L'Allemagne*, articulated a viewpoint that Jacques Maritain subsequently pushes further. She reported feeling that literary experience desensitizes one to the reality we actually live outside of reading, draining it of its surprise and wonder: "One can no longer experience anything without recalling having read about it" (On ne peut plus rien éprouver sans se souvenir de l'avoir lu).[19] Maritain sharpens the point by focusing upon the ultimate consequences of this desensitizing effect: one's sensitivity to the mysteriousness of the other is dulled and sullied by the fictional transformation of the heart into a "show."

O'Connor's fiction is interesting when viewed in the terms of this debate because her narratives suggest that she draws inspiration from both those critical and those in favor of a "modern" fictional treatment of the human heart. She is clearly critically engaged with the question of the fate of the heart in modern narration; indeed, she often uses it to create drama: in so many of her stories, a character blithely assumes a complete knowledge of the deepest attributes, or what she or he takes to be the deepest attributes, of the consciousness of others. Ruby Turpin in "Revelation," and Sheppard in "The Lame Shall Enter First," are among many good examples.

"Good Country People," in particular, contains several instances that are worth looking at. The three women in the story—Hulga, Mrs. Hopewell, and the wife of the hired farmer, Mrs. Freeman—are each convinced that they know the deepest motives of others, and Hulga's thought to this effect, in particular, is often made available to us through direct narration—"During the night she had imagined that she seduced him"—punctuated by free indirect discourse—"Some people might enjoy drain water if they were

19. *De L'Allemagne* II, 28, quoted in Chrétien, *Conscience et roman I*, 9.

told it was vodka."[20] The story conveys seeing into the life of others in other ways, as well. Mrs. Freeman is thought to be simple, "salt of the earth," "good country people" by Mrs. Hopewell, but Freeman sees everything that happens on the farm with "beady steel-pointed eyes" that always "[penetrate] far enough . . . to reach some secret fact" in those on whom she fixes them.[21] With such a gaze, she turns out to resemble the falsely naïve Manley Pointer, also thought by Mrs. Hopewell to be a simple "good country person," whose gaze is similarly described as "penetrating," with "eyes like two steel spikes."[22] The narration of the story is composed primarily of long retrospective passages that describe the characters, with special emphasis on what the three women think about themselves and one another, and that recount the visit the previous day by the traveling Bible salesman (Pointer). The present moment of the narration takes up only about two hours of the day (and nine out of the twenty pages that compose the story), from breakfast to the ten o'clock rendezvous of Hulga and Pointer, which culminates in his seduction of Hulga and the theft of her wooden leg.

Thus, the story's drama is structured by the clash between two sets of characters who each claim to be able to see into the hearts of others. Mrs. Hopewell and Hulga, respectively, fancy themselves able to narrate the inner lives of everyone else in their world while the two apparently simple and naïve "country" characters, Pointer and Mrs. Freeman, are endowed with a real ability to penetrate the secret pride and faulty claims to wisdom of the mother and the daughter. However, the *value* of this ability to penetrate to the heart is questionable: the overall tone of the story is one of danger and insecurity, which casts a shadow over this capacity to see into another's secrets. Although O'Connor is

20. Flannery O'Connor, *The Complete Stories*, ed. Robert Giroux (New York: Farrar, Straus and Giroux, 1971), 284, 286.

21. O'Connor, *The Complete Stories*, 275.

22. O'Connor, *The Complete Stories*, 288–289.

certainly right to claim that at the end of the story, "the reader realizes that [Pointer] has taken away part of [Hulga's] personality and has revealed her deeper affliction to her for the first time," it is also the case that there is no reason, based on the story's details alone, to believe that this apocalypse will lead Hulga to renewal and regeneration.[23] The world of the story is one in which another's knowledge of one's heart—knowledge of its "deceit" and "corruption," to paraphrase Jeremiah 17:9—is always something frightening and threatening. Mrs. Freeman's name, coupled with her ability to penetrate to the secret truth of other's lives, may call to the reader's mind the Gospel verse "You shall know the truth, and the truth shall make you free" (Jn 8:32), but the merciful and loving figure of Jesus, with his "*science sacerdotale*" or "priestly knowledge," in Maritain's words, seems conspicuously absent from the world of the story.

But, in a fascinating and, from a narrative point of view, provocative way, this mercy enters into a world similarly filled with danger for an exposed heart in "The Artificial Nigger," published in the same collection as "Good Country People" (*A Good Man is Hard to Find, and Other Stories*, 1955). As Ralph Wood has shown, O'Connor's approach in this story to the damaging impact of slavery and its legacy rejects the path of moral indignation, not because there is nothing to be indignant or scandalized about but precisely because she sees that at the root of racial hatred there lies a nihilistic will to power that views any moral appeal to one's self-restraint as a veiled attempt to control and oppress one's freedom.[24] This will to power is detailed in the story by the at-

23. Flannery O'Connor, *Mystery and Manners: Occasional Prose*, ed. Sally and Robert Fitzgerald (New York: Farrar, Straus and Giroux, 1969), 98.

24. The African American writer Alice Walker recognized this about O'Connor's work when she wrote that "*Essential* O'Connor is not about race at all, which is why it is so refreshing, coming, as it does, out of such a *racial* culture. If it can be said to be 'about' anything, then it is 'about' prophets and prophecy, 'about' revelation, and 'about' the impact of supernatural grace on human beings who don't have a chance of spiritual growth without it." Alice Walker, *In Search of Our Mother's Gardens* (New York: Harcourt, 1983), 53; quoted in Stanley Hauerwas and Ralph C. Wood, "How the

tempt of one character, the grandfather Mr. Head, to dictate to his grandson Nelson the truth of Nelson's innermost identity. Nelson, in turn, rebels, contesting whenever possible this attempt. The only way out of this vicious circle will be the surprising in-breaking of a mercy that seeks no recompense.

The role of "cardio-gnostic" narration in the story in communicating this mercy is my central concern here. More specifically, I want to zero in on the story's conclusion, with its famous narrative apocalypse of Mr. Head's heart as he and Nelson stand gazing at "the plaster figure of a Negro sitting bent over on a low yellow brick fence ... pitched forward at an unsteady angle because the putty that held him to the wall had cracked. One of his eyes was entirely white and he held a piece of brown watermelon."[25]

This is, of course, the famous "artificial nigger" of the story's title, and its effect on the two racists is startling. Finding himself reduced to the hell that his struggle for power has brought him to, Mr. Head is brought face-to-face with what, in fact, is a very complex figure. It is a kind of icon, what has been insightfully termed a "bent and harrowed emblem of the Suffering Servant,"[26] that allows him, paradoxically, to glimpse as idol the "nigger" that he has constructed as the means to gain power over his world and, especially, over the inner life of his grandson.[27] The narrator tells us, "They stood gazing at the artificial Negro as if they were faced with some great mystery, some monument to another's victory that brought them together in their common defeat. They

Church Became Invisible: A Christian Reading of American Literary Tradition," in *Invisible Conversations: Religion in the Literature of America*, ed. Roger Lundin (Waco, Tex.: Baylor University Press, 2009), 175–176.

25. O'Connor, *The Complete Stories*, 268.

26. Hauerwas and Wood, "How the Church Became Invisible," 174.

27. O'Connor masterfully conveys the control Mr. Head gains over Nelson's self-regard as a result of the lesson Mr. Head gives Nelson aboard the train in how to see a "nigger"—the episode concludes with Nelson's new feelings of hatred toward the Negro and toward himself as he gazes at his reflection in the train window: "He looked toward the window and the face there seemed to suggest that he might be inadequate to the day's exactions"; O'Connor, *The Complete Stories*, 256.

could both feel it dissolving their differences like an action of mercy."[28] The reader, along with Mr. Head, is thus brought gropingly toward a realization about the way in which the real, living, and breathing black figures in the story up to this point—first, the man on the train, and then the impressive woman in the black neighborhood where Mr. Head gets the pair lost—have been made to function, through Mr. Head's way of seeing "a nigger," as puppets in an elaborate attempt by Mr. Head to maintain his sense of being "too good" for mercy, which is to say too good for any definition of value external to the one within his own mind.[29] His is a world where all self-regard is wrested violently from others forced to recognize his power and his values or where he, on failing to maintain power, is forced in his turn to grovel in subjection to the power and values of others. The decaying, plaster, watermelon-eating "nigger" reveals to Mr. Head the decay within his own soul by confronting him with an externalization of the mercilessness that has filled his own head.

O'Connor concludes the story with the famous paragraph that has been criticized as a heavy-handed authorial intrusion into the drama, *telling* what should instead be *shown*.[30] Our focus on

28. O'Connor, *The Complete Stories*, 269.

29. O'Connor, *The Complete Stories*, 254–255, 260–262.

30. For an example of this sort of criticism, see John F. Desmond, *Risen Sons: Flannery O'Connor's Vision of History* (Athens: The University of Georgia Press, 1987), 29–30. In another context, O'Connor herself articulates the rule of modern fiction that dictates showing rather than telling. In her lecture "Writing Short Stories," she writes that "[t]he peculiar problem of the short-story writer is how to make the action he describes reveal as much of the mystery of existence as possible. He has only a short space to do it in and he can't do it by statement. He has to do it by showing, not by saying, and by showing the concrete—so that his problem is really how to make the concrete work double time for him"; O'Connor, *Mystery and Manners*, 98. She goes on to discuss the way in which Hulga's wooden leg, in "Good Country People," *shows* the state of the young woman's soul: "we perceive that there is a wooden part of her soul that corresponds to her wooden leg. Now of course this is never stated. The fiction writer states as little as possible"; O'Connor, *Mystery and Manners*, 99. O'Connor's copy of Percy Lubbock's *The Craft of Fiction* displays marginal markings of passages emphasizing that, to put it in Lubbock's words, "the art of fiction does not begin until the novelist thinks of his story as a matter to

the way in which O'Connor problematizes the tendency of modern people to believe that they can experience, through fictional narration, the inner workings and secrets of another's heart meets up here with what might seem to be a powerful contradiction to our thesis:

Mr. Head stood very still and felt the action of mercy touch him again but this time he knew that there were no words in the world that could name it. He understood that it grew out of agony, which is not denied to any man and which is given in strange ways to children. He understood it was all a man could carry into death to give his Maker and he suddenly burned with shame that he had so little of it to take with him. He stood appalled, judging himself with the thoroughness of God, while the action of mercy covered his pride like a flame and consumed it. He had never thought himself a great sinner before but he saw now that his true depravity had been hidden from him lest it cause him despair. He realized that he was forgiven for sins from the beginning of time, when he had conceived in his own heart the sin of Adam, until the present, when he had denied poor Nelson. He saw that no sin was too monstrous for him to claim as his own, and since God loved in proportion as He forgave, he felt ready at that instant to enter Paradise.[31]

On its face, this passage seems to be an egregious example of what Chrétien calls cardio-gnosy. Has O'Connor placed herself alongside "a Freud" in such a way as to earn Maritain's reproach?

In fact, O'Connor's choice to present Mr. Head's thoughts in this way fits properly with his human situation at the end of the story. For the story claims that Mr. Head has, in fact, encountered God through the idol-destroying effect of the statue. The knowledge of his own heart that Mr. Head is described as having here—for instance, his sudden capacity to "[judge] himself with the thoroughness of God, while the action of mercy [covers] his pride

---

be *shown*, to be so exhibited that it will tell itself." See Lubbock, *The Craft of Fiction* (New York: Peter Smith, [1921] 1945), 62. Cf. Kinney, *Flannery O'Connor's Library*, 109–110.

31. O'Connor, *The Complete Stories*, 269–270.

like a flame and [consumes] it"—can only be the result of a divine gift, "the action of mercy" that "touches" him. In other words, the reader is made to understand that Mr. Head's encounter with the "artificial nigger" has mediated an encounter with the divine that was present all along, especially in the living black figures he encountered during the day, and now that the divine has shattered his idol and his pride has been diminished, the contents of Mr. Head's head can be exposed and poured out before him and before us by the story's narrator, without any concern for how they might function in a game of power. In a *very* mysterious way, what Maritain called the *"science sacerdotale"* of Christ—essentially, the first sacrament, the Church—is present and active in the world of the story.[32] The attempts by Mr. Head to tell Nelson who he is through lessons about "niggers" and the city have ended; now, at last and before it is too late, something new and true can be thought in Mr. Head's head.

As for O'Connor's own relationship to the narrative voice at the end of this story, we know from two of her letters that, on re-reading the story, she discovered things in it that she did not fully understand.[33] This suggests that in some manner O'Connor herself had experienced something akin to what Mr. Head undergoes in the story. In a letter to Ben Griffith (May 4, 1955), O'Connor wrote, quite freely, "What I had in mind to suggest with the artificial nigger was the redemptive quality of the Negro's suffering

32. The *ecclesial dimension* of this story—that is, the role played by the Church as Body of Christ in mediating the divine touch of mercy experienced by Mr. Head, and with it, his newly gained self-knowledge—begs for exploration, something that I cannot pursue here. I will, however, point out that O'Connor's sensibility to mystery precluded an overly legalistic understanding of the Church's presence. See, for instance, O'Connor's January 17, 1956, letter to Betty Hester, in which she states her opinion that Hester was baptized into the Church by "desire," before she underwent a sacramental baptism by water; O'Connor, *The Habit of Being*, 130, 131. My suggestion here is that, for O'Connor, the *science sacerdotale* of Christ (to borrow Maritain's term) can be made present and effective in certain circumstances through Christians who are not full (sacramental) participants in the Church.

33. O'Connor, *The Habit of Being*, 78, 101.

for us all."[34] For many readers, a sentence like this one is offensive, because an attempt by a white person, especially a southerner of O'Connor's time, to define the meaning of black suffering potentially functions as an underhanded or unconscious attempt to excuse, unfairly justify, and/or minimalize that suffering. But we need to read this sentence as if it came from the mouth of the character Alyosha in Dostoevsky's *The Brothers Karamazov*: O'Connor is stating matter-of-factly an understanding of the redemptive power of innocent suffering that, it seems clear, she came to understand through her own Christian experience, as a southerner and as one who suffered.[35] Only someone who truly believed what she wrote about the meaning of African American suffering, and had herself experienced a merciful touch through the mysterious *"science sacerdotale"* of Christ, could have concluded the story "The Artificial Nigger" in the way she did, speaking of a heart that she herself had been given to know.

The final example I want to discuss displays what I take to be a key facet of O'Connor's most mature critical engagement with the modern novelist's tendency to engineer a knowledge of the heart that could in reality only ever be a divine gift. The example comes from *The Violent Bear It Away*, the second of O'Connor's two novels, published in 1960. I want to focus, albeit briefly, on how the novel

34. O'Connor, *The Habit of Being*, 78.

35. Indeed, Dostoevsky's masterpiece serves as a privileged reference point for O'Connor's meditations on the drama of innocent suffering, evoked in the penultimate paragraph of "The Artificial Nigger," quoted earlier recall the description of mercy that "[grows] out of agony, which is not denied to any man and which is given in strange ways to children"; O'Connor, *The Complete Stories*, 269. Five years later, O'Connor will link innocent suffering explicitly to *The Brothers Karamazov* in her introduction to *A Memoir of Mary Ann*, writing of the "suffering of children" as a stumbling block for faith (O'Connor, *Mystery and Manners*, 226–227). Given the historical context, the suffering of children evoked in the introduction, dated December 8, 1960, encompasses not only that of the white child Mary Ann but also the recently televised suffering of black children in the battles over desegregation, referred to that same year by Robert Lowell—"When I crouch to my television set / The drained faces of Negro school-children rise like balloons"—in his 1960 poem "For the Union Dead."

dramatizes young Tarwater's movement from Scripture to experience, where the drive for fictional knowledge of another's heart is counter-balanced by the human being's drive to be free from inscription. O'Connor will return to the question of the relation between Scripture and experience, but from a reverse angle, in "Parker's Back" (1964). In that story, Parker experiences what Scripture describes, but without having read it, while his wife Sarah Ruth fails to recognize the enacting of Scripture in her husband's experience, despite having committed the Scriptures to memory. As a result of this chiasmus, the reader is faced with the hypothesis that Scripture is, among other things, foremost a guide to experience, a help to recognize the action and presence of God in what is happening now, rather than a script to be read, and then moralistically enacted through application. Through young Tarwater, *The Violent Bear It Away* strikes another blow against the nihilistic imposition of values. Along with the initiating touch of mercy in the world, which makes it safe, in response, to accept as a gift the exposure of one's needs, and even of one's deceitfulness and corruption, there is the passion for freedom, which pushes one to verify personally the truth and fit of every account another attempts to give of who one is deep down.

   The Violent Bear It Away tells the story of fourteen-year-old Francis Marion Tarwater and his furious struggle to come to grips with his destiny. Young Tarwater has been raised on a backwoods farm by his great uncle, Mason Tarwater, a fire-and-brimstone preacher and prophet whose aim is to turn the ambivalent young Tarwater into the heir to his prophetic vocation. In particular, old Tarwater wants his charge to baptize Bishop, the young idiot son of his nephew, George Rayber, an atheist psychologist who has rebelled against his own baptism as a boy at the hands of his uncle. When old Tarwater dies suddenly, young Tarwater goes to the city to seek out Rayber and Bishop as a means to test himself and, especially, to test the destiny his great uncle has claimed was sown within him by baptism. Thus, for most of the novel, young

Tarwater is caught in a state of violent, tense rebellion against both his prophetic upbringing at the hands of his great uncle and the scornful atheism of his uncle—neither path seems fulfilling to young Tarwater because he doesn't see how either is truly made *for him*. The remainder of the novel dramatizes the teenager's discovery of *his own* need and of what it has to do with the needs of these two men who have shaped his life by articulating for him opposing destinies.

In the following half page from early in the novel, O'Connor expertly conveys young Tarwater's tense situation. His great uncle's witness moves him to recognize his own need for freedom, and yet, at the same time, a fear rises in him: if I settle upon something particular to fulfill me, he asks, what is there to keep what I've settled upon from disappointing me, and stealing my freedom in the process? What is truly worthy of my embrace? The passage begins as old Tarwater is telling young Tarwater how he outwitted Rayber and his attempts to publish a psychological case study of old Tarwater as a type of "religious fanatic." Note the way in which Tarwater describes being contained in another's cardiognostic narration—"inside" the narrator's "head":

"Where he [Rayber] wanted me was inside that schoolteacher magazine [said old Tarwater]. He thought once he got me in there, I'd be as good as inside his head and done for and that would be that, that would be the end of it. Well, that wasn't the end of it! Here I sit. And there you sit. In freedom. Not inside anybody's head!" and [old Tarwater's] voice would run away from him as if it were the freest part of his free self and were straining ahead of his heavy body to be off. Something of his greatuncle's glee would take hold of [young] Tarwater at that point and he would feel that he had escaped some mysterious prison. He even felt he could smell his freedom, pine-scented, coming out of the woods, until the old man would continue, "You were born into bondage and baptized into freedom, into the death of the Lord, into the death of the Lord Jesus Christ."

Then the child would feel a sullenness creeping over him, a slow warm rising resentment that this freedom had to be connected with Jesus and that Jesus had to be the Lord.

"Jesus is the bread of life," the old man said.

The boy, disconcerted, would look off into the distance over the dark blue treeline. . . . In the darkest, most private part of his soul, hanging upsidedown like a sleeping bat, was the certain, undeniable knowledge that he was not hungry for the bread of life. Had the bush flamed for Moses, the sun stood still for Joshua, the lions turned aside before Daniel only to prophesy the bread of life? Jesus? He felt a terrible disappointment in that conclusion, a dread that it was true. The old man said that as soon as he died, he would hasten to the banks of the Lake of Galilee to eat the loaves and fishes that the Lord had multiplied.

"Forever?" the horrified boy asked.

"Forever," the old man said.

The boy sensed that this was the heart of his great-uncle's madness, this hunger, and what he was secretly afraid of was that it might be passed down . . . might strike some day in him and then he would be torn by hunger like the old man, the bottom split out of his stomach so that nothing would heal or fill it but the bread of life.

He tried when possible to pass over these thoughts, to keep his vision located on an even level, to see no more than what was in front of his face and to let his eyes stop at the surface of that. It was as if he were afraid that if he let his eye rest for an instant longer than was needed to place something—a spade, a hoe, the mule's hind quarters before his plow, the red furrow under him—that the thing would suddenly stand before him, strange and terrifying, demanding that he name it and name it justly and be judged for the name he gave it. He did all he could to avoid this threatened intimacy of creation.[36]

The boy's horror here at two related things—the possibility that believing in Jesus Christ might require him to sell short his appetite and the felt, yet frightening, need he recognizes in himself to judge the things in front of him in terms of their capacity to fulfill him at his deepest level—sets the terms for the rest of

36. Flannery O'Connor, *Collected Works*, ed. Sally Fitzgerald (New York: Library of America, 1988), 342–343.

the novel. It also instantiates what I see as O'Connor's most fully worked-out critical stance with respect to the modern tendency to offer the reader a fictional experience of "divine" knowledge of the human heart. Just as old Tarwater refuses to be inscribed in Rayber's narrative because he doesn't recognize himself there, his grandson refuses to say that he wants Jesus unless he can truly discover within himself a hunger for the bread of life. Agreeing with Maritain, O'Connor shows repeatedly that true knowledge of the heart is only ever a gift from God; at the same time, like Mauriac, she emphasizes the individual's need freely to risk everything in searching and testing reality for what will truly satisfy.

What emerges, then, from an investigation of O'Connor's critical engagement with the modern drive for fictional knowledge of the heart is her counterbalancing emphasis on the human being's ineradicable attachment to freedom, and the need for mercy if that freedom is to be fully realized. Alongside the presence of mercy in the world, which makes it safe to accept as gift the exposure of one's neediness, is the human passion for freedom, which pushes one to verify personally the truth and fit of every account another might attempt to give of who one is deep down. Indeed, this need to verify the fit of every such account and of every presence encountered guarantees, in a story like "The Artificial Nigger" or the novel *The Violent Bear It Away*, that nihilism—the manufacture and attempted imposition of values or projects that dictate how to live and think—will never be the last word. O'Connor's fiction suggests to the modern reader craving to consume the fictional "divine" experience of another's consciousness that there is an even better experience to be had in the reading of literary narrative. Her fiction presents us dramatically with the hypothesis that there is a mercy to be encountered that can give us the capacity to face the truth about our hearts, and the accompanying assurance that embracing this newly dilated capacity will never impede our freedom.

CHAPTER 4

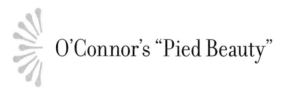

O'Connor's "Pied Beauty"

Gerard Manley Hopkins and the
Aesthetics of Difference

Mark Bosco, SJ

In a 2010 essay on the use of color in the works of Flannery
O'Connor, the scholar Bruce Gentry offers a striking list of words
that populate O'Connor's texts: rat-colored, chocolate purple, dead-
silver, dried yellow, fox-colored, freezing-blue, gold sawdust, gray-
purple, a green that was almost black or a black that was almost
green, green-gold, mole-colored, monkey white, polluted lemon
yellow, sticky-looking brown, sweet-potato-colored, toast colored,
and tobacco-colored. Gentry further highlights the way O'Connor

describes skin tones, white or otherwise: burnt-brown, cinna-
mon, coffee, gray, purple, red, tan, yellowish, mottled, speckled,
clay pink, purple-faced, and almost-gray.[1] O'Connor's palette recalls the powerfully evocative color spectrum of the Jesuit poet
Gerard Manley Hopkins: couple-coloured, brinded, rose-mole all
in a stipple, dapple-dawn, blue-bleak, gold-vermillion, speckled, clammyish, snowwhite, strawberry-breasted, sapphire-shot,
bugle blue, drop-of-blood-and-foam-dapple, silver-surfed cherry,
orchard-apple.[2]

Indeed, anyone who spends time reading O'Connor's stories
would agree that her work is "counter, original, spare, strange," to
borrow the phrase from Hopkins's poem "Pied Beauty." There is
undeniably something strange, spare, and original in O'Connor's
short stories, as characters maneuver their way through dark
and often impenetrable plots that seemingly lead to nowhere. Yet
there is something surprisingly *counter* to this surface nihilism,
for the ends of her stories repeatedly reveal a surplus of meaning
that redirects and reorders the reader toward a religious insight
about the mystery of human life. Her art is effective because her
readers—if not her characters'—experience a transformation of
consciousness in which the story is imbued with a new perspective, a deeper possibility of meaning. O'Connor explores the way
the shock of divine grace achieves what she calls the "essential
displacement" of the reader, a moment when the revelatory flash

1. Marshall Bruce Gentry, "O'Connor as Miscegenationist," in *Flannery O'Connor in the Age of Terrorism: Essays on Violence and Grace*, ed. Avis Hewitt and Robert Donahoo (Knoxville: University of Tennessee Press, 2010), 188–200. Gentry acknowledges that O'Connor was a painter, of course, as well as a writer, so she would have a sharp eye for the mixing of color, but Gentry argues rather provoca-
tively that this mixing of a wide range of colors in her fiction supports the claim of racial mixing more than O'Connor might be comfortable actually acknowledging herself. Although O'Connor never politically advocates this blurring of race, Gentry does propose that she endorses this in the apolitical, symbolic, and fantastical way that she writes.

2. Words and phrases are from the following poems by G. M. Hopkins: "Pied Beauty," "As Kingfishers Catch Fire," "The Blessed Virgin Compared to the Air We Breathe," "Ash-boughs," and "The May Magnificat."

of insight unexpectedly becomes the interpretive center of her stories.[3]

Hopkins's phrase "[a]ll things counter, original, spare, strange" is an apt way to describe O'Connor's effect on the reader. She greatly admired Hopkins throughout her adult life. The Jesuit priest and poet served as one among many literary and critical exemplars of the Catholic literary revival of the late nineteenth and early twentieth centuries. Fully engaged with Catholic theology and the cultural mores of his time, Hopkins's poetry offered a philosophical and artistic platform for O'Connor to test the mettle of her own literary aesthetic. She found affirmation for her creative imagination in Hopkins's rather distinctive, impulsive, visionary style of poetry. Like Hopkins, she would bring an intellectual depth to her craft, one that would go underappreciated by many of her early critics.

During Hopkins's short life (1844–1889), his friends, and later religious superiors, misunderstood his poetic innovations.[4] His poems were collected and published only decades after his death. In fact, the great Modernists of the twentieth century (Eliot, Pound, and later Auden) were the first to recognize and begin to think about Hopkins not as a Victorian but as one of "them," a poet whose radical excavation of the ancient sounds and expressions of Greek, Latin, Welsh, and Anglo-Saxon language accomplished something new, something modern. In a similar fashion, many of O'Connor's early reviewers misunderstood her art, cat-

3. Flannery O'Connor, *Mystery and Manners: Occasional Prose*, ed. Sally and Robert Fitzgerald (New York: Farrar, Straus and Giroux, 1969), 45.

4. See, for instance, the poet Coventry Patmore's letter to his friend Hopkins: "My dear Hopkins ... it seems to me that the thought and feeling of these poems, if expressed without any obscuring novelty of mode, are such as often to require the whole attention to apprehend and digest them; and are therefore of a kind to appeal only to a few. But to the already sufficiently arduous character of such poetry you seem to me to have added the difficulty of following several entirely novel and simultaneous experiments in versification and construction, together with an altogether unprecedented system of alliteration and compound words ... I often find it ... hard to follow you." Quoted in Philip A. Ballinger, *The Poem as Sacrament: The Theological Aesthetic of Gerard Manley Hopkins* (Louvain: Peeters Press, 2000), 187.

egorizing her stories as modern nihilistic satires of the southern
grotesque tradition, when, in fact, she was appropriating a medieval theological vision in radically new ways. Undeterred by this,
O'Connor remained hopeful that a wider audience would one day
grasp the Christian vision of her work.[5]

In *The Habit of Being* are several instances where O'Connor's
letters show that she is quite versed in Hopkins's poetry and
theological aesthetic. In a 1955 letter to Betty Hester, she makes a
rather profound reflection on Hopkins's poem "The Blessed Virgin Compared to the Air We Breathe," recalling that during the
early stages of her fight with lupus erythematosus, the large dos-
ages of the steroid ACTH prevented her from sleeping:

I once did without [sleep] almost all the time for several weeks. I had
high fever and was taking cortisone in big doses, which prevents your
sleeping. I was starting to go to sleep. Since then I have come to think
of sleep as metaphorically connected with the mother of God. Hopkins
said she was the air we breathe, but I have come to realize her most in
the gift of going to sleep. Life without her would be equivalent to me
to life without sleep and as she contained Christ for a time, she seems
to contain our life in sleep for a time so that we are able to wake up in
peace.[6]

In a 1956 letter to William Sessions, she alludes to a deeper investigation into Hopkins's life by mentioning the published correspondence of Hopkins and his friend Robert Bridges (a future
poet laureate and editor of Hopkins's poems). "Do you know the
Hopkins-Bridges correspondence?" she asks in her letter to Ses-

5. The early critical reception of O'Connor's work was negative, to say the
least. In the June 8, 1955, review of her first collection of short stories, *The New
Yorker* summarily derides them, missing the underlying Christian vision: "There
is a brutality in these stories, but since the brutes are as mindless as their victims,
all we have in the end, is a series of tales about creatures who collide and drown,
or survive to float passively in the isolated sea of the author's compassion, which
accepts them without reflecting anything."
6. Flannery O'Connor, *The Habit of Being: Letters of Flannery O'Connor*, ed. Sally
Fitzgerald (New York: Farrar, Straus and Giroux, 1979), 112.

sions. "Bridges wrote Hopkins at one point and asked him how he could possibly learn to believe, expecting, I suppose, a metaphysical answer. Hopkins only said, 'Give alms.'"[7] In a 1962 letter to Alfred Corn, she still has the same citation in mind, elucidating the point: "[Hopkins] was trying to say to Bridges that God is to be experienced in Charity (in the sense of love for the divine image in human beings). Don't get so entangled with intellectual difficulties that you fail to look for God in this way."[8] And in 1963, she writes to Sister Mariella Gable in commiseration over the dearth of good Catholic criticism: "I'll be glad when Catholic critics start looking at what they've got to criticize for what it is itself, for its sort of 'inscape' as Hopkins would have had it. Instead they look for some ideal intention, and criticize you for not having it."[9]

Recent studies by Sarah Gordon, Hank Edmondson, and Patrick Samway have elucidated ways in which O'Connor seems to have adopted Hopkins's radical language in some of her short stories, using his striking color palette to draw distinctive characters or to paint the setting of the natural world.[10] I would like to draw the exploration a bit further, considering Hopkins theory of inscape as a key to understanding more fully O'Connor's theological aesthetic of beauty. How does she understand the concept, the

7. O'Connor, *The Habit of Being*, 164.

8. O'Connor, *The Habit of Being*, 476.

9. O'Connor, *The Habit of Being*, 517. In one of her last letters from her hospital bed a few months before her death, O'Connor invokes Hopkins's poem about human mortality, "Spring and Fall: To a Young Child," as lines that bring her some comfort: "I like Hopkins (to answer one) particularly a sonnet beginning, Margaret, are you grieving / Over Goldengrove unleaving?" See O'Connor, *The Habit of Being*, 586.

10. Sarah Gordon, *Flannery O'Connor: The Obedient Imagination* (Athens: University of Georgia Press, 2000), 144–159; Hank T. Edmonson, "Flannery O'Connor, Gerard Manley Hopkins and Silence," *Gerard Manley Hopkins Archive*, accessed February 11, 2013, www.gerardmanleyhopkins.org/lectures_2003/flannery_oconnor .html; and Patrick Samway, "Jesuit Influence in the Life and Works of Flannery O'Connor," *Gerard Manley Hopkins Archive*, accessed February 11, 2013, www.gerard manleyhopkins.org/lectures_2004/jesuit_influence.html. Much of my analysis summarizes and builds on Gordon's fine reading of "A Good Man Is Hard to Find" and "The River" in light of Hopkins's language and theory of inscape.

place of Beauty in her art? If Hopkins's aesthetic depicts the soaring beauty and profound tragedy of God's presence, O'Connor's aesthetic depicts beauty irrupting forth within the ugliness of a fallen, sometimes profane world. I first look at what Hopkins is trying to accomplish in his poem "Pied Beauty" and then follow this with O'Connor's own texts. But first, the poem that acts as a guide to this exploration:

> Glory be to God for dappled things—
> For skies of couple-colour as a brinded cow;
> For rose-moles all in stipple upon trout that swim;
> Fresh-firecoal chestnut-falls; finches' wings;
> Landscape plotted and pieced—fold, fallow, and plough;
> And all trades, their gear and tackle and trim.
>
> All things counter, original, spare, strange;
> Whatever is fickle, freckled (who knows how?)
> With swift, slow; sweet, sour; adazzle, dim;
> He fathers-forth whose beauty is past change.
> Praise him.

Right away one notices Hopkins's generous aesthetic, seeing difference, not sameness, as the site where beauty resides. One can appreciate the poem as a poetic argument for a theological aesthetics of difference—dappled things—an intense acknowledgment of divine presence at the heart of the diversity of matter. Hopkins was well aware how provocative this was, taking a philosophical stand that straddles the centuries-old conflict between two historical polarities, objectivist and subjectivist, in the development of Western aesthetic theory. Prior to and through the Renaissance, the classical or objective pole dominated, grounded as it was in Platonic Idealism. Artistic production was understood in terms of mimesis, as an imitative art. This theory of art was expressed in the phrase, *ars simiae naturae*, art imitates nature. The creation of a work of art was a limited (and thus imperfect) reflection of metaphysical beauty, a transcendental quality that nonetheless could be detected in all things. Bernard Bosanquet suggests that the classical art of the Greek and Roman world was "not merely a consideration of the object to be represented, but a consideration of the art of imaginative production by which [beauty] is born again under the new conditions imposed by another medium."[11] By copying a thing of Beauty, the artist produced a beautiful work of art that shared in a new way some universal quality of life. Beauty, as a metaphysical attribute of being, shared with and illuminated the other qualities of being, Truth and the Good. The objectivity of Beauty, Truth, and Goodness could thus be discovered in the way a work of art conformed to these metaphysical attributes.

The eighteenth century began a shift in thinking about the ontological claims of Beauty. With the Enlightenment's "turn to the subject," philosophical aesthetics shifted from emphasizing the objectivity of Beauty to its subjective creation and reception as the beautiful. Following Immanuel Kant's relegation of aesthetics to the sublime, the emphasis moved from a metaphysics of Beauty to a transcendental analysis of the subjective process within human experience. The foundational assumption is expressed in the phrase *de gustibus non est disputandum*, one must not dispute what is a matter of taste, or, in the more evocative paraphrase, "beauty is in the eye of the beholder." With this move to subjective analysis, that which we find beautiful is no longer tethered to any metaphysical reality that might ground it in rational or moral truth. That which is beautiful could make no universal claims on us.

The theologian Alejandro Garcia-Rivera argues that this conflict in contemporary aesthetics between the formal quality of Beauty and the subjective reception of what is beautiful ultimately ends in a standoff: "One is forced to choose between the mistaken, primitive discussion that had Beauty as purely objective

11. Bernard Boscanquet, *A History of Aesthetics* (Cleveland, Ohio: World Publishing, Meridian, 1957), 12.

(from the modern perspective) over the irrational, modern over-emphasis on the subjectivity of the beautiful (from the classicist perspective). These two perspectives coexist in contemporary philosophical aesthetics but only as irreconcilable differences."[12] Thus, one is forced to choose between a supposedly flawed, classical discussion of Beauty or the more modern stress on the subjectivity of the beautiful. Yet, neither pole seems to suffice. Garcia-Rivera invokes the need to turn to a theological aesthetics as a solution as a way to bring together the objective encounter with beauty and the transformation it has on the subject as the receptor of such beauty.

We see this in the movement through Hopkins's poem, where the two poles become rather a two-part experience. In the first line, "Glory be to God for dappled things," and throughout the entire first stanza of the poem, we get acknowledgment of the play of Beauty, of the unique and dynamic ways in which beauty is everywhere in the material world. For Hopkins, this revelation is immediate and unavoidable, a simple instantiation. Hopkins privileges the pied beauty of life, giving us a catalogue of "dappled things." Yet by the end of the poem, the poet's descriptions cannot be contained any longer as merely a list of "things." The poet is so moved by the power beyond his own subjectivity, by the power of the strangeness of what he sees, that he ends the poem simply praising God as the only viable reply. In the final line of the poem, "Praise him," the poet responds to such beauty, for Beauty is, in the Christian tradition, the first name for God.[13] What Hopkins's aesthetic vision makes room for, in the words of

12. Alejandro Garcia-Rivera, *The Community of the Beautiful: A Theological Aesthetics* (Collegeville, Minn.: Liturgical Press, 1999), 13–14. Garcia-Rivera's scholarship is dedicated to forging a robust theological aesthetic that builds on both objective and subjective discourses of philosophy.

13. Beauty as a name for God resonates throughout the Christian tradition, from the Psalms to the book of Revelation in scripture, in the theology of Augustine and Aquinas, and in the Russian Orthodox vision of Dostoevsky. Perhaps the church father Hilary of Poitiers says it most succinctly: "Surely the author of all created beauty must himself be the beauty in all beauty." For a concise introduc-

Flannery O'Connor, is *mystery*. And mystery irrupts within the human imagination, moving the human heart. Hopkins's theological aesthetic allows for the interplay of a Beauty "past change" radiating out in the particularity, the uniqueness of the natural world, the objective and subjective realms of experience organically connected.

But more to the point of O'Connor's aesthetic strategies, Hopkins's "Pied Beauty" is an exploration, an explosion into difference, an aesthetics of contrast, not sameness. All things counter, original, spare, and strange reveal themselves. This strangeness, for Hopkins, points to the presence of a God, a Beauty past change. Like God, the *strange* is hard to categorize. Language fails, and the human person is forced to break its boundaries. Hopkins breaks every grammatical rule in the book in an effort to get at this reality, "Fresh-firecoal chestnut-falls." Adjective, noun, and adverb mix as he tries to name that which cannot be named even as he strives to do so. He transforms language to startle us, to confront us, to stop us in our tracks, to wake us up.

With Hopkins, we are far from Plato's vision of a changeless world of forms that exists independent of the world of appearances. Whereas Plato would say that true Beauty requires the uncompromising white light of the intellect with absolutely no shadows or color, Hopkins finds Beauty not *in spite of* the shadows and the colors but *because of* them. In his discovery of the medieval theologian of Oxford, Duns Scotus, Hopkins found a philosopher who validated his own poetic instincts.[14] Scotus celebrated difference over sameness, what he called *haeccitas*, the

---

tion, see Bruno Forte, *The Portal of Beauty: Towards a Theology of Aesthetics* (Grand Rapids, Mich.: Eerdmans, 2008).

14. Hopkins dedicated a poem, "Dun Scotus's Oxford," in celebration of his kinship with Scotus's thought. Yet that Hopkins's neologisms such as inscape, instress, and the "thisness" of things preceded his discovery of the Subtle Doctor should be noted. The attraction for Hopkins was finding in Scotus a thinker that could affirm his theories of poetry. On Hopkins's reading of Scotus, see Ballinger, *Poem as Sacrament*, 108–110.

thisness-and-not-thatness in all things, the property that makes each thing individual and unique. Rather than Plato's metaphor of Beauty as a colorless white light, one might describe Scotus's understanding as a beautiful spectrum of a rainbow, Beauty differentiated as if through a prism, white light arrayed across a color continuum. The metaphor of the rainbow is a sound analogy of the deep incarnationalism found throughout Scotus's theology. The divine Logos is found within all creation, various in its depth and realization in and through Christ's Incarnation. For Scotus, as for Hopkins, the doctrine of the Incarnation changes everything—conceptually, materially, spiritually—about being. The world is "charged with the grandeur of God."

Confirmed by Scotian philosophy, Hopkins fashions his own neologisms, *inscape* and *instress*, to describe his aesthetic. Walter Ong describes these terms in the following way: "the inscape of being is the distinctive controlling energy that makes a being itself and connects it distinctively with all else. Instress is the action that takes place when the inscape of a given being fuses itself in a given human consciousness."[15] Instress brings the human self, this particularized, subjective human being, into the dynamics of the otherwise objective inscape. Subject and object are given a moment of contact. Only then can one see a larger, cosmic connection at play within reality. If discerning the inscape of a thing is, in part, the experience (the instress) of Christ's Incarnation, then all art has the possibility of being sacramental, a unique mediation of the glory of God. Hopkins's poems provide a moment that makes present and felt the unprocessed, primeval nature of a thing in a way that discursive argument cannot comprehend. The poetic stress of a poem forces an encounter with the "givenness" of a thing in its self-expressive power.

However, for all the wonder of it, Hopkins thought that in his own time the experience of inscape was not common. He notes

15. See Walter Ong, *Hopkins, the Self, and God* (Toronto: University of Toronto Press, 1986), 17. See especially pages 15–21 for further development.

in his journal how difficult the perception of inscape can be for most people: "I thought how sadly beauty of inscape was unknown and buried away from simple people and yet how near at hand it was if they had eyes to see it."[16] Hopkins lived in a time overshadowed by the tedium and grime of his industrial age. He found the undifferentiated experience of city life dehumanizing and monotonous. He was interested in the experience of a beauty "past change" but always revealed in a particular, fallen, sinful, and suffering world. It is what Garcia-Rivera notes about the foundational proposition of a theological aesthetics of difference: we always experience beauty only in the context of "the garden of good and evil," in and within the backdrop of shadows and sin in the world.[17] To hold for an aesthetics of pied beauty, then, suggests that the discerning eye is in search of the beautiful, of a way of seeing that wades through the catalogue of material life to discover the good, or better stated, a way of uncovering what is behind or within the fallenness of the world. It is, in the end, a sacramental aesthetic, the objective glory of God in things revealed in the quotidian, in everyday differences, as ordinary as bread and water, or as ordinary as a woodlark, a cloud-fleeced sky, a piece of music, or even a poem.

For O'Connor, steeped in the same Catholic intellectual tradition as Hopkins, the doctrine of the Incarnation is the fundamental reality that allows the beautiful to be revealed in such grotesque ways throughout her fiction. The Incarnation is not merely a momentary event in history but the ultimate expression of human history, an event that marks the unique nature of human flourishing. In orthodox Christian theology, the birth of Christ, "according to the flesh," brings the universal form of the divine into the particular and finite realities of all life. In Christ's resur-

16. Gerard Manley Hopkins, *The Journals and Papers of Gerard Manley Hopkins*, ed. Humphrey House, 2nd ed. (London: Oxford University, 1959), 221. Cited in Ballinger, *Poem as Sacrament*, 137.

17. Garcia-Rivera uses this phrase in reference to the American philosopher, Josiah Royce. See *Community of the Beautiful*, 34–37, 155–186.

rection, the sacredness of each and every person is transformed and uniquely participates in this renovation of nature. "For me it is the virgin birth, the Incarnation, the resurrection which are the true laws of the flesh and the physical" she observes in a letter to Betty Hester. "Death, decay, destruction are the suspension of these laws. I am always astonished at the emphasis the Church puts on the body.... The resurrection of Christ seems the high point in the law of nature."[18]

Without a doubt O'Connor's own vision finds congruence, and oftentimes amplification of, Hopkins's aesthetics of contrast and difference. The following excerpt from "The Nature and Aim of Fiction" is directly in line with Hopkins: "The longer you look at one object, the more of the world you see in it; and it's well to remember that the serious fiction writer always writes about the whole world, no matter how limited his particular scene. For him, the bomb that was dropped on Hiroshima affects life on the Oconee River, and there's not anything he can do about it."[19] The particular and the universal, the passing and that which is past change, are held in creative tension in the artist. Furthermore, O'Connor's level of specificity in her narratives gives her an opportunity to hone in on the strangeness and originality of both nature and the human person. Farrell O'Gorman describes the aesthetic as an "emphasis on the concrete and a faith that the immediate world itself holds a mystery and a meaning that does not have to be imposed by the artist but is already present, if only recognized."[20] Often, the function of her grotesque characters is to engage the reader in this present mystery. O'Connor says as much in her essay "Some Aspects of the Grotesque in Southern Fiction," affirming that "what he [i.e., the writer] sees on the surface will be of interest to him only as he can go through it into an

18. O'Connor, *The Habit of Being*, 100.

19. O'Connor, *Mystery and Manners*, 77.

20. Farrell O'Gorman, *Peculiar Crossroads: Flannery O'Connor, Walker Percy, and Catholic Vision in Postwar Southern Fiction* (Baton Rouge: Louisiana State University Press, 2004), 108.

experience of mystery itself" so that her art "will always be push-
ing its own limits outward toward the limits of mystery . . . until it
touches that realm which is the concern of prophets and poets."[21]
   O'Connor is indeed in the realm of prophets and poets and
the particularity of her vision of the natural world is often placed
center stage in her texts. Her violent endings, almost all of which
end with some reference to the natural world, break narrative expectations much like Hopkins enjambed use of language
does in his poetry. In a recent essay on O'Connor's ecological vision, Mark Graybill notes that O'Connor's texts always "decried
the separation of the physical world from the spiritual" and that
"throughout her *oeuvre*, she seeks to break down barriers between
the human and the natural."[22] The natural world—the tree line,
the sky, the clouds, and especially the sun—becomes like a chorus
in a Greek tragedy, bearing witness to a Beauty past change, and
a beauty certainly past the consciousness of her characters, but
made alive to the reader. The natural landscape reveals what her
characters cannot see, the particularity of place as a manifestation of the cosmic and the transcendent. Just as Hopkins's poetic landscapes are neither mythological nor romantically ideal,
O'Connor's forests and clouds have a primeval literalism to them,
a "brute beauty" that expresses the presence or power of something greater at stake. We see this especially in O'Connor's use of
language. She metaphorically paints the natural world as oddly
colored, ready and waiting for a moment of grace to be violently
revealed to characters with their delusions of grandeur or myopic
vision.
   In "A Good Man Is Hard to Find" O'Connor writes with a
Hopkins-like catalogue of colors as the grandmother and her family drive out of Georgia and into Tennessee, a vacation that will
end in their death: "the blue granite that in some places came up

   21. O'Connor, *Mystery and Manners*, 41, 45.
   22. Mark S. Graybill, "O'Connor's Deep Ecological Vision," *The Flannery
O'Connor Review* 9 (2011): 3.

to both sides of the highway; the brilliant red clay banks slightly streaked with purple, and the various crops that made rows of green lace-work on the ground." This description of the surrounding landscape ends with "The trees were full of silver-white sunlight and the meanest of them sparkled."[23] None of the protagonists in the story seem to notice this, still unaware that God's redeeming presence can occur even after an encounter with the radical evil of The Misfit. These mean-sparkling trees that the author depicts are reminders, if you will, of "the pure thisness-and-not-thatness in all things," as explored in "Pied Beauty." The grandeur of God sparkles even in the lowest of the most threatening of the trees as a rebuke, a transcendent choral witness to the disordered and deadly performances of humankind. After the grandmother witnesses each member of her family escorted out to the woods to be killed by the Misfit's fellow convicts, she gathers all her strength to plea a religious case for not shooting her: "Jesus! . . . You've got good blood! I know you wouldn't shoot a lady!"[24] In "turning to Jesus," both the grandmother and the Misfit stumble on a truth that climaxes in a gesture of beauty. O'Connor stretches the notion of a startling grace to the breaking point as the grandmother's disequilibrium allows her to see what she did not see before—that the Misfit is a person in need. He is "one of her babies."[25] The grandmother sees in this extreme moment a pied beauty—the Misfit as a pained child—something strange, certainly, and original. She is left dead but with "her face smiling up at the cloudless sky," affecting an intimacy with the heavens above and the earth below. The story ends with the slightest echo of Hopkins's poem "Praise Him" as the dead woman's gaze effects a knowing smile.

If there is the echo of worship at the end of "A Good Man Is Hard to Find," then a liturgical discourse on baptism structures

23. Flannery O'Connor, *The Complete Stories*, ed. Robert Giroux (New York: Farrar, Straus and Giroux, 1971), 119.

24. O'Connor, *The Complete Stories*, 132.

25. O'Connor, *The Complete Stories*, 132.

the dramatic ending of "The River." O'Connor suggests that the young Harry Ashfield's drowning is a spiritual encounter of baptism, and the reader is startled by any staid associations he or she might have about its significance to a Christian life. The story climaxes when the young boy returns to a river where his babysitter Mrs. Connin has previously brought him to be baptized. Through these waters the revival minister had assured him that he would now count where he didn't count before, and that he could now enter the Kingdom of God. Harry's four-year-old logic is simple and direct, at least in his naïve spiritual economy. If, as the boy feels, his parents do not want him, then why not go "home" to God's Kingdom under the river? Sarah Gordon's analysis of the story offers an insightful illustration of O'Connor's use of Hopkins's aesthetic vision. O'Connor describes Mrs. Connin as a "speckled skeleton," the word *speckled* echoing Hopkins's inscape and emphasizing Mrs. Connin's uniqueness.[26] Her own children on the farm are described as having "identical speckled faces," perhaps signifying both their sameness and their own particularity.[27] On their way to the river with Harry and her children, we get O'Connor's homage to Hopkins's poetry:

They walked on the dirt road for a while and then they crossed a field *stippled with purple weeds* and entered *the shadows of a wood* where the ground was covered with thick pine needles. He had never been in woods before and he walked carefully, looking from side to side as if he were entering a strange country. They moved along a bridle path that twisted downhill through *crackling red leaves*, and once, catching at a branch to keep himself from slipping, he looked into two *frozen green-gold eyes* enclosed in the darkness of a tree hole. At the bottom of the hill, the woods opened suddenly onto a *pasture dotted here and there with black and white cows* and sloping down, *tier after tier*, to a broad orange stream where the reflection of the *sun was set like a diamond.*[28]

26. O'Connor, *The Complete Stories*, 157; and Gordon, *Obedient Imagination*, 147.
27. O'Connor, *The Complete Stories*, 160.
28. O'Connor, *The Complete Stories*, 164; emphasis added.

Sarah Gordon notes that the last image resonates with the line from "A Good Man Is Hard to Find"—"The trees were full of silver-white sunlight and the meanest of them sparkled"—suggesting God's imminence, the charge of God's glory, just as the black-and-white cows echo the "brinded cows" of "Pied Beauty." We even can imagine the sloping tiers of land to be a vision of "landscape plotted and pieced," all of God's handiwork incarnated within the particularity of the world. Finally, as Harry listens to the preacher, his eyes follow "drowsily the slow circles of two silent birds revolving high in the air," and we are told that there is a "low red and gold grove of sassafras with hills of dark blue trees behind it and an occasional pine jutting over the skyline."[29] With this image of birds conjuring the Holy Spirit, we have the unmistakable influence of Hopkins on O'Connor. Here the natural world does not stand so much as a cosmic, choral witness of the tragedy at hand but as the site of redemption, the beautiful arrayed on a walk toward the "River of Life."

Yet who registers this poetic inscape? It is the reader. Rarely ever is it the characters, except perhaps at the moment of their absolute crisis, which, for O'Connor's stories, is often the moment right before death. Just as the grandmother and her family do not seem to notice the sky and the sun as a revelation of pied beauty, neither do they see it in the particularity of each other. Just as Harry walks almost unaware "into a strange country" of speckled and brinded beauty, neither does he quite understand how all of a sudden he counted when he didn't count before. It is up to the reader to sense, to feel this contrast, this difference. It is as if we are reading a text amid the monotony of grayness, in a world intermixed with the color palette of sin and redemption. O'Connor invites the reader to have the discerning vision, to see the difference between the two. What to do with little Harry as he gets pulled under by the river's current? What to do with Mr. Paradise, touched by the mystery before him while staring with "dull

29. Gordon, *Obedient Imagination*, 148–149.

eyes as far down the river as he could see"? Is not the reader sum-
moned to sense the strange beauty in this ending? The tragedy
of the boy's drowning is literally *countered* by the reader's sense
that his naïve faith has somehow led him to God, just as surely as
Mr. Paradise emerges from the river empty-handed.

Perhaps only in her story "Revelation" do the character and
the reader both get to see the same pied beauty at work. The self-
indulgent Ruby Turpin, who confuses the righteousness of faith
with the pride she feels as a white Christian lady, is wrapped up in
the moral superiority of her race and economic class. O'Connor
builds Ruby's spiritual deformity in the first part of the story
as the characters sit in a doctor's office, assessing the worth of
various representatives of the South's class structure in terms of
sameness: how similar or dissimilar they are to her. Ruby's habit
of "naming the classes of people" turns the dissimilarity of each
human person into a liability.[30] Difference is not a celebration
of a pied beauty—the variety of the beautiful—but a threat to her
own understanding of herself. Instead of leading Ruby to praise,
difference causes anxiety of the Other. As she falls asleep thinking about the complexity of human diversity "moiling and roil-
ing around in her head," she dreams that the classes of people
"were all crammed in together in a box car, being ridden off to
be put in a gas oven."[31] Ruby's vision of reality forces Beauty into
sameness. A univocal imagination, it prescribes what is beautiful from the abstractions of race and class. Just as Beauty is co-
erced into the prevailing manners of a privileged class, so, too,
are the notions of goodness and truth, the other attributes of being. Ruby's aesthetic judgment about the people in the room assumes that a good woman is not so hard to find; she is right there
in her own skin.

When the Wellesley girl, Mary Grace, has had enough of Ruby's talk of her "good disposition," she hits Ruby in the eye with a

---

30. O'Connor, *The Complete Stories*, 491.
31. O'Connor, *The Complete Stories*, 492.

book and tries to strangle her, telling her, "Go back to hell where you came from, you old wart hog."[32] Ruby finds this violent revelation hard to understand but cannot deny the force of truth in it. The aesthetic question for Ruby, and for the reader, is, how can I be a hog and me both, how can I be saved and from hell, too? In the theological language of Hopkins, Ruby is saved precisely because of the particular blemish, the dappled quality of her life. She can be "a hog and me both" only in Christ, the inscape that presses on her worldview. Quoting Hopkins, only then can Christ "play in ten thousand places, / Lovely in limbs, and lovely in eyes not his / To the Father through the features of men's faces."[33] Ruby will be lovely—beautiful—the more she comes to reflect Christ.

As Ruby wrestles with this revelation in the final scene of the story, we return to the natural world as Ruby marches out to her pig parlor. O'Connor's use of the realistic, natural setting reinforces a Hopkins-like moment in the story, as if a transformative light shines on her. From the brightness of the afternoon setting to the deepening blue hue of evening, Ruby rages at God for giving her such a revelation, as she angrily hoses down her pigs: "The color of everything, field and crimson sky, burned for a moment with a transparent intensity.... Mrs. Turpin stood there, her gaze fixed on the highway, all her muscles rigid.... Then like a monumental statue coming to life, she bent her head slowly and gazed, as if through the very heart of mystery, down into the pig parlor at the hogs. They had settled all in one corner around the old sow who was grunting softly. A red glow suffused them. They appeared to pant with a secret life."[34] O'Connor literally paints with words the final revelation where the heavens and the earth open up before the reader: "There was only a purple streak in the sky, cutting through a field of crimson and leading, like an extension of the highway, into the descending dusk.... A vision-

32. O'Connor, *The Complete Stories*, 500.
33. G. M. Hopkins, "As Kingfishers Catch Fire."
34. O'Connor, *The Complete Stories*, 507–508.

ary light settled in her eyes. She saw the streak as a vast swinging bridge extending upward from the earth through a field of living fire."[35] We reach an overwhelming moment in which the pied beauty of nature and the pied beauty of Ruby collide into one another and the only response is praise. The story ends with O'Connor's version of Hopkins's poem: "In the woods around her the invisible cricket choruses had struck up, but what she heard were the voices of the souls climbing upward into the starry field and shouting hallelujah."[36]

Most readers are drawn to O'Connor's strangeness, what is counter, original, and spare, as part of the glory of her work, a kind of radiance of careful observation. In the words of the poet Richard Wilbur, she "calls us to the things of this world." We might even say she calls us into the dappled things of this world. This is the glory of her aesthetic, a recognition of objective Beauty, of the *inscape* in each and every thing. And what about our own subjective grasp, our own *instress*? Is this not the surplus of meaning that lingers with us in the endings of her texts? I think this is analogous to Hopkins's final exhortation: Praise. Praise God whose beauty is past change. The reader senses exaltation but not through the usual path of triumph but in a counter-path, an original path. Our subjective encounter with the text moves us. O'Connor's characters lead us paradoxically to praise, as each of them is drawn into the swift; slow; sweet; sour; adazzle dim of beauty.

35. O'Connor, *The Complete Stories*, 508.
36. O'Connor, *The Complete Stories*, 509.

CHAPTER 5

 "The Baron Is in Milledgeville"

Friedrich von Hügel's Influence on O'Connor

Michael Bruner

Which brings me to the embarrassing subject of what I have not read and been influenced by. I hope nobody ever asks me in public. If so I intend to look dark and mutter, "Henry James Henry James"—which will be the veriest lie, but no matter. I have not been influenced by the best people.

—Flannery O'Connor, in a letter to
Betty Hester, August 28, 1955[1]

1. Flannery O'Connor, *The Habit of Being: Letters of Flannery O'Connor*, ed. Sally Fitzgerald (New York: Farrar, Straus and Giroux, 1979), 98.

Sunday, May 17, '59

Dear Fannie,

The Baron is in Milledgeville and I am highly obliged to you. I have almost finished the first volume and will send it along when I finish it. You are contributing greatly to my education. I see nobody has checked these books out since 1954. Them Tennessee theologians must all be Baptists.

Cheers,

Flannery[2]

Flannery O'Connor was in the midst of revising her soon-to-be-published second and last novel, *The Violent Bear It Away*, when she wrote the letter highlighted above to Fannie Cheney in May 1959.[3] She was clearly in a less sardonic mood than when she wrote to Betty Hester in 1955, highlighted at the chapter opening. Baron von Hügel's writings had already proved to be an invaluable companion to, and crucial influence on, O'Connor's growing storehouse of theological knowledge, and her latest foray into his first book, *The Mystical Element of Religion as Studied in Saint Catherine of Genoa and Her Friends*, would serve as a capstone of that influence during what was arguably her busiest and most productive writing period, from around 1954 to 1959.[4]

2. C. Ralph Stephens, ed., *The Correspondence of Flannery O'Connor and the Brainard Cheneys* (Jackson: University Press of Mississippi, 1986), 86. Fannie Cheney had sent O'Connor a two-volume work by Baron Friedrich von Hügel titled *The Mystical Element of Religion as Studied in Saint Catherine of Genoa and Her Friends* (London: J. M. Dent, 1908, 1923), considered a classic study on mysticism and the definitive historical study of St. Catherine of Genoa (1447–1510).

3. Flannery O'Connor, *The Violent Bear It Away* (New York: Farrar, Straus and Giroux, 1960).

4. O'Connor's professional writing career can be divided into three periods that parallel the publication of her four major works: 1949–1955, during which she began her career as a professional writer and published her first novel, *Wise Blood* (New York: Harcourt, Brace and Co., 1952), and her first collection of short stories, *A Good Man is Hard to Find* (New York: Harcourt, Brace and Co., 1955); 1955–1960, when her novel *The Violent Bear It Away* was both written and published and many of her essays and reviews were published (and some short stories were written); and 1960–1964, when her last collection of short stories, *Everything That Rises Must*

In this chapter, my central claims focus on two apparently contradictory truths: that Baron von Hügel is ignored by most of O'Connor scholarship and that he was a major influence on O'Connor and her writing.[5] On one level, I am simply extending an argument put forth in a preliminary manner by William Kirkland for the *Flannery O'Connor Bulletin* in 1989, which is the only extended study I am aware of regarding von Hügel's influence on O'Connor.[6] But given the limitations of length, the aims of this study are necessarily modest, focusing almost exclusively on O'Connor's nonfiction—her reviews, essays, and letters—and drawing only general lines of influence from von Hügel. Evidence of his influence can be found in her fiction, to be sure, but it is one of theme more than content. A separate study will need to be done to more fully address this crucial but neglected piece in O'Connor studies.[7]

The neglect of von Hügel by the consensus of O'Connor scholarship is curious indeed, given O'Connor's frequent and effusive praise of the man and her consistent and comparatively frequent references to him and his work. But when one considers the cen-

---

Converge (New York: Farrar, Straus and Giroux, 1965), and some additional essays were written and published. In spite of the fact that the period from 1955 to 1960 represents only about one-third of O'Connor's writing career, it accounts for almost two-thirds of her published correspondence in *The Habit of Being* and nearly half of the essays published in *Mystery and Manners: Occasional Prose*, ed. Sally Fitzgerald (New York: Farrar, Straus and Giroux, 1969).

5. Even if my second proposition were found to be false, the first would still merit attention, given the comparatively frequent (and sometimes almost fulsome) references O'Connor makes about von Hügel and about his writings in her letters, book reviews, public lectures, and published essays.

6. William Kirkland, "Baron Friedrich von Hügel and Flannery O'Connor," *The Flannery O'Connor Bulletin* 18 (1989): 28–42. Kirkland's essential argument in this essay, besides the fact that von Hügel was a major influence on O'Connor, was that O'Connor was a Catholic humanist of the von Hügel, de Chardin, and Guardini variety, "individuals who, like her character Haze Motes,... had difficulty with the Church. 'If they are good they are dangerous,'" he quotes O'Connor as saying (about de Chardin). O'Connor, *The Habit of Being*, 571.

7. I include von Hugel's influence on O'Connor's fiction in a series, Studies in Art and Theology, IVP Academic Press.

tral themes in O'Connor's fiction and nonfiction, themes I argue were either borrowed directly from or influenced heavily by von Hügel, this silence becomes "curiouser and curiouser." As a result, I have had to depend largely on material that has either not been examined closely enough or, in some cases, not previously accounted for at all—in other words, "facts of the past."[8]

My working assumption is that O'Connor's theological and literary intentions and sympathies are likely to be more obvious and transparent in her personal correspondence, book reviews, essays (some of them unpublished), private diaries, and the marginalia of her personal library than they would be in her published fiction, the latter of which was written with a wary eye toward what she believed to be a mostly hostile audience.[9] What she published, then, as well as the literary artifacts never intended for public consumption, is grist for the mill in this study.

Having said this, I share William Session's caution regard-

8. I am borrowing from historian E. H. Carr's distinction between "facts of the past" and "historical facts." The former, Carr claimed, are facts that are true regardless of what attention they may have garnered from historians, whereas the latter are those facts that historians have deemed important about a particular subject. Carr advocated for the former and argued at the time he wrote his seminal *What Is History?* that a methodological hegemony had crept into historical research that favored an uncritical dependence on the latter—on "historical facts."

9. Some of the material used for this study is only available at the Ina Dillard Russell Library's Flannery O'Connor Collection at Georgia College and State University, the staff of which I owe a debt of gratitude. A personal diary, written while she was a young graduate student in Iowa, has only recently come to light, discovered by William Sessions among her extensive papers. Portions of the diary (later published as *A Prayer Journal* [New York: Farrar, Straus and Giroux, 2013]) were read for the first time to a group of O'Connor scholars at a conference in Chicago in the fall of 2011, which I was fortunate enough to have attended. None of the content of the diary, written before she had read any of von Hügel, pertains directly to this study. What is noteworthy, however, is the degree to which the diary shows a young woman (age twenty-one to twenty-two at the time) of remarkably deep theological and spiritual perspicacity and Christian commitment. In this regard, O'Connor was no average fiction writer whose theological sympathies and spiritual concerns might merely be incidental to her output. Clearly, for this prodigious student of writing, matters of theology would play a central and fundamental role in her work as a fiction writer. William Sessions is Regent's Professor Emeritus at Georgia State University and was a personal friend of O'Connor.

ing the biographical fallacy, which is "akin to the mistaken belief that if we know where William Wordsworth and his sister Dorothy went for their walks in the Lake District, we can ... understand 'Tintern Abbey.'"[10] This study is not so much concerned, then, with precise interpretations as it is with acknowledging the proper source of some of O'Connor's iconic themes. Indeed, accounting for the host of paradoxes and crosscurrents at play in O'Connor's situation as a Roman Catholic in the rural South in the 1950s—and given someone of her intellectual acuity, spiritual depth, and physical limitations, all of which had a profound effect on her person as well as her art—makes the task of tracing precise lines of theological influence from von Hügel's to O'Connor's work difficult at best.

Von Hügel was no incidental figure of twentieth-century Catholicism. His monumental work on the life of St. Catherine of Genoa remains one of the definitive studies on mysticism, and he was spiritual mentor to Evelyn Underhill, one of the clarion voices of the mystical tradition of the twentieth century. He was the first Catholic since the Reformation to be awarded an honorary doctorate from Oxford, and he was invited to give the Gifford Lectures of 1924 through 1926. O'Connor understood von Hügel's importance as a thinker and theologian and wrote in a book review that "Friedrich von Hügel is frequently considered, along with Newman and Acton, as one of the great Catholic scholars."[11] Although he only began to be published later in his life—in his mid-fifties—von Hügel nonetheless managed to pen some of the

10. Jan Nordby Gretlund and Karl-Heinz Westarp, eds., *Flannery O'Connor's Radical Reality* (Columbia: The University of South Carolina Press, 2007), 58–59. Sessions goes on to say, "At the moment this generic fallacy and faulty historicist analysis appears with some frequency in O'Connor studies. To this kind of analysis, including my own, I pose the following question: If we know where O'Connor garnered her ideas of prophecy, choice, and the fundamental horror of the human condition, do we automatically understand O'Connor's dense and violent texts? ... I doubt it."

11. Leo Zuber and Carter W. Martin, eds., *The Presence of Grace and Other Book Reviews by Flannery O'Connor* (Athens: The University of Georgia Press, 2008), 21.

seminal books of the Catholic Intellectual Renaissance of the
twentieth century, among them *The Mystical Element of Religion*;
Essays and Addresses on the Philosophy of Religion; and *Letters To A
Niece.*[12] O'Connor wrote glowing reviews for the latter two but
considered *Mystical* his finest work.

Von Hügel's notion of the "three elements of religion," considered perhaps to be his main contribution to Catholic theology and
which became a literary trope in his work, suggests that the life of
a person, and the religious life, in particular—even, finally, history itself—could be divided into three elements or stages: (1) the
historical/institutional/sensible, (2) the scientific/intellectual/
rational, and (3) the mystical/experiential/spiritual. Each element
represents a stage in development, but none replaces the others as
development progresses. Von Hügel believed that all three must be
in tension to maintain a healthy balance of creative forces within a
person or period in history, yet precisely this balance of tensions
gives rise to difficulties in life and history, particularly as such
tensions manifest themselves in the religious life.

O'Connor's interest in von Hügel grew out of her fascination
with the third element of von Hügel's schema, the mystical/ex-
periential/spiritual, particularly as the phenomenon of mysticism was reflected in various female religious figures of the
past.[13] In fact, her early interest in St. Catherine of Genoa, dating back to at least 1949 when she acquired Catherine's *Treatise*

12. *The Mystical Element of Religion*, considered von Hügel's magnum opus (see
note 2 in this chapter); *Essays and Addresses on the Philosophy of Religion* (London:
J. M. Dent and Sons, Ltd., vol. 1, 1921; vol. 2, 1925); and *Letters To A Niece* (Chicago:
Henry Regnery, 1955; first published in 1931), a collection of von Hügel's correspondence with his niece from 1918 until his death in 1924. Another of von Hügel's
books, *The Reality of God and Religion and Agnosticism: Being the Literary Remains of
Baron Friedrich von Hügel* (London: J. M. Dent and Sons, Ltd., 1931), was the published version of his Gifford Lectures of 1924–25 and 1925–26, although serious
illness prevented him from attending in person.

13. I use the term *figures* deliberately because in O'Connor's case, it is quite
literally true: "I got interested in St. Catherine of Genoa," O'Connor writes, "when
I saw her picture—a most beautiful woman"; O'Connor, *The Habit of Being*, 113.
O'Connor was also interested in St. Catherine of Siena, Simone Weil, and Edith

on Purgatory, was likely the catalyst that eventually led O'Connor to von Hügel.[14] (Evelyn Underhill was another likely catalyst.) But O'Connor herself was too much a pessimistic southerner, too invested a sacramental Catholic, and too stubbornly pragmatic to be fully taken in by mysticism on its own, much less become a mystic herself.[15] In a letter to Ted Spivey in 1958, she writes, "I got a double dose of the mystics, mostly Spanish and Italian, and I haven't had a taste for them since."[16] Yet in the very next line she expresses an interest in reading von Hügel's *The Mystical Element*.

Whatever her disposition might have been at the time toward mysticism, many of O'Connor's fictional characters see visions and dream dreams and generally carry on in ways that might be considered the twentieth-century southern backwoods version of medieval mysticism. O'Connor herself was drawn, likely in spite of herself, to the mystic tradition. She had read about the deep fount of divine experience that mysticism provided for those who practiced it, and she wanted something like that for herself, as her early diary entries at Yaddo, the books in her personal library related to mysticism, and her trip to Lourdes all seem to indicate.[17] But what she needed was someone to systematize and

Stein, writing of the latter two, "[Weil] and Stein are the two 20th-century women who interest me most"; O'Connor, *The Habit of Being*, 93.

14. Catherine, Charlotte C. Balfour, Helen Douglas-Irvine, and Battistina Vernazza. *Treatise on Purgatory: The Dialogue* (London: Sheed and Ward, 1946). O'Connor's signature and the year "1949" is written on the inside cover. Von Hügel figures prominently in this edition, given his place as the principal biographer of St. Catherine.

15. Some scholars claim that O'Connor was, indeed, a mystic. See, for example, Cecilia McGowan, "The Faith of Flannery O'Connor," *Catholic Digest* (February 1983): 74–78. Ted Spivey writes that O'Connor "was no less a visionary than earlier Catholic mystics who looked to the sky for inspiration," but adds that "[h]er mysticism was directed at nature and society." Ted Spivey, *The Woman, the Thinker, the Visionary* (Macon, Ga.: Mercer University Press, 1997), 103. William Kirkland thinks that O'Connor's "deep sense of mystery and her Thomistic reliance on reason *and* revelation came together in a nonpietistic mysticism that was peculiarly Catholic"; Kirkland, *Bulletin*, 30.

16. O'Connor, *The Habit of Being*, 297.

17. Perhaps the urgency of her disease also led to a heightened interest in such

incarnate mysticism and, by doing so, to make it more accessible to a "sensible" Catholic. She found this in von Hügel, who served as the bridge between O'Connor's interest in mystical spirituality, on one hand, and her thoroughgoing commitment to the material, sensible world, on the other. With von Hügel's systematic treatment of mysticism, O'Connor could more readily create the theological stage upon which her characters wrestled with God. The South became O'Connor's literary *Is/ra/el* (*one who / contends with / God*).

Like O'Connor, von Hügel was suspicious of the *merely* spiritual and insisted that the religious life must be marked by a commitment to—and balance of—the sensible, material world, a point he goes to great lengths to defend in virtually all his writing: "Indeed, the Spiritual generally, whether natural or even supernatural, is always preceded or occasioned, accompanied or followed, by the Sensible—the soul by the body."[18] O'Connor quotes this very line, in fact, in "Catholic Novelists and Their Readers," where she, too, argues for the inseparability of such realities: "Baron von Hügel, one of the great modern Catholic scholars, wrote that 'the Supernatural experience always appears as the transfiguration of Natural conditions, acts, states . . . ,' that 'the Spiritual generally is always preceded, or occasioned, accompanied or followed, by the Sensible. . . . The highest realities and deepest responses are experienced by us within, or in contact with, the lower and the lowliest.'"[19] O'Connor believed that the

matters, but what we see in the diaries prior to her diagnosis is a young woman with an incredibly sensitive spiritual disposition yearning for a mystical connection to God. Her trip to Lourdes as a reluctant pilgrim appears on the surface to be quite another matter, given her sardonic assessment of the trip; she quipped to many a friend that "the miracle at Lourdes is that there are no epidemics . . ."; O'Connor, *The Habit of Being*, 286. And yet later, and quite poignantly, O'Connor expressed gratitude for the place after her doctor told her that there had been a significant improvement in her condition. "Maybe this is Lourdes," she wrote. "Anyway, it's something to be thankful to the same Source for"; O'Connor, *The Habit of Being*, 305.

18. Von Hügel, *Essays*, 292.

19. Flannery O'Connor, *Mystery and Manners: Occasional Prose*, ed. Sally and

mystery of God is mysterious largely *because* it is embodied in the material. The Incarnation, in other words, is precisely what gives God's divine mystery its peculiar vitality, and to separate the two is to do injury to both; it would be to fall into either one of two egregious but opposite errors of rank materialism, on one hand, or dualistic Manichaeism, on the other.

But von Hügel's influence extended further than notions of the spiritual made manifest in and through the material, or of their essential and indivisible union in this world, or of the central mystery of God being heightened precisely because the Word became flesh. In her essays, letters, and reviews, O'Connor spoke of the "cost" of Christianity, of how faith and obedience cannot be easy things if they are to be of any lasting value, and that such a cost was, in fact, part and parcel of what it means to be a Christian.[20] That O'Connor acknowledges von Hügel as the source of these ideas, which lie at the heart of her fiction, serves to confirm von Hügel's influence on O'Connor as no mere theological balustrade but as belonging to the spiritual center of her foundation as a Catholic writer. This brings up the obvious question: Why has there been such little acknowledgment of von Hügel's influence, he who verily led O'Connor to the wellspring of the mystical tradition and gave her the theological scaffolding to incorporate that tradition into her fictional landscape?

Perhaps the most conspicuous example of this curious neglect of von Hügel in O'Connor scholarship is evidenced by the fact that Neil Scott's exhaustive account of articles, essays, books, and monographs written about O'Connor between 1975 and 2002 includes only a single entry on von Hügel.[21] Other examples of such neglect include Ted Spivey's *The Woman, the Thinker, the Vi-*

Robert Fitzgerald (New York: Farrar, Straus and Giroux, 1969), 176. See also von Hügel, *Essays*, 292. The convergence of these two realities is, of course, the very "mystery and manners" to which the title of her collection of essays refers.

20. O'Connor, *Mystery and Manners*, 112; and *The Habit of Being*, 336.

21. The entry mentioned is William Kirkland's essay, referenced earlier.

sionary; David Eggenschwiler's *The Christian Humanism of Flannery O'Connor*; and Ralph Wood's *Flannery O'Connor and the Christ-Haunted South*, which are merely representative of the whole of O'Connor scholarship.[22] My intention in singling these books out is that each makes a distinct argument for the provenance of O'Connor's thought. Spivey argues that O'Connor's worldview comes from "continental novelists, philosophers, and theologians"; Eggenschwiler traces O'Connor's thought to twentieth-century Catholic humanism; and Wood casts a wider net of influence, which he calls "a veritable compendium of Pre-Vatican II theologians and writers."[23] Von Hügel fits comfortably into any of

22. Many other examples of such neglect exist: Richard Giannone's *The Spiritual Writings of Flannery O'Connor* (Fordham University Press, 1999) includes a lengthy introduction that highlights O'Connor's extensive reading of Catholic writers, and it lists the usual suspects: Chardin, Guardini, Yves Congar—even Protestant writers like Karl Barth, Rudolf Bultmann, and Paul Tillich make the cut. Von Hügel is not included, despite the fact that O'Connor read more of von Hügel's published pages than she did of virtually any other single writer. Von Hügel's name does come up, ironically, in a footnote that quotes O'Connor bemoaning the fact that the Baron "has not been widely read in American Catholic circles" (77).

23. Spivey writes that O'Connor's "Catholic worldview was based on her discovery of certain continental novelists, philosophers, and theologians." He then includes a quote by her from *The Habit of Being* that mentions "Bloy, Bernanos, Mauriac ... Gilson, Maritain and Gabriel Marcel ... Max Picard, Romano Guardini and Karl Adam"; Spivey, *The Woman*, 69. Spivey goes on to talk about the seminal influence of Picard and Bernanos on O'Connor's writing, calling them "the two most important writers for her, among the above." He also includes Teilhard de Chardin and Thomas Merton in that company of those who exacted a profound influence on O'Connor's Catholic vision. Von Hügel is never mentioned in Spivey's book, a curious omission for a number of reasons, not least of which because von Hügel is mentioned a number of times by O'Connor in her correspondence with Spivey; in fact, she sends Spivey her only other copy of *Letters to a Niece*; O'Connor, *The Habit of Being*, 330. David Eggenschwiler's *The Christian Humanism of Flannery O'Connor* (Detroit, Mich.: Wayne State University Press, 1972) does not mention von Hügel a single time, a particularly odd omission given von Hügel's place as one of the leading Catholic Humanists of the twentieth century, while Ralph Wood's *Flannery O'Connor and the Christ-Haunted South* (Grand Rapids, Mich.: William B. Eerdmans, 2004), his groundbreaking theological and cultural examination of O'Connor's place in, and contribution to, the southern literary scene, includes a paragraph dedicated to her extensive reading of Catholic luminaries. He lists Romano Guardini, Jacques Maritain, Etienne Gilson, Tielhard de Chardin, Ga-

these categories. The fact that he makes none of them shows how he remains a minor figure at best in a broad sampling of O'Connor scholarship. Indeed, no book, monograph, article, or dissertation written since her death, with only two exceptions, makes more than a few cursory references to von Hügel and his influence on O'Connor, and most never mention him at all.

Apparently, this neglect of von Hügel was true even prior to O'Connor's death, as she expresses chagrin and surprise at the lack of interest in the man. In her review of his *Letters to a Niece*, she writes, "A protestant minister once remarked to the reviewer that he had never met an American Catholic priest who had read Baron von Hügel. Since Friedrich von Hügel is frequently considered, along with Newman and Acton, as one of the great Catholic scholars, it is to be hoped that the minister's acquaintance with priests was limited. With the publication of Baron von Hügel's letters to his niece, this great man and his vigorous, intelligent piety may become better known to Americans."[24] In another review a year later, this time of von Hügel's *Essays*, O'Connor continues her lament regarding von Hügel's relative obscurity, even among Catholics: "The writings of Baron von Hügel have apparently been little read in this country by Catholics in spite of the reissue of his 'Letters to a Niece.' ... This is unfortunate because a consideration of the always measured and intellectually just tone of his essays on religious subjects would serve as an antidote to the frequently superficial methods by which many popular American Catholic writers approach and sidestep the problems of faith or meet them with the Instant Answer."[25] Of the few scholars who do mention him, Robert Brinkmeyer exemplifies this dubious relationship that von Hügel has had with O'Connor

---

briel Marcel, Léon Bloy, Charles Peguy, Martin D'Arcy, Christopher Dawson, Eric Voegelin, Bruce Vawter, John McKenzie, and Claude Tresmontant. Von Hügel does not make the list.

24. Zuber, *Presence*, 21.

25. Zuber, *Presence*, 41.

scholarship through the years, which amounts to an admixture of nods to his significant influence along with a simultaneous neglect of any substantive acknowledgment of that influence. Brinkmeyer mentions von Hügel in a single passage: "At the center of O'Connor's thinking was her conviction that the writer of fiction can express the mysteries of existence only as embodied in concrete human experience. In 'Catholic Novelists and Their Readers' she cites several observations by Baron Friedrich von Hügel on the concreteness of spiritual experience [and] then notes the relevance of von Hügel's insights to the artist."[26] Brinkmeyer then immediately discusses O'Connor's insistence that "only by making their stories believable on a dramatic level can Christian writers suggest what she frequently called the 'added dimension'—the Christian mysteries."[27] In a single citation, in other words, Brinkmeyer distills von Hügel's immense influence on O'Connor to a single salient passage, mentioning what is arguably the key characteristic of all of O'Connor's fiction—namely, its deeply incarnational quality—and rightly acknowledges the provenance of this key characteristic as being von Hügel. Then he simply moves on without another mention of the Baron at all.[28]

To be sure, any study written prior to the publication of *The Habit of Being* (1979) can perhaps be excused for underestimating von Hügel's influence, because O'Connor's effusive regard for the man and his writing becomes clearly evident in her published letters. But what of the studies since 1979? And what are we to do with the fact that in her collection of essays, *Mystery and Manners* (1989), the second-longest quotation is from a passage in von

26. Robert Brinkmeyer, *The Art and Vision of Flannery O'Connor* (Baton Rouge: Louisiana State University, 1989), 167.

27. Brinkmeyer, *The Art and Vision of Flannery O'Connor*, 167.

28. Christine Bieber-Lake confirms Brinkmeyer's position when she writes that O'Connor's notion of grace working through nature comes from von Hügel. See Bieber-Lake's *The Incarnational Art of Flannery O'Connor* (Macon, Ga.: Mercer University Press, 2005), 12f. Bieber-Lake is one of the few O'Connor scholars who refers to von Hügel a few times, but still, she does not acknowledge his central contribution to O'Connor's incarnational art.

Hügel?[29] Von Hügel's writings are, in fact, alluded to or directly quoted more times in *Mystery and Manners* (at least six) than any other writer. Evidence of von Hügel's influence, in other words, has been readily available to those with eyes to see.

Two who did see were William Kirkland and Anne Ebrecht, both of whom wrote about von Hügel's influence on O'Connor. Ebrecht argues that von Hügel's main contribution to O'Connor's thought involved the notion that the material and spiritual planes are of a piece and cannot be separated without doing violence to both.[30] She writes about von Hügel, that his "Catholicism is essentially a 'twice-born temper, a moving indeed into the visible and sublunar; yet this in order to raise the visible ... to the invisible and transcendent.'"[31] The same can be said of O'Connor, and Ebrecht acknowledges her debt to von Hügel in this regard: "It is easy to understand why O'Connor valued von Hügel's ideas so highly. For a central idea in each of the pieces in his Essays and Addresses is the complex nature of man—flesh and spirit, one half incomplete without the other. For von Hügel, man is not simply mind. He is also sense, imagination, feeling, and will. Human personality holds and harmonizes all these forces in a difficult but [thorough?] interpenetration. Throughout his writings he emphasizes the richness of the interrelated elements of the unique creature man and the richness of this relation to [the] physical world."[32]

William Kirkland saw O'Connor's debt to von Hügel even more clearly than does Ebrecht. Kirkland, an Anglican priest who moved to Milledgeville in the spring of 1954 and met Flannery later that summer, writes that what stood out in their first meeting was their mutual admiration of von Hügel, which sur-

29. O'Connor, *Mystery and Manners*, 176.

30. Ann Ebrecht, "Flannery O'Connor's Moral Vision and 'The Things of This World'" (PhD diss., Tulane University, 1982).

31. Ebrecht, *Moral Vision*, 34.

32. Ebrecht, *Moral Vision*, 29. See, for example, O'Connor, *Mystery and Manners*, 41f.

prised them both because he was so little-known outside of England. He remembers her exclaiming at that first encounter, "He's wonderful!"[33] They each owned a well-worn copy of von Hügel's *Letters to a Niece*, so well worn, apparently, that O'Connor tells Betty Hester in a letter the following year that she intended to order up another copy of the book, which, incidentally, she would send on to Ted Spivey five years later, in the spring of 1959.

Kirkland argues that von Hügel's influence on O'Connor was more of a personal rather than professional one: "[A]s important as the von Hügel legacy was to Flannery O'Connor the artist, it must have had a more profound meaning in her personal life . . . and in the strengthening of her religious faith."[34] Yet O'Connor herself claimed that writers write with their entire being, their whole personality: "For the writer of fiction, everything has its testing point in the eye, and the eye is an organ that eventually involves the whole personality," and "[i]t is a fact that fiction writing is something in which the whole personality takes part—the conscious as well as the unconscious mind."[35] Kirkland's claim, in other words, introduces a dichotomy that O'Connor herself rejected. She believed that the person and the writer, although distinct, were finally inseparable.

Kirkland nevertheless acknowledges von Hügel's influence on O'Connor's craft, writing that "from about 1954 . . . to the end of her life, the Baron was one of her mentors" and that O'Connor "was significantly influenced by the man and his writings."[36] He goes on to spell out this significance, claiming, for instance, that O'Connor's belief "that the supernatural is known in and through the natural: the God of Grace is also the God of Nature" was taken

33. Kirkland, *Bulletin*, 28. I suspect Kirkland might be the Protestant minister O'Connor refers to in her review of von Hügel's *Letters* who states that he's "never met an American Catholic priest who had read Baron von Hügel." Zuber, *Presence*, 21.

34. Kirkland, *Bulletin*, 37.

35. O'Connor, *Mystery and Manners*, 91, 101.

36. Kirkland, *Bulletin*, 29.

directly from von Hügel.[37] Von Hügel talks of the God of the heavens interpenetrating the whole of the cosmos, including "his little planet," and although the heavens seem infinitely distant, they are yet "near, near at least to the complete and fundamental Jesus; for it is assuredly part of, it is penetrated by, the spirit of Christ living in the Church to bless and to purify all the gifts and calls of the God of Nature by the calls and gifts of the God of Grace."[38] He also writes, "The dispensation under which we men actually live is not a dispensation of Simple Nature but a dispensation of Mingled Nature and Supernature."[39] Repeatedly in *Mystery and Manners*, O'Connor makes a similar if not identical point, that "the fiction writer presents mystery through manners, grace through nature"; that the two are ineluctably related and "the more a writer wishes to make the supernatural apparent, the more real he has to be able to make the natural world"; and that "if [the novelist] is going to show the supernatural taking place, he has nowhere to do it except on the literal level of natural events."[40] O'Connor consistently warns against separating the two because one "cannot show the operation of grace when grace is cut off from nature" and "as grace and nature have been separated, so imagination and reason have been separated, and this always means an end to art."[41]

O'Connor's choice to connect the inseparability of grace and nature (an idea she finds over and over again in von Hügel) with the inseparability of "mystery and manners" is brought up again in her complaints about her readers' need for easy solutions wherein they are "transported, instantly, either to mock damnation or a mock innocence."[42] She extends this temptation to all Catholics, writing, "We Catholics are very much given to the Instant Answer. Fiction doesn't have any. It leaves us, like Job, with

---

37. Kirkland, *Bulletin*, 29.
38. Von Hügel, *Essays*, 143.
39. Von Hügel, *Essays*, xiv.
40. O'Connor, *Mystery and Manners*, 116, 153, 176.
41. O'Connor, *Mystery and Manners*, 82, 166, see also 184.
42. O'Connor, *Mystery and Manners*, 49.

a renewed sense of mystery."[43] Her curious use of the phrase "Instant Answer" is used only one other time in her writing, in her review of von Hügel's *Essays*.[44]

In "Catholic Novelists and Their Readers," after she spends the first few pages talking about the talent necessary to be a decent novelist of any kind, O'Connor moves to a long discussion about the necessity of mystery in fiction—the essay's central point and one of the singular emphases of O'Connor's entire approach as a Catholic writer: "the main concern of the fiction writer is with mystery and how it is incarnated in human life."[45] She immediately cites von Hügel and, for the next few pages, builds this argument using his ideas as her foundation. She then laments the Christian instinct to dispense with mystery, and again she quotes von Hügel, again regarding the particular temptation of Catholic novelists to want to "tidy up reality."[46]

What is apparent in all of these examples is how O'Connor attaches von Hügel, either explicitly or implicitly, to central and controlling ideas of her vocation as a Catholic writer. Much of the rest of "Catholic Novelists and Their Readers" is an homage to von Hügel's ideas. Kirkland contends that such ideas—the inseparability of grace and nature and their connection to the "costingness" of faith (see the following discussion) and to the whole world of mystery and manners; the need to dispense with the Instant Answer and not fall prey to the compulsion to tidy up reality—were crucial for O'Connor "as a believer and as a writer of a unique kind of fiction."[47]

As an example of such an influence, one need only examine the use and purpose of violence in O'Connor's stories. O'Connor

43. O'Connor, *Mystery and Manners*, 184.

44. See Zuber, *Presence*, 41.

45. The fact that O'Connor cites von Hügel twice in this essay, which she wrote just before her death in 1964, tells us that O'Connor meant what she said when she told Hester almost a decade earlier that von Hügel was "something for a lifetime and not any passing pleasure"; O'Connor, *The Habit of Being*, 165.

46. O'Connor, *Mystery and Manners*, 177–178. Von Hügel, *Essays*, 288.

47. Kirkland, *Bulletin*, 29.

scholars generally fall into one of two camps regarding such
violence: that it is the result of the devil's—or sinful human nature's—actions, which God then inscrutably turns to his divine
purposes when he (or O'Connor) sees fit, or that the violence reflects the cosmic battle between good and evil, God and the devil,
whose designs are variously ordained for divine or evil purposes.[48] However, I suggest a third alternative, which seeks to understand the violence in her stories in relation to whether grace
and nature are held together or separated.[49]

48. This difference is perhaps most palpably seen in the competing interpretations of the verse from which the title of O'Connor's second novel comes: "From
the days of John the Baptist until now, the kingdom of Heaven suffereth violence,
and the violent bear it away" (Mt 11:12). Some interpret the "violent" as the malevolent who try to steal the Kingdom of Heaven away from the righteous, while
others understand the violent to be the saints themselves, who protect and ultimately fulfill the Kingdom of God by violent means. The former, like John Traynor
Jr., thus see Old Tarwater as a malevolent creature and Francis' subsequent murder of Bishop as an experience of "catharsis" because the boy "has been uprooted
from the fiery brimstone patch of his great-uncle's planting"; John Traynor Jr.,
"Books," Extension 55 (July 1960): 25. Stanley Hyman agrees, concluding that "the
verse's clear meaning is that the violent are enemies of the kingdom, capturing it
from the righteous"; Hyman, Flannery O'Connor (St. Paul: University of Minnesota
Press, 1966), 26. The latter camp, represented in John May's essay "The Violent Bear
It Away: The Meaning of the Title" in Flannery O'Connor Bulletin 2 (1973), 83–86,
understands the violence of Old Tarwater's fierce visions and Bishop's subsequent
baptism by Francis "as a mark of the enthusiast," rather than enemies of the kingdom of God and such deeds as "a sign of intensity of belief" (84). In effect, the two
camps disagree on which of the two—the baptism or the drowning—deserves existential priority.

49. It should be noted that violence seen in this light does not follow the
conventional understanding of violence as something primarily physical and/or
obviously destructive. Rather, it indicates a disruptive and unwanted experience
in a person's life that often (though not always) leads to a dramatic or unexpected
change. Such a definition of violence, I believe, reflects not only a more inclusive
and realistic understanding of how most people experience violence in their lives
but a more biblical understanding, as well. One need only consider the social and
emotional (not to mention physical) ramifications of the Annunciation, for example, where a young betrothed Jewish girl learns in a vision that she's been im-
pregnated by the Holy Spirit; or the devastating economic implications of Jesus's
calling of the disciples away from their means of supporting their families; or
the imprisonment of Paul. Each event is predicated on an understanding of God's
severe mercies, which not only lead through violent means for the purpose of redemptive ends but whose means are themselves redemptive (Gabriel's announce-

The table on the following page draws on such a distinction between divine violence, on one hand, which keeps grace and nature together, and demonic violence, on the other, which separates them. Von Hügel and O'Connor both insisted that the impulse to separate the two—which finds its origins in the Fall and the desire to see the fruit not as a means for communion with God but as an end in itself—was demonic.[50] O'Connor makes use of both kinds of violence prior to her formal introduction to von Hügel in or around 1954, but this particular idea of divine violence—to which von Hügel himself was drawn and which would become a controlling motif in his biography of St. Catherine of Genoa—is a central preoccupation in St. Catherine's *Treatise on Purgatory*, which O'Connor had read as early as 1949 (see p. 136). The violence in O'Connor's stories, it should be noted, is not always or even primarily physical.

This O'Connor axiom, that grace and nature are separated only at our peril, an idea that she explicitly borrows from and credits to von Hügel, turns out, I believe, to be a reliable guide for delineating the two kinds of violence present in O'Connor's fiction. Demonic violence separates grace from nature and, in so doing, becomes an end in itself, which, in O'Connor's world, always resulted, in one form or another, in an abject denial of a person's status as *imago Dei*. The person becomes a thing, or a

---

ment not only to Mary but to Joseph, Jesus's compassion for his disciples' willingness to commit to his summons in the opening words of his Sermon on the Mount, Paul's access to sympathetic prison guards and the quite literal forcing of his hand to pen and pen to paper as the only means of communication to his churches).

50. Original sin, Alexander Schmemann contends, came by way of the first Adam's partaking of the one food that was an end in itself and not something blessed by God and given as a gift to us. The effect was that we began to see the world as an end in itself and not as a gift from God, and when such a separation occurs—when we see life as an end in itself—everything loses value because nothing has significance outside of itself, because "only in God is found the meaning (value) of everything and the world is meaningful only when it is the 'sacrament' of God's presence." "The world of nature, cut off from the source of life," Schmemann avers, "is a dying world." From *For the Life of the World* (New York: St. Vladimir's Seminary Press, 1973), 17.

	DIVINE VIOLENCE (Grace and Nature Together)	DEMONIC VIOLENCE (Grace and Nature Separated)
Wise Blood	Self-blinding and subsequent death of Hazel Motes	Killing of pedestrian; sleeping with prostitute
A Good Man Is Hard to Find	The threat of violence and subsequent murder of the Grandma	The murder of the family; the Grandma's sentimental faith; the Misfit's recalcitrance
The River	The drowning of Bevel	The neglect of Harry's (Bevel's) parents
The Life You Save May Be Your Own	Shiftlet's leaving Lucynell with the waiter who saw her as an angel	The mother's objectifying "love" of her daughter; Shiftlet's kidnapping of Lucynell
A Stroke of Good Fortune	Ruby's pregnancy	Ruby's treatment of Bill Hill and Rufus
A Temple of the Holy Ghost	The response of the child to the hermaphrodite	The response of the girls to the hermaphrodite
The Artificial Nigger	Mr. Head's and Nelson's mind-altering epiphany at the lawn jockey	Mr. Head's denial of Nelson
A Circle in the Fire	The boys burning down of Ms. Copes' woods	
A Late Encounter with the Enemy	General Sash's death after his revelation	Sally's objectifying her grandfather
Good Country People	Manley's theft of Hulga's wooden leg	Manley's scheming ways; Hulga's cynicism; her mother's gentrified religion
The Displaced Person	Mrs. McIntyre's epiphany	The objectification and subsequent murder of Guizac
The Violent Bear It Away	The drowning baptism of Bishop; the collapse of Rayber; the kidnappings	The rape of Tarwater; Rayber's treatment of Bishop; the Friend's counsel
Everything That Rises Must Converge	The mother's collapse, her revelation, and her death	Julian's and his mother's racism; their distorted love
Greenleaf	Mrs. May's death by (papal) bull	Mrs. May's view and treatment of Mrs. Greenleaf and her family
A View of the Woods		Fortune's treatment of nature and of his progeny; his murder of Mary
The Enduring Chill		Asbury's view of the world and of himself
The Comforts of Home		Thomas's shooting of his mother; his attempted murder of Star Drake
The Lame Shall Enter First	Rufus's truth telling; Sheppard's conversion; Norton's death	Sheppard's distorted love for Norton and concern for Rufus; Rufus's distorted will
Revelation	The teenage girl's assault of Ruby; Ruby's pigsty (Prodigal?) conversion	Ruby's racism and classism; Claud's passivity
Parker's Back	Parker's tattoo	Sarah Ruth's rejection of him; her disembodied faith
Judgment Day	Tanner's being attacked and his subsequent revelation	Tanner's racism; the neighbor's complicity in his death; the daughter's distorted love

type, or part of a class. Thus, to objectify is to kill, literally or figuratively; it is, in either case, to render a person something less than who he or she is, less than *imago Dei.*

Divine violence, on the other hand, sees the whole person for who he or she is and, in doing so, refuses to separate grace from nature, and in such a refusal, grants the recipient of such violence access to redemptive truth, goodness, and beauty, whether in the form of a teenage prank or a bull's upending horn. The spirit and the material conspire together in a kind of divine hermeneutic, uncovering the hidden truth beneath the distorted surface of things. If such a scheme seems far-fetched, it is well to remember that Jesus reevaluates true violence as a metaphysical category that includes one's thoughts and intentions as well as one's actions. The reader of O'Connor's stories, in like manner, must be prepared to look at the violence of her stories with Jesus's eyes. One has to be willing to get ahold of the right horror, in other words.[51]

Another of von Hügel's ideas that Kirkland suggests was an influence on O'Connor is the terrible "cost" of one's faith. Kirkland writes, "'Friction' and 'costingness' were, von Hügel thought, the sine qua non of healthy growth for the individual and for institutional religion."[52] A typical example of such "costingness" is found in his *Essays,* where he argues that "there is, finally, no such thing as appurtenance to a particular religious body without cost—cost to the poorer side of human nature and cost even, in some degree and way, to the better side of that same nature."[53] O'Connor, in

51. If O'Connor believes that sentiment can lead to the gas chambers and Jesus reevaluates murder to include what we say and not just what we do, then readers of O'Connor must be willing to look at the violence in her stories with a similar bias. In this connection, von Hügel distinguishes between *consolation* and *desolation* and insists that one follows the other, "and the latter is when and where God sends it, and we have not ourselves brought it on ourselves by laxness and dissipation . . ."; von Hügel, *Letters,* 105. So there is the abomination of desolation in Jesus's Olivet discourse, but then there is a desolation wrought by God, and von Hügel thought this the better way to God than consolation. So did O'Connor.

52. Kirkland, *Bulletin,* 32.

53. Von Hügel, *Essays,* 15. See also his *Mystical Element,* 47, 256, 281, 358, 382; and *Letters,* 21, 26, and this from page 62, "I want, then, to wish you a very rich,

fact, remarked on von Hügel's frequent use of the word *cost* and its grammatical variants in a letter to Ted Spivey where she castigates Beat writers for being too self-consciously and *conveniently* countercultural: "They seem to know a good many of the right things to run away from, but to lack any necessary discipline. They call themselves holy but holiness costs and so far as I can see they pay nothing. It's true that grace is the free gift of God but in order to put yourself in the way of being receptive to it you have to practice self-denial. I observe that Baron von Hügel's most used words are derivatives of the word *cost*."[54]

In the composite essay "On Her Own Work," O'Connor acknowledges that this notion of cost is crucial for her fiction; that we the readers, like her characters, usually have such hard heads that "reality is something to which we must be returned at considerable cost"; and that although this cost can often involve violent means, it is a cost that is nonetheless "implicit in the Christian view of the world."[55] It was certainly implicit in O'Connor's worldview as well as in her theology, and her characters were not spared its implications. And neither was she.

In O'Connor's own life, this cost of obedience found its most poignant expression in her fourteen-year struggle with lupus, which set limits on her that she never wanted but which she nevertheless eventually relented as a blessing. One never senses that she deeply resented her condition or that she blamed God for such things, and in this, too, she found a kindred spirit in von Hügel, who was sick much of his own life but bore this fact with the same equanimity that O'Connor appears to have mustered in the face of her own illness.[56]

Besides Kirkland and Ebrecht, other scholars acknowledge O'Connor's debt to von Hügel. According to Lorine Getz, von Hü-

---

deep, true, straight and simple growth in the love of God, accepted and willed gently but greatly, *at the daily, hourly, cost of self*"; emphasis original.

54. O'Connor, *The Habit of Being*, 336.

55. O'Connor, *Mystery and Manners*, 112.

56. See de la Bedoyere, *The Life*, 342f.

gel is "among the most heavily annotated of her holdings,"[57] a fact confirmed by Arthur Kinney's study of O'Connor's library and marginalia, where the single longest theological or philosophical citation of O'Connor's marginalia is of von Hügel's *Essays*.[58]

Jean Cash speculates as to why O'Connor, "with her dedication to writing fiction, her extensive correspondence with numerous friends, and her desire to lecture as widely as she was able," took on "the added responsibility of becoming a regular reviewer for *The Bulletin*." Cash argues that "[w]riting regular reviews gave [O'Connor] the opportunity both to read and comment on books that she probably would have found and read anyway [and] writing about them helped her to focus her understanding of the ideas of the Catholic theologians whom she most admired, among them Romano Guardini, Baron Friedrich von Hügel, Karl Adam, Gustave Weigel, and Pierre Teilhard de Chardin."[59]

If one is to accept von Hügel's crucial role as the catalyst that helped develop these ideas in O'Connor, overestimating his decisive influence on her as a writer seems, indeed, difficult. The inseparability of grace and nature and their connection to the whole paradox of mystery and manners; the need to dispense with the Instant Answer and to accept the "costingness" of Christian belief; the centrality of mystery as a critical reality in religious life, as well as a controlling device in fiction—if these were not central themes and devices in O'Connor's writing, she would have been a different writer, if not a different person altogether. And all of these iconic O'Connor themes found, if not their source, then at the very least their theological imprimatur, in Baron von Hügel's writings.

In *The Habit of Being*, O'Connor mentions von Hügel more than

57. Lorine Getz, *Flannery O'Connor: Her Life, Library and Book Reviews* (New York: The Edwin Mellen Press, 1980), 70.

58. Arthur Kinney, *Flannery O'Connor's Library: Resources of Being* (Athens: The University of Georgia Press, 1985), 29–32.

59. Jean Cash, *Flannery O'Connor: A Life* (Knoxville: University of Tennessee Press, 2004), 67.

either Maritain or Chardin, as many times as Mauriac and Guardini, and more effusively and favorably than any of them. For example, she writes to Hester in 1956 about von Hügel's *Essays*, "I didn't know the essays existed where they could be got hold of, and I can think of nothing that I am gladder to be reading.... The old man I think is the most congenial spirit I have found in English Catholic letters, with more to say, to me anyway, than Newman.... They [von Hügel's essays] require to be read many times and you have given me something for a lifetime and not any passing pleasure."[60] In a letter to Spivey in 1958 (not included in *The Habit of Being*), in response to his question about her influences and favorite Catholic novelists and theologians, O'Connor lists five writers: Bernanos, Guardini, Karl Adam, Marcel, and von Hügel.[61]

O'Connor first mentions von Hügel in a letter to Betty Hester in November of 1955, saying that she'd "like to read Baron von Hügel's book, *The Mystical Element in [sic] Religion*."[62] Two weeks later in another letter to Hester, O'Connor writes that she intends "to order off after his *Letters to a Niece*."[63] In this same letter, O'Connor refers to St. Catherine of Genoa's meditations on purgatory. By May 1956, she has already reviewed *Letters to a Niece* for the Bulletin and asks Hester if she'd like to read it, telling her that it is "absolutely finer than anything I've seen in a long time,"[64] high praise from someone of O'Connor's prodigious reading prowess who had digested in that year alone books by Kristen Undset, Romano Guardini, Simone Weil, Raissa Maritain, William Michelfelder, Eric Gill, and Marcel Proust, among others. In her review, she expresses her hope that with "the publication of Baron von Hügel's letters to his niece, this great man and his vigorous, intelligent piety may become better known to

60. O'Connor, *The Habit of Being*, 165.
61. Spivey, *The Woman*, 45.
62. O'Connor, *The Habit of Being*, 116.
63. O'Connor, *The Habit of Being*, 119.
64. O'Connor, *The Habit of Being*, 155–156.

Americans."[65] As a way of characterizing the book, O'Connor chooses to focus on von Hügel's warning to this niece not to read "only religious literature, however good, and [thus allow] the fascinations of Grace to deaden the expressions of nature and thereby 'lose the material for Grace to work on.'"[66] As discussed earlier, this oft-quoted phrase of O'Connor's expresses one of the central motifs in her writing, and it is an idea that she attributes explicitly to von Hügel in this review.

Von Hügel comes up again in another letter to Hester in July 1956, where O'Connor writes that she's "too busy reading the Baron's essays" and adds that she'll "finish the biography, after which I may go back and read the Baron's essays again." She tells Hester that von Hügel's "*Essays* are better than his *Letters*" and that she's "marked up the first three essays thoroughly."[67]

A week or so later she is offering yet more praise for von Hügel, this time in a letter to Bill Sessions,[68] and a week after that, again in a letter to Hester, she tells her that she's finished the biography of von Hügel and that it has helped her understand his *Essays* better. Barely a week after that she tells Hester that she's "finished the biography of the Baron" and is about to embark on volume 2 of the Baron's essays. "Vol. 1," she says, "is much marked up."[69] In her last letter of 1956, she writes to Hester, "Well, a happy new year and more thanks than I can tell you for the many things you have done for me, for Baron von Hügel and Simone Weil, but even more for your own letters."[70]

Eight months later, in August 1957, O'Connor writes that she has just sent off a review of both volumes of *Essays*,[71] and in September 1958 tells Hester once again that she'd like to read von

---

65. Zuber, *Presence*, 21.
66. Zuber, *Presence*, 21.
67. O'Connor, *The Habit of Being*, 165.
68. O'Connor, *The Habit of Being*, 166.
69. O'Connor, *The Habit of Being*, 168.
70. O'Connor, *The Habit of Being*, 192.
71. O'Connor, *The Habit of Being*, 236.

Hügel's book on Catherine of Genoa but that it is unobtainable. Apparently not that unobtainable, as nine months later, in June of 1959, she tells Hester all about the book and says, "I am more than ever impressed with the greatness of von Hügel."[72] In a letter to Spivey written around the same time, she writes that von Hügel's spirit is "an antidote to much of the vulgarity and rawness of American Catholics,"[73] and a few weeks after that sends Spivey a copy of *Letters to a Niece*, which she encourages him to read.[74] Her last mention of von Hügel in *The Habit of Being* comes in another letter to Spivey where she mentions von Hügel's repeated use of the word "cost,"[75] and the rest of the letter is a recapitulation of von Hügel's central ideas.

Later that year (1959), O'Connor sends a letter to the Cheneys after having just sent them a copy of her novel *The Violent Bear It Away* to look over prior to its publication:

Thank you both for reading [*The Violent Bear It Away*]. About the end: I meant that Tarwater was going to the city to be a prophet and the "fate" that awaits him is the fate that awaits all prophets or as the old man said, "the servants of the Lord can expect the worst." I reckon on the children of God doing Tarwater up pretty quick. What he means by the speed of mercy is that mercy burns up what we are attached to, the word is a burning word to burn you clean (see Vol. II Baron Von Hügel, *The Mystical Element of Religion*).[76]

O'Connor is likely referring not to a single passage but to the whole of volume 2 of the book because it references God's burning love, mercy, and grace numerous times, for example, when "Catherine, since her mind has perceived Love to be the central character of God, and has adopted fire as love's fullest image, cannot but hold,—God and Love and Christ and Spirit being all

72. O'Connor, *The Habit of Being*, 335.
73. O'Connor, *The Habit of Being*, 331.
74. See note 23.
75. O'Connor, *The Habit of Being*, 336.
76. Stephens, *Correspondence*, 93.

one and the same thing,—that Christ-Spirit-Fire is in her and she in It."[77]

Not incidentally, only after O'Connor had read von Hügel's *The Mystical Element* do her working drafts of *The Violent Bear It Away* include burning imagery and the terrible nature of God's mercy.[78] It is interesting to note, simply by way of comparison, that the words *mercy, grace, fire, burn,* and *Lord* do not appear a single time in *Wise Blood*, a novel written prior to O'Connor's introduction to von Hügel.[79] It is a story preoccupied with a more *religious* sensibility, or as von Hügel might have put it using the schema of his three elements, a more *sensual* as opposed to a properly *spiritual*, element in mind. *Wise Blood* is largely a physical novel of religious impulses and distractions related to questions of institutional religion and the institutional church; the word *church*, in fact, occurs thirty times in *Wise Blood* whereas it is entirely absent from *The Violent Bear It Away*. Questions of a more spiritual nature—attendant visions, dreams, and prophecies—are the central concern of O'Connor's second novel, and, in this regard, it is a completely different *kind* of novel from *Wise Blood* and seems to indicate not only O'Connor's changing theological preoccupations but, according at least to von Hügel's elemental perspective, her growth in faith.[80]

77. Von Hügel, *Mystical Elements*, vol. 2, 70. See also pages 124–125 and 158 of volume 2 for von Hügel's references to God's grace and mercy being burning realities.

78. Language about Tarwater being sent as a prophet to Mason "to burn [his] eyes clean" appears for the first time in draft (183b), a draft that was written (as far as I could surmise) in the summer of 1959, and an even later addition (189b) has the entry: "GO WARN THE CHILDREN OF GOD, . . . OF THE TERRIBLE SPEED OF JUSTICE, OR THE TERRIBLE SPEED OF MERCY. WHO WILL BE LEFT? WHO WILL BE LEFT WHEN THE LORD'S MERCY STRIKES?"

79. Obtained by a word search in Google Books.

80. I am convinced that similar differences can be found between her two collections of short stories, written before and after her introduction to von Hügel (respectively), but more work needs to be done to show this definitively. Frederick Asals writes about the essential differences between Hazel Motes and Francis Tarwater in *The Flannery O'Connor Bulletin* 4 (1975): 57–58, writing how Motes decides that life is not worth living and "that the best thing to do is get out of it as

But speculations of this sort must wait for another study, one that focuses exclusively on O'Connor's fiction after 1954–1955 and her introduction to von Hügel. Indeed, a fuller comparison of her writing both before and after this period, with deliberate attention being paid to von Hügel's influence, would yield tremendous insight into the development of the themes and rich imagery of O'Connor's fiction as she moved through the second stage of her writing career and into her third. There is much promise in such a study, I believe, but only to the degree that O'Connor scholarship realizes it can no longer neglect von Hügel's influence on O'Connor.[81]

It seems clear that O'Connor's debt to von Hügel was immense. It was, as I hope I've shown here, also fairly obvious, which makes his almost complete neglect in O'Connor scholarship both mystifying and unfortunate. For von Hügel, as for O'Connor, mystery and manners, grace and nature, were two sides of the same coin, each strictly unthinkable without the other and each informing not merely the contours but the essence of the other. Indeed, the incarnation of divine realities was the fact that made their connection necessary and, thus, so mysterious. God's mercy and love, so often presented by the church in sentimental—even tawdry—ways (particularly as they are kept separate from God's judgment and wrath), become, in the hands of O'Connor's genius, burning fixities of the religious life that exact a tremendous cost, a point that her spiritual mentor, Baron von Hügel, went to great lengths to emphasize.

Such a fundamental paradox, long celebrated by the church in the image of the cross, O'Connor compellingly encounters in, and then fully adopts from, von Hügel's writings. It is practi-

---

soon as possible. And that seems to me to be very different from what is implied towards the ending of *The Violent Bear It Away*, and, in fact, all the way through [that novel], in which the whole thrust of the novel is to return the action to this world . . . Tarwater finds that, little as he may like it, he's doomed to live."

81. See note 7.

cally considered a truism in O'Connor studies that these central paradoxes—these "tensions," to use a term of von Hügel's—form the crux (cross) of her writing's mysterious depth and vitality. Would it be too much to say that this tension, so present also in O'Connor's own life, may indeed be the defining characteristic of her legacy both as a writer and as a woman writing in the heart of twentieth-century American South?

CHAPTER 6

The "All-Demanding Eyes"

St. Augustine and the Restless Seeker

Andrew J. Garavel, SJ

"Parker's Back," which Flannery O'Connor wrote as she was dying at the age of thirty-nine, is a story of conversion in which God's grace overwhelms the title character, O. E. Parker, after years of wandering, denial, and dissatisfaction. The present reading points out significant affinities between this narrative and the conversion of St. Augustine of Hippo (354–430) recounted in his *Confessions*, a text that exerts a considerable influence on O'Connor's story.[1] "Parker's Back," in its author's words, "dramatiz[es] a heresy" that

1. The author wishes to acknowledge with gratitude the comments and suggestions received from Professors Francis T. Hannafey, SJ (Fairfield University) and Lawrence A. Vitulano (Yale Child Study Center).

figures importantly in Augustine's work.[2] In addition, the theory of illumination set forth in *The Confessions* can help us to understand Parker's conversion, the crucial moment of which involves light. Consonant with O'Connor's deeply sacramental imagination,[3] the story is informed by Augustine's conviction that we are at least partially able to see the true light of God shining through creation.

It is perhaps the failure to see a theological purpose behind the narrative that has led some critics to regard "Parker's Back" as incoherent or nearly so; for example, Carol Shloss asserts that it is "contrived, its message offered at the expense of credibility ... [there is] the sense of meaning being forced into the unwilling mold of unrelated events."[4] A number of critics have paid attention to the importance of scripture in the story (the allusions to Adam, Moses, Jonah, and Paul; the significance of Parker's given names "Obadiah" and "Elihue"; the tattooed Christ, etc.).[5] However, none of the previous criticism of this work recognizes to any great extent the influence of *The Confessions*. Michel Feith does at one point connect "Augustine's famous '*Tolle, lege*' (Take and read)" to Parker flipping through the tattoo artist's book of

2. Flannery O'Connor, *The Habit of Being: Letters of Flannery O'Connor*, ed. Sally Fitzgerald (New York: Farrar, Straus and Giroux, 1979), 593.

3. Or, as a recent critic observes, O'Connor's "theology is sacramental, her fiction incarnational"; Susan Srigley, *Flannery O'Connor's Sacramental Art* (Notre Dame, Ind.: University of Notre Dame Press, 2004), 16.

4. Carol Shloss, *Flannery O'Connor's Dark Comedies: The Limits of Inference* (Baton Rouge: Louisiana State University Press, 1980), 113, 118.

5. See Debra Romanick Baldwin, "Augustinian Physicality and the Rhetoric of the Grotesque in the Art of Flannery O'Connor," in *Augustine and Literature*, ed. Robert P. Kennedy, Kim Paffenroth, and John Doody (Lanham, Md.: Lexington, 2006), 322; Leon V. Driskell and Joan Brittain, *The Eternal Crossroads: The Art of Flannery O'Connor* (Lexington: University Press of Kentucky, 1972), 115–123; Lorine M. Getz, *Nature and Grace in Flannery O'Connor's Fiction* (Lewiston, N.Y.: Edwin Mellen, 1982), 74–82; John R. May, *The Pruning Word: The Parables of Flannery O'Connor* (Notre Dame, Ind.: University of Notre Dame Press, 1976), 117–120; Ralph C. Wood, *Flannery O'Connor and the Christ-Haunted South* (Grand Rapids, Mich.: William B. Eerdmans, 2004), 45n; and Jacqueline A. Zubeck, "Back to Page One in 'Parker's Back': An Orthodox Examination of O'Connor's Last Story," *Flannery O'Connor Review* 8 (2010): 96–97.

images and hearing a voice telling him to "GO BACK," and Richard Giannone briefly compares Augustine's flight from himself and from God to Parker's.[6] Debra Romanick Baldwin discusses the story in light of the anti-Manichaeism or antidualism shared by Augustine and O'Connor but does not directly relate "Parker's Back" to *The Confessions*; in fact, she holds that "Parker's Back" represents "O'Connor's divergence from Augustine." However, in speaking of the grotesquerie found throughout O'Connor's fiction, Baldwin points out that the writer "adopts the rhetorical force of Augustine's *Confessions* when she appeals to the vivid sensations of sin in order to jar her readers into a deeper encounter with reality."[7]

Augustine was undeniably significant for O'Connor. Although St. Thomas Aquinas is usually considered a more obvious presence in her writings, Frederick Asals argues that "the essential cast of her imagination was far more Augustinian than Thomistic. Reconciliation and synthesis, the congruity of faith and human reason, the harmonious hierarchy of the faculties—the great accommodations of Thomistic thought seem curiously irrelevant to the central experience of O'Connor's fiction; whereas Augustine's disposition of the major contraries—grace and sin, spirit and flesh, God and self, the heavenly city and the earthly—immediately evokes the tensions and dualities of her work."[8] In a similar vein, Andre Bleikasten says that in O'Connor's writings, "[i]nstead of grace coming to complete and crown nature—as the mainstream Catholic tradition would have it—it breaks in on it," an understanding of grace closer to Augustine than to Thomas.[9]

6. Michel Feith, "The Stained-Glass Man: Word and Icon in Flannery O'Connor's 'Parker's Back,'" *Journal of the Short Story in English* 45 (Autumn 2005): paragraph 33, accessed July 25, 2011, http://jsse.revues.org/index447.html. Richard Giannone, *Flannery O'Connor, Hermit Novelist* (Urbana: University of Illinois Press, 2000), 250.

7. Baldwin, "Augustinian Physicality," 302–303.

8. Frederick Asals, *Flannery O'Connor: The Imagination of Extremity* (Athens: University of Georgia Press, 1982), 200.

9. Andre Bleikasten, "The Role of Grace in O'Connor's Fiction," in *Readings*

The figure of Augustine the restless seeker after truth appealed to O'Connor. As Sister Kathleen Feeley points out, "the book on Augustine which best reveals his influence on her is Jean Guitton's *The Modernity of Saint Augustine*. . . . In discussing the timelessness of Augustine's search for truth through the byways of error and sin, Guitton says, 'Sometimes by secret stirrings, sometimes by the promptings of circumstance, God recalls the soul to itself. . . . He makes it aware of its wretchedness . . . he orders [human sinfulness] to the good.' Flannery O'Connor marked this passage, and [her] stories show how deeply the idea embedded itself in her mind."[10] "[S]ecret stirrings" and the "promptings of circumstance" impel both Augustine and Parker toward their true selves and, hence, toward God. Of course, "Parker's Back" is not simply a retelling of *The Confessions* in the twentieth-century South, nor does O'Connor employ Augustine's text in a programmatic or mechanical fashion. In a 1957 essay she observes that

the serious fiction writer will think that any story that can be entirely explained by the adequate motivation of its characters, or by a believable imitation of a way of life, or by a proper theology, will not be a large enough story for him to occupy himself with. This is not to say he does not have to be concerned with adequate motivation or accurate references or a right theology; he does; but he has to be concerned with these only because the meaning of his story does not begin except at a depth where these things have been exhausted. The fiction writer presents mystery through manners, grace through nature, but when he finishes there always has to be left over that sense of Mystery which cannot be accounted for by any human formula.[11]

---

on *Flannery O'Connor*, ed. Jennifer A. Hurley, The Greenhaven Press Literary Companion to American Authors (San Diego, Calif.: Greenhaven, 2001), 78.

10. Sister Kathleen Feeley, SSND, *Flannery O'Connor: The Voice of the Peacock* (New Brunswick, N.J.: Rutgers University Press, 1972), 50. O'Connor wrote a brief, favorable review of Guitton's book for *The Bulletin*, the newspaper of the Diocese of Atlanta; see Leo J. Zuber, *The Presence of Grace and Other Book Reviews by Flannery O'Connor*, ed. Carter W. Martin (Athens: University of Georgia Press, 1983), 90–91.

11. Flannery O'Connor, *Mystery and Manners: Occasional Prose*, ed. Sally and Robert Fitzgerald (New York: Farrar, Straus and Giroux, 1969), 153.

As a story of conversion, "Parker's Back" has strong affiliations with Augustine's work, and although an appreciation of how *The Confessions* informs O'Connor's text does not "entirely explain" the story, it does, I believe, offer the reader a useful avenue to approach the mystery she sets out. That the saint's story captured her imagination is borne out by her brief 1961 review of *The Conversion of Augustine*:

Msgr. [Romano] Guardini notes two approaches in dealing with his subject, both of which he has tried to avoid. One of these sees the Confessions as a record of conversion from evil to good, the outcome only being of interest, the hesitations along the way of no real significance. This view leaves out of account the living man, ignores his psychology and ends with merely theoretical insights. The other approach goes to the opposite extreme and makes psychology and the living process everything and ends seeing the subject as a case history. Msgr. Guardini has steered well in between these two approaches and has produced a psychological study well informed on spiritual realities.[12]

O'Connor adopts this method in writing "Parker's Back," ignoring neither the gradual and tumultuous psychological stages her character undergoes nor what she identified as the subject of her fiction, the mysterious "action of grace in territory held largely by the devil."[13]

Augustine addresses God at the beginning of *The Confessions*: "Thou madest us for Thyself, and our heart is restless, until it repose in Thee."[14] Restlessness as the result of alienation from God figures in both texts: Ralph C. Wood calls Parker's discontent "an Augustinian ache at the core of his unquiet soul, a restlessness seeking the rest that only God can grant."[15] O'Connor

12. O'Connor, quoted in Zuber, *The Presence of Grace*, 113–114.

13. O'Connor, *Mystery and Manners*, 118.

14. Augustine of Hippo, *The Confessions*, trans. E. B. Pusey (Mount Vernon, N.Y.: Peter Pauper, n.d.), Book I, 9. Subsequent quotations are also taken from Pusey's 1838 translation, which O'Connor had in her library; see Arthur F. Kinney, *Flannery O'Connor's Library: Resources of Being* (Athens: University of Georgia Press, 1985), 73.

15. Wood, *Flannery O'Connor*, 44.

describes O.E. Parker as continually dissatisfied: with his wife, with his job, and with the appearance of the tattoos he habitually collects on his body, but mostly with himself. The character brings to mind O'Connor's description of the "type of modern man who can neither believe nor contain himself in unbelief and who searches desperately, feeling about in all experience for the lost God."[16] Of course, Augustine is also dissatisfied in his sinfulness, his wanderings, and his doubts. But whereas *The Confessions* gives an intellectual account of the progress of a troubled soul, of how Augustine proceeds from one inadequate idea or way of life to another, the short story renders its protagonist's anxiety in visual terms: sight, blindness, light, darkness, eyes, and pictures are all integral to the movement he makes toward conversion.

In an address given the year before she wrote the story, O'Connor cites the importance of the "sensible world" for Augustine, and for her own fiction: "St. Augustine wrote that the things of the world pour forth from God in a double way: intellectually into the minds of the angels and physically into the world of things. To the person who believes this—as the western world did up until a few centuries ago—this physical, sensible world is good because it proceeds from a divine source. The artist usually knows this by instinct; his senses, which are used to penetrating the concrete, tell him so.... The artist penetrates the concrete world in order to find at its depths the image of its source, the image of ultimate reality."[17] On another occasion, O'Connor makes clear that sight is the predominant sense in her attempt to get at this source: "For the writer of fiction, everything has its testing point in the eye, an organ which eventually involves the whole personality and as much of the world as can be got into it. Msgr. Romano Guardini has written that the roots of the eye are in the heart."[18] Second only to the face, the eye is the human fea-

16. O'Connor, *Mystery and Manners*, 159.
17. O'Connor, *Mystery and Manners*, 157.
18. O'Connor, *Mystery and Manners*, 159.

ture most frequently alluded to in O'Connor's stories,[19] in which
a character's ability to see often functions as a marker of his or
her moral integrity. That O'Connor's primary avocations—painting and the raising of that most visually arresting of birds, the
peacock—involved sight is not surprising.

Parker's journey starts when he has a vision of a tattooed man at
a fair: "a single intricate design of brilliant color" on the skin, "men
and beasts and flowers" that seem to come alive with the motion
of the man's muscles. The fourteen-year-old Parker is strangely
moved at the sight: prompted by wonder at the beauty of the created universe, the men and beasts and flowers coming together in
a unified design, he begins to feel a previously unknown wonder at
the fact of his own existence. But the created world "writ small" on
the tattooed man's skin is still insufficient and leaves Parker with
a "peculiar unease.... It was as if a blind boy had been turned so
gently in a different direction that he did not know his destination
had been changed."[20] Blind to the light shining through created
reality, Parker does not realize he has been turned, in the sense
that the word *conversion* literally implies a turning.

Augustine would at first seem to be antagonistic to the sense
of sight: although he deems it the primary of the senses, it is also
in a way the most dangerous. Relentlessly curious, insatiable
and fickle, the eyes lead the weak astray: "The eyes love fair and
varied forms, and bright and soft colors. Let not these occupy my
soul; let God rather occupy it, who made these things, very good
indeed, yet He is my good, not they.... What innumerable toys,
made by divers arts and manufactures ... in pictures ... and divers images, and these far exceeding all necessary and moderate
use and all pious meaning, have men added to tempt their own
eyes withal." Yet in the same passage he asserts that reflections

19. See Donald E. Hardy, *The Body in Flannery O'Connor's Fiction: Computational Technique and Linguistic Voice* (Columbia: University of South Carolina Press,
2007), 95–96.

20. Flannery O'Connor, *Collected Works*, ed. Sally Fitzgerald (New York: Library of America, 1988), 658.

of God are to be found in created beauties and he praises the Creator "because those beautiful patterns which through men's souls are conveyed into their cunning hands, come from that Beauty, which is above our souls, which my soul day and night sigheth after."[21] Augustine testifies that he himself has been, and continues to be, assailed by temptations of the senses, yet (at times without his being aware of it) he is saved by God's grace. Even though "the framers and followers of the outward beauties" do not recognize God's presence in the beautiful objects they behold, nonetheless, "He is there, though they perceive Him not, that so they might not wander, but keep their strength for Thee, and not scatter it abroad upon pleasurable weariness."[22] Augustine warns against pursuing beauty for its own sweet sake; rather, it should be sought only insofar as it leads one to God, the source of all beauty. For example, he worries about the effects of beautiful music, even in the liturgy: one should be "moved, not with the singing, but with the things sung.... Yet when it befalls me to be more moved with the voice than the words sung, I confess to have sinned penally, and then had rather not hear music."[23] More than once he emphasizes that the Creator is not to be identified with creation, yet God draws sinful humanity in and through created things. For Augustine, Paul's image of the clouded mirror in 1 Corinthians 13:12 ("For now we see through a glass darkly; but then face to face") is, as Carol Harrison points out, "a powerful metaphor of human life following the Fall.... The vision of Divine Beauty, which man has lost, can ... be grasped in the mirror of created reality, albeit obscured by a veil of temporality and corporeity (indeed, this is precisely the reason it *can* be grasped by fallen man). This is most especially the case with the revelation of divine beauty within that realm, which serves to reform ... deformed or ugly man by inspiring his faith, hope and love,

21. Augustine, *Confessions*, X:214.
22. Augustine, *Confessions*, X:215.
23. Augustine, *Confessions*, X:213.

not simply to look *at* it, but *in* and *through* it, to bring him to vision face to face."[24] At first, Parker is one of those "followers of the outward beauties" who do not perceive God revealed in created things. He tries to replicate on his own skin the "bright and soft colors" in "beautiful patterns" but without any clear direction or sense of his own motivations. As Augustine is first attracted by and then disappointed in various relationships, places, sensual experiences, and ideas, so Parker "did not care much what the subject was so long as it was colorful. . . . [He] would be satisfied with each tattoo about a month, then something about it that had attracted him would wear off."[25] He does not know what the "something" is that first drew him to a particular tattoo, why he no longer finds it attractive, or what is behind his need to collect tattoos in the first place. Nonetheless, his fascination with tattoos is positive as it shows his recognition of the (limited) good to be found in God's creation, and as it moves him towards the final tattoo which will be instrumental in his conversion.

When he gets his first tattoo at the age of fifteen, "[i]t hurt very little, just enough to make it appear to Parker to be worth doing. This was peculiar too for before he had thought that only what did not hurt was worth doing."[26] This sense that there might be something beyond his own pleasure is another moment in his turning. For Augustine, his theft of pears from an orchard "in [the] sixteenth year of my age" also produces a change of view. The reason he stole plagues him years afterward: he neither needed nor wanted the fruit but delighted in the wickedness of the act itself. In part, both experiences suggest an adolescent rite of passage, perhaps an attempt to define oneself by rebelling against adult constraints. However, the thrill of the transgression soon dissipates, leaving one more dissatisfied than before. Although Parker's get-

24. Carol Harrison, *Beauty and Revelation in the Thought of Saint Augustine* (Oxford: Clarendon, 1992), 1–2.

25. O'Connor, *Collected Works*, 659.

26. O'Connor, *Collected Works*, 658.

ting a tattoo is not sinful, unlike the theft, both acts contribute to the unease that moves the two protagonists. Both leave school at the age of sixteen (although Augustine returns after some time) and begin to live riotously. Augustine is blinded by his unchaste desires: "I could not discern the clear brightness of love from the fog of lustfulness."[27] Parker "found out that the tattoos were attractive to the kind of girls he liked but who never liked him before. He began to drink beer and get in fights. His mother wept over what was becoming of him." St. Monica famously sheds tears over her son's misbehavior, and both mothers try to bring their sons back to God: Monica by prayers and entreaties, Betty Jean by dragging her son to a revival meeting in a "big lighted church."[28] The young men escape their mothers by remarkably similar ruses: both lie in order to get away by ship. Augustine relates that his mother "followed me as far as the sea. But I deceived her, holding me by force.... And I lied to my mother ... and escaped."[29] When Parker's mother tries to restrain him at the revival, "he jerked out of her grasp and ran. The next day he lied about his age and joined the navy."[30]

Parker wanders over sea and land as Augustine travels over much of the Roman world. But with both protagonists, the movement from place to place is less important than the inner wandering, the attempted flight from God rendered in terms of seeing and of being seen: "Let the restless, the godless, depart and flee from Thee; yet Thou seest them, and dividest the darkness.... For whither fled they, when they fled from Thy presence? or where dost Thou not find them? But they fled, that they might not see Thee seeing them, and, blinded, might stumble against Thee (because Thou forsakest nothing Thou hast made)." Furthermore, the blind wanderer is separated from his true self, as well as from

27. Augustine, *Confessions*, II:29.
28. O'Connor, *Collected Works*, 658.
29. Augustine, *Confessions*, V:85.
30. O'Connor, *Collected Works*, 658.

God: "but I had gone away from Thee; nor did I find myself, how much less Thee!"[31] Before Parker's conversion, images of sight indicate how he wishes to avoid introspection and to stay with surface appearances: "long views depressed Parker. You look out into space like that and you begin to feel as if someone were after you, the navy or the government or religion."[32] The sense of being pursued contributes to his drifting and the further indulgence of his peculiar obsession.

In addition to mirroring Augustine's journey through the world of the senses, Parker's choice of tattoos imitates the traditional "chain of being," although he is unaware of any such pattern. He starts with inanimate objects such as anchors and rifles, moves upward to animals (tigers, panthers, snakes, hawks, etc.), then to human beings ("Elizabeth II and Philip over where his stomach and liver were respectively"), and finally to manifestations of the spiritual, a figure of the Buddha and twin peacocks, which can represent the immortal soul or "the psychic duality of man."[33] These last symbols can be seen to correspond to Augustine's interest in non-Christian religions and schools of thought, particularly the Neoplatonism that helped to move him beyond a purely materialist stance.[34] On the other hand, the peacock, although a proverbial image of pride, has also been appropriated as a Christian symbol by some, including both Augustine and O'Connor: in her story "The Displaced Person," the elderly priest Father Flynn sees a peacock spread its tail and exclaims, "Christ will come like that!"[35] As Parker tries to turn his body into a microcosm of the created world, "his eyes ... reflected the immense

31. Augustine, *Confessions*, V:77.

32. O'Connor, *Collected Works*, 661.

33. O'Connor, *Collected Works*, 558. J. E. Cirlot, *A Dictionary of Symbols*, trans. Jack Sage (London: Routledge and Kegan Paul, 1962), 251.

34. See Frederick Copleston, SJ, *A History of Philosophy*, vol. 2, *Mediaeval Philosophy, Part I: Augustine to Bonaventure* (Garden City, N.Y.: Image, 1962), 42–43.

35. See Marshall Bruce Gentry, *Flannery O'Connor's Religion of the Grotesque* (Jackson: University Press of Mississippi, 1986), 25. See also O'Connor's "The Displaced Person," in *Collected Works*, 317.

spaces around him as if they were a microcosm of the mysterious sea."[36] This openness to mystery and to the infinite is hopeful, despite his attempt to replicate creation without the presence of its Creator, an absence that affects him, even though he does not realize what is missing:

Whenever a decent-sized mirror was available, he would get in front of it and study his overall look. The effect was not of one intricate arabesque of colors but of something haphazard and botched. A huge dissatisfaction would come over him and he would go off and find another tattooist and have another space filled up. The front of Parker was almost completely covered but there were no tattoos on his back. He had no desire for one anywhere he could not readily see it himself. As the space on the front of him for tattoos decreased, his dissatisfaction grew and became general.[37]

Parker's viewing himself in the mirror is not fundamentally narcissistic: it is positive to the extent that he recognizes the "haphazard and botched" nature of the "world" he has appropriated to himself, a realization that impels him to "patch it up" with yet another tattoo. This, of course, only adds to the bungled effect and leads to further discontent, but his problem at this point lies not in what he sees but in what he cannot or will not see. The tattoos consist of visible things placed only where he can see them: at this point Parker is a complete materialist, valuing nothing but what can be experienced directly and immediately. When he meets Sarah Ruth, his future wife, he slyly says of his tattoos, "You ought to see the ones you can't see."[38] Here he speaks more truth than he knows: he himself should be focusing on the things he cannot see.

This concentration on the material at the expense of the spiritual is reflected in Augustine's life at about the same period. Both men are twenty-eight years old when they begin to seek greater

36. O'Connor, *Collected Works*, 658–659.
37. O'Connor, *Collected Works*, 659.
38. O'Connor, *Collected Works*, 657.

meaning in their lives. From his nineteenth year till the end of his twenty-eighth, Augustine is an adherent of Manichaeism, which held that all matter is evil; in his own words, the Manicheans denied "that the good God produced a good creation."[39] Under the influence of the sect, Whitney J. Oates observes, Augustine's "thought had been inveterately concrete. It was difficult for him to conceive of existence apart from material embodiments, or to move easily on a level of abstraction. During the Manichaean period, God to Saint Augustine could only exist in some kind of material terms."[40] Similarly, at this stage he could only conceive of evil as material (instead of the Neoplatonic understanding of evil as a privation of the good), hence his attraction to Manichaean dualism.

Eventually, however, the concrete alone cannot satisfy, and the protagonists find it necessary to search elsewhere. Both seem to be attracted to people, places, and ideas largely against their wills. Doubts, appetites, and anxieties contend against one another within the two men, just as the outward signs of Parker's haphazard soul seem to struggle: "His dissatisfaction, from being chronic and latent, had suddenly become acute and raged in him. It was as if the panther and the lion and the serpents and the eagles and the hawks had penetrated his skin and lived inside him in a raging warfare."[41] Soon after, Parker weds Sarah Ruth, but marriage only intensifies his dissatisfaction: "Whenever Parker couldn't stand the way he felt, he would have another tattoo, but the only surface left on him now was his back. To see a tattoo on his own back he would have to get two mirrors and stand between them in just the correct position and this seemed to Parker a good way to make an idiot of himself."[42] Again there is the reluctance

39. Augustine, *The City of God*, trans. Marcus Dods (New York: Modern Library, 1950), 366.

40. Whitney J. Oates, introduction to *Basic Writings of Saint Augustine* (New York: Random House, 1948), xvi.

41. O'Connor, *Collected Works*, 659.

42. O'Connor, *Collected Works*, 663.

to see, rendered here as the refusal to look at his back, or to "look back" at all, which would involve confronting whatever or whomever he feels is pursuing him: "Once or twice he found himself turning around abruptly as if someone were trailing him."[43] To look back also means examining his life, which bewilders and disenchants him, as Augustine depicts the blind sinner fleeing not only from God but also from himself. By standing between two mirrors, Parker would be forced to see himself front and back, past and present, and to recognize the botched, haphazard, and incomplete nature of the tattooing job. To do this is to see the radically imperfect state of the world and of his own soul, particularly because he has tried to make a "world" without God. In addition, two mirrors placed opposite one another produce a seemingly unending series of images which in the field of optics is called an "infinite regress." So Parker, in refusing to look at himself between the two mirrors (until the tattoo artist forces him to) refuses to put himself in "just the correct position" to see himself in relation to the infinite, to see his life as it really is and as it might be: a refusal to turn back or regress to his true self and to God.

But eventually "dissatisfaction began to grow so great in Parker that there was no containing it outside of a tattoo . . . it had to be his back . . . but as urgent as it might be for him to get a tattoo, it was just as urgent that he get exactly the right one to bring Sarah Ruth to heel." But the true reason is not to placate his wife: although that idea is a "dim half-formed inspiration," he is heading in the right direction when he realizes that the tattoo should be "a religious subject" and that "[h]e needed something better even than the Bible!" He is being drawn closer to the understanding that he needs the Word made flesh, indeed, the Word shown forth on his own flesh. Two lines later we are told, "He was already losing flesh—Sarah Ruth just threw food in the pot and let

43. O'Connor, *Collected Works*, 664.

it boil."[44] He gets no life or nourishment from his wife or from anything else, and he has not yet found another source of sustenance.

"In addition to her other bad qualities [Sarah Ruth] was forever sniffing up sin. She did not smoke or dip, drink whiskey, use bad language or paint her face, and God knew some paint would have improved it, Parker thought."[45] With her contempt for the created world and strict asceticism, Sarah Ruth is a latter-day Manichaean, giving voice to a dualistic, antisacramental attitude and ignoring God's providential goodness revealed in and through matter, above all by the Incarnation. As O'Connor remarks in a letter, "Sarah Ruth was the heretic—the notion that you can worship in pure spirit."[46] Sarah Ruth insists on being married "in the County Ordinary's office" because she thinks a church, or any form of mediation, "idolatrous," and she is "against color.... When [Parker] attempted to point out especial details of [his tattoos], she would shut her eyes tight and turn her back as well. Except in total darkness, she preferred Parker dressed and with his sleeves rolled down."[47]

Along with her prudery (another connection with Manichaeism, which abjured sex and procreation), her refusal to see the beauty and color of the world makes it impossible for her to see the true light that illuminates created objects. Her vision is consistently clouded: on meeting Parker, she mistakes his tattooed eagle for a chicken and, at the end of the story, fails to recognize "Christ, who is the image of God" (2 Corinthians 4:4) on her husband's back. Her gray eyes, twice compared to ice picks, are as much weapons as organs of sight. While Parker is being pursued by God, she is absolutely certain she has the divine in her possession and can even speak on God's behalf: "At the judgment

44. O'Connor, *Collected Works*, 664.
45. O'Connor, *Collected Works*, 655.
46. O'Connor, *The Habit of Being*, 594.
47. O'Connor, *Collected Works*, 663.

seat of God, Jesus is going to say to you, 'What you been doing all your life besides have pictures drawn all over you?' she said ... 'Parker did nothing much when he was at home but listen to what the judgment seat of God would be like for him if he didn't change his ways.'"[48] Sarah Ruth seems to embody Augustine's observation that "all heresy begins with excessive holiness."[49] Guilty of spiritual pride, she has sternly severed nature and grace, cutting herself off from the divine, while Parker, like Augustine, struggles to allow grace to build on nature, a reality made literal when, on his own flesh, he puts on the Lord Jesus Christ.

Parker desperately wants to get the tattoo that will make him complete but finds himself unable to act, exactly Augustine's state at the analogous stage of his narrative, when he wants to will his acceptance of Christianity but finds he cannot. Then suddenly, through God's grace, his impotent will is made capable of action. This transformation of the will often occurs when the sinner is moved by something in the created realm: as Augustine states in an earlier work, *Ad Simplicianus*, "the will itself can have no motive unless something presents itself to delight and stir the mind. That this should happen ... is not in any man's power."[50] This is what happens to Parker when, baling hay in the field, he crashes the tractor, falls to the ground and immediately runs off to acquire the final tattoo. In accordance with Augustine's theology, Parker has done nothing to earn the grace he receives, but is at least favorably disposed to receive it. Before he hits the tree, "his mind was on a suitable design for his back. The sun ... began to switch from in front to behind him, but he appeared to see it in both places as if he had eyes in the back of his head."[51]

That Parker, circling the field, seems to see both forward and backward indicates that he is on the point of turning toward the

48. O'Connor, *Collected Works*, 663–664.
49. Augustine, *De Haeresibus (Heresies)*, trans. Rev. Liguori C. Muller (Washington, D.C.: Catholic University Press, 1956), 12.
50. Augustine, *Ad Simplicianus*, quoted in Harrison, 52.
51. O'Connor, *Collected Works*, 665.

Light instead of turning his back to it.[52] However, we are still in the conditional: Parker sees *as if* he had eyes in the back of his head, whereas he still lacks the eyes which will allow him to see behind so that he might turn back. Parker's action, after being knocked to the ground, to fly off immediately to be tattooed with the image of Christ has an analogue in *The Confessions*, when Augustine prays that the unjust, blind and fleeing, "might stumble upon Thee, and justly be hurt; withdrawing themselves from thy gentleness, and stumbling at Thy uprightness, and falling upon their own ruggedness.... Let them then be turned, and seek Thee."[53] Having fallen, Parker "scrambled backwards, still sitting, his eyes cavernous, and"—desperate for a Christ sign—"if he had known how to cross himself he would have done it." On his subsequent drive to the city, Parker "only knew that there had been a great change in his life, a leap forward into a worse unknown, and that there was nothing he could do about it."[54] This corresponds to Augustine's sense that in a way he does not even wish for, let alone deserve, the grace he has been given.

Like Augustine at the moment of his conversion, Parker feels compelled to turn to the book "with all the pictures of God in it . . . the religious one." (Augustine, of course, opens the Bible when he seems to hear a voice repeating, "Take up and read," and comes to Romans 13:14: "put on the Lord Jesus Christ.") The tattooist asks Parker, "'Who are you interested in? . . . saints, angels, Christs, or what?' 'God,' Parker said. 'Father, Son or Spirit?' 'Just God,' Parker said impatiently. 'Christ. I don't care. Just so it's God.'"[55]

52. The sun is particularly important to Augustine as an analogue of the "divine light, which illumines the mind," a light which "comes from God, who is the 'intelligible light', in whom and by whom and through whom all those things which are luminous to the intellect become luminous"; Copleston, *A History of Philosophy*, 2:77.

53. Augustine, *Confessions*, V:77.

54. O'Connor, *Collected Works*, 665–666.

55. O'Connor, *Collected Works*, 666. This affirmation of the Trinity reflects one of Augustine's major concerns, the danger posed by heresies that tried to deny or compromise Christ's divinity. See Copleston, *A History of Philosophy*, 2:77.

For both Augustine and Parker, the experience with the book is an intensely emotional one: the former weeping in a "torrent of ... tears," the latter's heart beating faster and faster. Parker "flipped the pages quickly, feeling that when he reached the one ordained, a sign would come.... On one of the pages a pair of eyes glanced at him swiftly.... His heart ... appeared to cut off; there was absolute silence. It said as plainly as if silence were a language itself, GO BACK. Parker returned to the picture—the haloed head of a flat stern Byzantine Christ with all-demanding eyes." The "one ordained" by the Father is, of course, Jesus Christ. Parker has finally come back to himself, as "his heart began slowly to beat again as if it were being brought to life by a subtle power." And the silence can only be answered with silence: "'You found what you want?' the artist asked. Parker's throat was too dry to speak." When he insists that the image be tattooed on his back "just like it is or nothing," the artist replies, "It's your funeral," evoking the notion that putting on Christ entails dying to the old, sinful self.[56]

Like Augustine's simultaneous desire for, and resistance to, conversion, Parker feels ambivalent about the step he is to take: "He wanted to go look at the picture again but at the same time he did not want to." However, he does look at the first stage of the artist's work by positioning himself between two mirrors, so he seems disposed to look into the infinite. But just as *The Confessions* shows a soul returning to itself and to God only by gradual steps, so Parker at this point is not ready to see all, or to see clearly. Although he sees "a flashing burst of color reflected from his back ... the face was empty; the eyes had not yet been put in."[57] When the tattoo is completed, the artist must force him to look at the image infinitely reflected in the two mirrors: "Parker looked, turned white and moved away. The eyes in the reflected face continued to look at him—still, straight, all-demanding, enclosed

56. O'Connor, *Collected Works*, 667.
57. O'Connor, *Collected Works*, 668.

in silence."[58] As he writes in *Confessions*, Augustine, too, feels his "countenance altered," and when he reads from Romans, "by a light ... of serenity infused into my heart, all the darkness of doubt vanished away."[59] He prays, "Thou didst stream forth Thy beams of light upon me most strongly ... and Thou madest my soul to consume away like a spider."[60] After Parker gets the tattoo of Christ, he examines his soul and finds it "a spider web of facts and lies."[61] Later, at the door of his house, he turns and a "tree of light burst over the skyline.... Parker fell back against the door ... all at once he felt the light pouring through him, turning his spider web soul into a perfect arabesque of colors, a garden of trees and birds and beasts."[62] The combination of light pouring through the soul and the spider imagery links this passage with Augustine's description of divine illumination. For Augustine, the human mind, although rational, is temporal and mutable and, therefore, unable to comprehend transcendent and immutable truth; the mind is not "lighted of itself, but is lighted by participation of eternal Truth."[63] Parker now knows he is unable to save himself; he needs the experience of illumination, especially the "new eyes" which make this possible, to return to himself and to God.

This is a return denied to Sarah Ruth, however. When Parker takes off his shirt to show her the tattoo, her distaste for the physical asserts itself once more: "And you ain't gonna have none of me this near morning." She does not want to look at the tattoo, and when Parker forces her, she completely rejects it, saying that the image of Christ "ain't anybody I know." Dismayed at her reaction, Parker says that it is a picture of God, to which she angrily responds, "He don't *look*.... He's a spirit. No man shall see

58. O'Connor, *Collected Works*, 670.
59. Augustine, *Confessions*, VIII:157–158.
60. Augustine, *Confessions*, VII:131.
61. O'Connor, *Collected Works*, 672.
62. O'Connor, *Collected Works*, 673.
63. Augustine, quoted in Copleston, *A History of Philosophy*, 2:78.

his face." Accusing him of idolatry, she beats her husband across the shoulders with a broom, raising "large welts ... on the face of the tattooed Christ."[64] He stumbles out the door and begins to cry under a pecan tree, not unlike Augustine, who in *Confessions* weeps beneath a fig tree when he hears the voice tell him to "take up and read."[65] Sarah Ruth watches her husband, and "her eyes hardened still more."[66] Parker, on the other hand, can see clearly at last although, as the tattooist foretold, it has cost him plenty—indeed, it has cost him everything. But he has followed the vision he had first glimpsed in seeing the tattooed man at the fair and, through the light given to him by God, the vision has become a transformative reality: he now embodies Christ on his own flesh, a profound image of what it is to be a Christian. Finally, we are left with the wordplay of the story's title ("Parker is back"), and with Parker "crying like a baby," having "put on the Lord Jesus Christ" like Augustine, his restless fellow wanderer.

64. O'Connor, *Collected Works*, 674.
65. Augustine, *Confessions*, VIII:15.
66. O'Connor, *Collected Works*, 675.

CHAPTER 7

Mrs. May's Dark Night in O'Connor's "Greenleaf"

George Piggford, CSC

O burn that burns to heal!
O more than pleasant wound!
And O soft hand, O touch most delicate,
That dost new life reveal,
That dost in grace abound
And, slaying, dost from death to life translate.[1]

1.This chapter was originally published in *Christianity and Literature* 65, no. 4 (2016): 397–412.

Epigraph from John of the Cross, "Llama de amor viva" ["Flame of Love"], trans. Arthur Symons, quoted in Evelyn Underhill, *Mysticism: The Nature and Development of Spiritual Consciousness* (New York: Noonday/Meridian, 1955), 236.

Shortly before her baptism into the Catholic Church on March 31, 1956, Elizabeth Hester received from her friend Flannery O'Connor a present in the mail: the final copy of O'Connor's latest short story, "Greenleaf," which would be published that summer by John Crowe Ransom in the *Kenyon Review*.[2] My intention in this essay is to situate the composition of that story in the context of O'Connor's burgeoning friendship with Hester, to note the powerful influence of Evelyn Underhill's *Mysticism* (1910) on O'Connor and most especially O'Connor's understanding of St. John of the Cross, and to trace the interconnectedness of O'Connor's short story with the spiritual insights of the Spanish mystic. Underhill presents these in her synthesis of mysticism, and they are found in St. John's poem "On a Dark Night," as well as in its source text the Song of Songs chapters two and three. In "Greenleaf," the character Mrs. May undergoes her own, somewhat ironized, version of the "dark night," and not at her own behest. Rather, the experience of spiritual union is almost wholly imposed on her by the structure of the narrative in "Greenleaf" and through the free indirect discourse of O'Connor's "sacralizing" narrative voice.[3]

In the summer of 1955, just a few months before O'Connor would start work on "Greenleaf," Elizabeth Hester initiated a correspondence with her, and by mid-October of that year, "Miss Hester" and "Miss O'Connor" had become in the letters' greetings "Betty" and "Flannery." The increased intimacy in this epistolary friendship was brought about through exchanges in the mail on the topics of faith, theology, the church, and, notably, books. Within the first three months of their letter writing, O'Connor had managed to recommend to Hester works by authors as diverse as Simone Weil, Romano Guardini, Céline, and Wyndham Lewis. She had also embarked on a nonsystematic explanation of Catho-

2. Brad Gooch, *Flannery: A Life of Flannery O'Connor* (New York: Little, Brown, 2009), 275.
3. Gilles Deleuze, *Cinema 1: The Movement-Image*, trans. Hugh Tomlinson and Barbara Habberjan (Minneapolis: University of Minnesota Press, 1986), 75.

lic theology and spirituality through the exchanges with Hester, and although in one of these letters one finds O'Connor's famous comment "I am not a mystic," she also regularly mentions the ideas of Catholic mystics, including those of Saints Catherine of Genoa, Teresa of Avila, Catherine of Siena, and John of the Cross.[4]

This last figure is first mentioned in an August 28, 1955, letter, and in another dated September 6, O'Connor explicitly engages with the notion of the "dark night" in John of the Cross. After noting that the existentialist philosopher Jean-Paul Sartre "finds God emotionally unsatisfactory in the extreme," O'Connor points out the profound influence of Sartre's atheism on "most of my friends of less stature than he." The influence after World War II of works such as Sartre's *Existentialism Is a Humanism* (1946) cannot be underestimated, especially its exploration of the experience of forlornness, or abandonment in a godless universe. Beyond such feelings, however, is a "higher paradox" that "confounds emotion as well as reason." She continues: "[T]here are long periods in the lives of all of us, and of the saints, when the truth as revealed by faith is hideous, emotionally disturbing, downright repulsive. Witness the dark night of the soul in individual saints. Right now the whole world seems to be going through a dark night of the soul."[5] Owing to this "dark night," O'Connor consciously wrote for "the people who think God is dead."[6] In the fall of 1955, Elizabeth Hester was not one of those people, but it would take some careful intellectual and spiritual exchanges before O'Connor's new friend would accept the sacrament of Baptism and entrance into the Catholic Church.

4. Flannery O'Connor, *The Habit of Being: Letters of Flannery O'Connor*, ed. Sally Fitzgerald (New York: Farrar, Straus and Giroux, 1979), 92. This disavowal of mysticism contrasts with O'Connor's earlier expressions of a desire to become a mystic found in the 1946–1947 *Prayer Journal*; for example, "Please help me to get down under things and find where you are," and "Oh Lord, I am saying ... make me a mystic, immediately." See Flannery O'Connor, *A Prayer Journal*, ed. W. A. Sessions (New York: Farrar, Straus and Giroux, 2013) 4, 38.

5. O'Connor, *The Habit of Being*, 100.

6. O'Connor, *The Habit of Being*, 92.

Although there is no way to confirm that O'Connor had read any of the writing of St. John of the Cross by the fall of 1955, she does, by 1959, imply familiarity with Roy Campbell's translation of the sixteenth-century saint's spiritual masterpiece *La Noche Oscura del Alma*, commonly translated as *The Dark Night of the Soul*.[7] Judging from the letters to Hester from fall 1955, however, she had at least a basic understanding that St. John defined the "dark night of the soul" as an experience of "the sorrowful soul" who "thinks that God has abandoned it, and, in His abhorrence of it, has flung it into darkness; it is a grave and piteous grief for it to believe that God has forsaken it."[8] Such is the state of the postwar world for O'Connor, that those "who think that God is dead" are therefore very much like those abandoned in the dark night of the soul for St. John of the Cross. In an unpublished book review she insists that Friedrich Nietzsche's formula from *The Gay Science* (1882) that "God is dead" is "the gospel in reverse": it is bad news rather than good, announcing not only an atheistic era but one in which life is radically lonely and ultimately meaningless as well.[9] O'Connor's point is cultural: the West, which was once in a state of illuminated belief, was beginning quickly to descend, owing partly to the influence of Nietzsche, Sartre, and other atheist existentialists, into a profoundly dark night.[10] Night, however, leads—perhaps inevitably—to day, just as an experience of utter forlornness might presage union with the divine.[11]

7. O'Connor, *The Habit of Being*, 339.

8. John of the Cross, *Dark Night of the Soul*, ed. and trans. E. Allison Peers (New York: Image, 1959), 104.

9. Flannery O'Connor, *The Presence of Grace and Other Book Reviews*, ed. Carter W. Martin (Athens: University of Georgia Press, 1983), 168. See also Farrell O'Gorman, *Peculiar Crossroads: Flannery O'Connor, Walker Percy, and Catholic Vision in Postwar Southern Fiction* (Baton Rouge: Louisiana State University Press, 2004), 82.

10. For the definitive study of O'Connor's engagement with Nietzsche's atheist nihilism, see Henry T. Edmondson, III, *Return to Good and Evil: Flannery O'Connor's Response to Nihilism* (Lanham, Md.: Lexington, 2002), 19–34.

11. After her reading of the work of the Jewish philosopher Martin Buber in 1958, O'Connor embraced his phrase "the eclipse of God" as a needful correction of the Nietzschean formulation "the death of God." This is so because the metaphor

Even if we cannot confirm that O'Connor had read John of
the Cross while she was composing "Greenleaf" by the beginning of 1956, we do know that she had read in spring 1955 Evelyn
Underhill's monumental and influential study *Mysticism*, which
she recommended to Hester in November 1955 as "a mine of
information."[12] Underhill pointedly records writing the preface
to that work on *"The Feast of John of the Cross 1910"* and that saint is
regularly mentioned and quoted throughout Underhill's encyclo-
pedic study.[13] Underhill also quotes Arthur Symons's translation
of the poem that gives its name to *The Dark Night of the Soul* in a
section on mystical contemplation (see the appendix).[14] Underhill defines mysticism as "the science of ultimates, the science of
union with the Absolute, and nothing else."[15] For her mysticism
is not about knowing but about *being* and particularly about being loved, allowing oneself to be loved by this Absolute, by what
she regularly terms the "Divinity." For her, humans are not as in
the classical formation "rational animals" but are contemplative,
"vision-making" animals.[16] She divides her book into two sec-

---

of an "eclipse" acknowledges (1) the Judeo-Christian God's continued existence;
(2) the difficulty in the West of maintaining faith after the atrocities of World War II,
most particularly the Holocaust; and (3) the transitory nature of the world's atheistic
and existentialist dark night. On Buber's influence on O'Connor, see George Piggford, "'A Dialogue Between Above and Below': Flannery O'Connor, Martin Buber,
and 'Revelation' after the Holocaust," *Flannery O'Connor Review* 13 (2015): 90–91.

12. O'Connor, *The Habit of Being*, 116. O'Connor's personal copy of Underhill's
Mysticism can be found in the archives of Georgia College and State University. According to my own inspection of that text, it was read thoroughly, judging from the
copy's concave and creased spine, which is broken between pages 206 and 207. I
could locate only one marking in the text, an ink smudge on page 430 in the left
margin, next to a passage about St. Teresa of Avila that reads: "A chronic invalid
over fifty years of age, weakened by long ill-health and the mortifications of the
Purgative Way, she deliberately breaks with her old career in obedience to her inward Voice . . ."; Underhill, *Mysticism*, 430. This marking is not noted by Arthur F.
Kinney in *Flannery O'Connor's Library: Resources of Being* (Athens: University of
Georgia Press, 1985), 61.

13. Underhill, *Mysticism*, xv.

14. Underhill, *Mysticism*, 352.

15. Underhill, *Mysticism*, 72.

16. Underhill, *Mysticism*, 17.

tions, "The Mystic Fact" and "The Mystic Way." The latter is most powerfully influenced by John of the Cross, especially states two, "Purification" or the dark night of the senses, and four, "The Dark Night of the Soul," of the five that she outlines as comprising the "Way."

It is important to note that Underhill outlines five "states" rather than stages of the mystic way. She resists too linear a model for progress in the contemplative life both because each mystic is different "one from another" and because for some mystics "stages which have been regarded as essential are entirely omitted: in others, their order appears to be reversed."[17] Her model is, however, essentially dialectic; a positive state is invariably followed by a negative until the fifth and final state is achieved. The first state, "Awakening" to "consciousness of Divine Reality," represents the moment of "conversion" and is considered, in the words of the psychologist of religion Edwin Diller Starbuck, an experience of "unselving."[18] According to Underhill, such experiences are followed by a period of purgation or purification. She calls St. John of the Cross "the classic authority on this portion of the mystic quest," which is typically associated with his phrase "dark night of the senses," which he describes in the book *Subida del Monte Carmelo* or *The Ascent of Mt. Carmel*. Underhill quotes St. John at some length in her "Purification" chapter: "In order to overcome our desires . . . and to renounce all those things, our love and inclination for which are wont to inflame the will that it delights therein, we require a more ardent fire and a nobler love—that of the Bridegroom."[19] The "Bridegroom" here is, of course, both Christ and the one addressed as "my love" "who is "like . . . a young hart" in the Song of Songs (Song 2:9).[20] This scene provides the

17. Underhill, *Mysticism*, 168.
18. Underhill, *Mysticism*, 169, 176.
19. Quoted in Underhill, *Mysticism*, 203.
20. Throughout this chap., I employ quotations from the 1899 American ed. of the Douay-Rhiems Bible, which calls this book the "Song of Solomon." Most commonly it is titled the "Song of Songs" in contemporary translations.

inspiration for St. John's "On a Dark Night," and, as is shown in the following, O'Connor's "scrub bull" in "Greenleaf."[21] The heart of the dark night of the senses is for both St. John and Underhill detachment from material things and even the world itself. "The soul," says the saint, "is not empty, so long as the desire for sensible things remains," and this is true whether one's attachment to worldly things might be likened to a "slender thread" or to "a rope."[22]

The processes of detachment and mortification in the second mystic state often lead—or allow the mystic to be led—to state three, "Illumination." On this state Underhill quotes St. John's "*Llama de Amor Viva*" or "Flame of Love." In the stanza cited by Underhill, the burns and wounds of the purgative state culminate in healing, pleasure, "new life" and abounding "grace" in the illuminative experience.[23] This is the "'contemplative state' *par excellence.* . . . It is a state of happiness." Here, according to Underhill, those trapped in the spiritual equivalent of Plato's Cave are able after much effort on the part of both mystic and Divinity to arrive at the mouth of this "Cave of Illusion" and to look "upon the sun." Some never proceed beyond this state. In the case of the "great and most strenuous seekers," however, this consoling experience is eventually eclipsed by that second dark night for which John of the Cross is best known.[24]

There, in St. John's words, "The soul . . . sees itself in the midst of opposite evils, miserable imperfections, dryness and emptiness of the understanding, and abandonment of the spirit in darkness."[25] This fourth state provides the profoundest experience of desolation and abandonment; John of the Cross likens it to "[t]he pain . . . endured by weak or diseased eyes when suddenly

21. Flannery O'Connor, *The Complete Stories*, ed. Robert Giroux (New York: Farrar, Straus and Giroux, 1971), 311.
22. Quoted in Underhill, *Mysticism*, 211–212.
23. Quoted in Underhill, *Mysticism*, 236.
24. Underhill, *Mysticism*, 169.
25. Quoted in Underhill, *Mysticism*, 391.

struck by a strong light." This light is "cleansing," but in this experience, the soul of the mystic realizes that it was not as totally pure as he or she had believed during the illuminative phase.[26] In his book on O'Connor's *Response to Nihilism*, Henry T. Edmondson has associated this second dark night with the "sanctifying nihilism" that "serves as a means of greater intimacy, indeed union with God."[27]

For Underhill the final state of the mystic way is exactly "Union." This occurs when the dark night of the soul ends and the soul is given "its footing in Eternity."[28] John of the Cross describes this experience as the "houses of the soul"—the "sensual" and the "spiritual"—being unified and at "peace."[29] The unified life now lived by such mystics is difficult to characterize, and in fact largely eludes language, but Underhill does provide some examples, including St. John of the Cross, who "wrote love songs to his Love."[30] The most familiar and powerful of these love songs is, of course, that reinterpretation of the Song of Songs from *The Dark Night of the Soul* titled "On a Dark Night," sometimes also titled "Stanzas of the Soul." As noted earlier, O'Connor was definitely aware of Arthur Symons's translation of the poem; the first six and the eighth stanzas—that is, all except the seventh—are found in Underhill.[31] This poem by St. John of the Cross, along with Underhill's com-

26. Quoted in Underhill, *Mysticism*, 399.

27. Edmondson, *Return to Good and Evil*, 69.

28. Underhill, *Mysticism*, 402.

29. Quoted in Underhill, *Mysticism*, 402.

30. Underhill, *Mysticism*, 440.

31. In a December 27, 1956 letter to William Sessions, O'Connor mentions that she was "highly enjoying the beautiful book [*Three Mystics*] about St. Theresa and St. John and El Greco and so for that matter has my mother" (O'Connor, *The Habit of Being*, 189). That book includes Fr. Bruno de Jésus-Marie's translation of "On a Dark Night" (109), but it seems unlikely that O'Connor was aware of this version while she was writing "Greenleaf," given the impression in this quotation that she is discovering *Three Mystics* for the first time late in 1956. She knew the same author's *St. John of the Cross* (1936) well enough to review it, negatively, in the Atlanta diocesan *Bulletin* in December 1957 (see O'Connor, *The Presence of Grace*, 46–47). This biography incorporates English translations of sections of St. John's poem. It seems equally unlikely that O'Connor knew of this book before that year, espe-

mentary on mysticism, informed O'Connor's imagination both before and during the writing of "Greenleaf."

A number of critics have noted that the opening scene of the story is reminiscent of what Frekerick Asals calls "the erotic-allegorical Canticle of Canticles," or Song of Songs, with God coming as a Bridegroom to his Betrothed (Song 3:4). In "Greenleaf," O'Connor calls the Bridegroom "a patient God come down" and "an uncouth country suitor" who arrives in the form of a bull "to woo" Mrs. May.[32] George Kilcourse has gone so far as to claim that the opening scene of the scrub bull beneath the window of Mrs. May "parodies the biblical text, frequently read in marriage liturgies, of the lover who gazes through the windows in search of the beloved."[33] This section of the Song of Songs, chapter two, offers a prelude to the chapter that provides the foundation for St. John's poem. In that third chapter of the Song of Songs, after a fruitless search of her own bed, the soul rises and seeks her lover in the night. She encounters "watchmen ... as they made their rounds of the city," and she asks them, "Have you seen him, whom my soul loveth?" They are of no help, but the speaker soon finds the one she is looking for: "I held him: and I will not let him go, till I bring him into my mother's house" (Song 3:3, 4). Likewise, the speaker of St. John's poem departs from her home in search of the "lover" whom she eventually finds in a "night of wandering."

---

cially since she often received volumes to review relatively close to the date of a review's publication.

32. O'Connor, *The Complete Stories*, 311–312. Frederick Asals, "The Mythic Dimensions of Flannery O'Connor's 'Greenleaf,'" *Studies in Short Fiction* 5 (1968): 317–330; see also David Havird, "The Saving Rape: Flannery O'Connor and Patri-archal Religion," *Mississippi Quarterly* 47, no.1 (1993): 18. Other critics have noted less specifically that "Greenleaf" employs bride and bridegroom imagery famil-iar in Christian spirituality; see David Eggenschwiler, *The Christian Humanism of Flannery O'Connor* (Detroit, Mich.: Wayne State University Press, 1972), 63; Sarah Gordon, *Flannery O'Connor: The Obedient Imagination* (Athens: University of Geor-gia Press, 2000), 194; and Marshall Bruce Gentry, *Flannery O'Connor's Religion of the Grotesque* (Jackson: University Press of Mississippi, 1986), 15.

33. George A. Kilcourse Jr., *Flannery O'Connor's Religious Imagination: A World with Everything Off Balance* (New York: Paulist, 2001), 254.

He "wounds her in the side / And," she says, "in my body all my senses died."[34] This emphasis on the suspension of senses represents an innovative reinterpretation of the Song of Songs on the part of John of the Cross.

The critic's strong inclination at this point is to read the narrative of O'Connor's "Greenleaf" as an ironic allegory or peculiarly grotesque reinterpretation of St. John's poem "On a Dark Night." In a recent essay Denise T. Askin has reminded us that O'Connor's preferred literary genre was "satiric comedy" on the model of Aristophanes and that "Greenleaf" follows this model remarkably well even though it refuses an unambiguously liberatory, and therefore traditionally comic, ending.[35] If we imagine that Mrs. May represents in this comic mode both *senex*, or "opposer of the new order" represented by the Greenleafs, and *alazon*, or pompous (Christian) imposter, the idea of her as a novel reiteration of the lover in the Song of Songs chapter three and St. John's is in fact humorously satiric.[36] Although she spends much of the narrative searching for her scrub bull/lover, and even though the Greenleafs, particularly Mr. Greenleaf, might be understood as standing in for the unhelpful town "watchmen" of the Song of Songs, she is certainly no mystic seeker, at least consciously, no true lover of the Divine (Song 3:3). O'Connor's narrator informs us, with a bathetic twist, that Mrs. May "was a good Christian woman with a large respect for religion, though she did not, of course, believe any of it was true."[37] Like the soul in St. John's poem, however, Mrs. May treats the bull as an idée fixe, and it is her obsession with first "penn[ing] up" the bull before having Mr. Greenleaf "shoot" him that drives the story's plot.[38]

34. Quoted in Thomas Walsh, ed., *Hispanic Anthology: Poems Translated from the Spanish by English and North American Poets* (New York: Putnam, 1920), 248.

35. Denise T. Askin, "Anagogical Vision and Comedic Form in Flannery O'Connor: The Reasonable Use of the Unreasonable," *Renascence* 57, no. 1 (2004): 51.

36. Askin, "Anagogical Vision," 55.

37. O'Connor, *The Complete Stories*, 316.

38. O'Connor, *The Complete Stories*, 313, 331.

This obsession unwittingly leads Mrs. May to her final, abrupt, and violent union with the creature at the end of the narrative.

If there is a candidate for the mystic seeker in "Greenleaf" it is surely Mrs. Greenleaf, whom Ralph Wood describes as a "writhing Pentecostal."[39] In a March 24, 1956, letter to Hester, O'Connor labels Mrs. Greenleaf "a sympathetic character" who is "connected" to "the sun and the bull."[40] Richard Giannone has pointed out the Christlike role of Mrs. Greenleaf, who "heals by assuming the affliction of the victims."[41] These include victims of rape, "criminals who had escaped and children who had been burned," those involved in "train wrecks and plane crashes," and even "divorce[d] movie stars." It is Mrs. Greenleaf who seeks to heal others through her peculiar swaying "back and forth on her hands and knees" and groaning "Jesus, Jesus." It is Mrs. Greenleaf, dirty and crying and rolling on the ground, who begs Jesus, "[S]tab me in the heart!" For her part, Mrs. May abjures this showy and emotionally intense spiritual practice. After witnessing one of Mrs. Greenleaf's attempts at Pentecostal healing, she tells Mrs. Greenleaf that "Jesus ... would be *ashamed* of you."[42] Nevertheless, it is Mrs. May, the nonbelieving Christian to whom the "patient god" that is the bull comes at the beginning of the story, who searches for this "beloved one"[43] throughout the narrative and who will literally "pierce" the heart of his beloved.[44]

One of the great contributions of Underhill's work on mysticism is that anyone might become a mystic, might follow the mystic way. As she puts it, "mysticism may be looked upon as the final term, the active expression of a power latent in the whole

39. Ralph Wood, *Flannery O'Connor and the Christ-Haunted South* (Grand Rapids, Mich.: Eerdmans, 2004), 87.

40. O'Connor, *The Habit of Being*, 148.

41. Richard Giannone, "'Greenleaf': A Story of Lent," *Studies in Short Fiction* 22, no. 4 (Fall 1985): 425.

42. O'Connor, *The Complete Stories*, 315–317.

43. Quoted in Underhill, *Mysticism*, 352.

44. O'Connor, *The Complete Stories*, 311, 333.

race: the power, that is, of perceiving transcendent reality. Few people pass through this life without knowing what it is to be at least touched by this mystical feeling."[45] Mrs. May comes across as a most unlikely candidate for potential mystic. Still, the bull with its Christlike "prickly crown"[46] arrives in the night to help this woman's "consciousness ... across the gap which separates it from its Home," and that proper human Home, for Underhill, is "union with the Divinity."[47] Mrs. May arguably finds this "Home" at the story's end in the arms of her "wild tormented lover" the bull.[48] This creature represents a peculiar manifestation of the Christian Divinity and has, indeed, been associated by many critics with classical myth, notably the story of Europa and the Bull.[49]

Denise Askin has most helpfully linked the bull in "Greenleaf" to the "sacrificial carnival ox of the Middle Ages," which according to Mikhail Bakhtin, was often "decorated with multicolored ribbons."[50] Perhaps an emblem of *kenosis* or divine emptying, this "god" comes not as a proper bull but as a "scrub," as insignificant and even contemptible. Certainly the bull comes originally in an interplay of moonlight and darkness suggesting the dialectical light and dark states of Underhill's five-part mystic way. The bull is first "silvered in the moonlight" under Mrs. May's "bedroom window"; it is then enshrouded in the "dark" while "the moon blackened him." Again for a second time he "appears" illuminated in the dim light, then once more is invisible while the "moon drifted

45. Underhill, *Mysticism*, 73.

46. O'Connor, *The Complete Stories*, 312.

47. Underhill, *Mysticism*, 355.

48. O'Connor, *The Complete Stories*, 333.

49. For interpretations of the scrub bull in relation to Eastern and classical myth, see Asals, "The Mythic Dimensions," 319; and Nancy Ann Gidden, "Classical Agents of Christian Grace in Flannery O'Connor's 'Greenleaf,'" *Studies in Short Fiction* 23, no. 2 (Spring 1986): 201. On "Greenleaf" and the myth of Europa and Zeus, see John C. Shields, "Flannery O'Connor's 'Greenleaf' and the Myth of Europa and the Bull," *Studies in Short Fiction* 18, no. 4 (Fall 1981): 421–431.

50. Askin, "Anagogical Vision," 53; and Mikhail Bakhtin, *Rabelais and His World*, trans. Hélène Iswolsky (Bloomington: Indiana University Press, 1984), 201.

into retirement." Finally, light comes from inside Mrs. May's bedroom in the form of a "pink glow," which shines "bars of light" on
the bull through slit pink blinds. These suggest the stairs by which
the soul seeks its lover in the night in St. John's poem as well as the
states of light and darkness of Underhill's mystic way.[51]

In the morning, Mr. Greenleaf comes to Mrs. May's home, not
on the "secret stair" that the soul takes to its lover in the night
in St John's poem but to the bottom of her "three back stairs."[52]
He comes to her as a potential vessel for Christ in the form of
the Precious Blood given that Mr. Greenleaf's face is "shaped
like a rough chalice."[53] After emotionally unsatisfying interactions with Mrs. May's sons, the narrator connects the bull to the
Greenleafs with the report that Mrs. May considers the Greenleaf family in their entirety—Mr., Mrs., and the adult sons O. T.
and E. T.—to be "scrub-human."[54] She also thinks of the Greenleafs, in an allusion to the Sermon on the Mount (Mt 6:28), as "lilies of the field" who live "off the fat that she struggled to put into
the land."[55] Mrs. May fails to fathom the theological import of
this phrase—after all, the lilies of the field are contrasted in the
Gospel of Matthew to "ye of little faith" (Mt 6:30). Also "among
the lilies," the soul will eventually forget her "cares and shame"
at the end of St. John's "On a Dark Night."[56] Mrs. May herself is
associated with lilies. The narrator informs us that her son Scofield would often "grab her arm" and hold up her hand "so that
her blue-veined little hand would dangle from her wrist like the
head of a broken lily."[57] The implication is that she has allowed
herself to lose any sense of the pure faith traditionally associated

51. O'Connor, *The Complete Stories*, 310–311.
52. Quoted in Underhill, *Mysticism*, 352; and O'Connor, *The Complete Stories*, 331.
53. O'Connor, *The Complete Stories*, 314.
54. O'Connor, *The Complete Stories*, 317.
55. O'Connor, *The Complete Stories*, 319.
56. Quoted in Underhill, *Mysticism*, 371.
57. O'Connor, *The Complete Stories*, 322.

with the lily and has focused her attention on financial gain and a narrow definition of respectability.

Nevertheless, "some violent unleashed force" or a "violent black streak" that is associated both with Mrs. Greenleaf and with the scrub bull pursues Mrs. May persistently throughout the story just as she stubbornly maintains her search for the errant bull.[58] Shortly after associating the Greenleafs with the "lilies of the field," Mrs. May learns from Scofield that the owners of the "scrub bull" are actually O. T. and E. T. Greenleaf.[59] This makes the bull both legally and spiritually a Greenleaf bull. The second time that Mrs. May encounters this animal it is described as "a darker shape" among grazing cows on a bright day, and the bull "might have been" the sun's "shadow cast at an angle, moving among them."[60] This odd description situates the bull as a shadow image of the sun. This void or shadow associated with the beast might be a representation of the "Divine Dark" of Pseudo-Dionysius and the apophatic tradition, of what mystics call "dim contemplation."[61] Another way to understand this is as the bull inviting Mrs. May into a dark night of the senses or a renunciation of the things of the world, of materiality and sensuality. The danger that John of the Cross points out for someone on the mystic way is what he calls "spiritual gluttony," that is, interpreting all things in relation to the self and to self-interest.[62] This gluttony relates both to Mrs. May's self-satisfaction when seeing herself reflected in a window, and perceiving only "the reflection of her own character," and to her dream of an all-consuming force that she connects to the bull.[63] She projects onto this animal her own desire to consume, which is to say her own proclivity to gluttony.

58. O'Connor, *The Complete Stories*, 316, 333.

59. O'Connor, *The Complete Stories*, 320.

60. O'Connor, *The Complete Stories*, 322.

61. Underhill, *Mysticism*, 354.

62. Quoted in Underhill, *Mysticism*, 92.

63. O'Connor, *The Complete Stories*, 311–312.

After her second encounter with the bull, which begins with
the animal being described as the sun's shadow and ends with
her staring out of a window at the "ambling" animal, Mrs. May is
determined to track down its owners and insist that they retrieve
the creature.[64] She fails to locate O. T. and E. T. on their farm
but does enter the templelike space of the twins' modern, empty
milking parlor, where she feels she may "lose her breath." It is
"spotless" and "white," a purity associated with lilies, and filled
"with sunlight that came from a row of windows head-high along
both walls." On departing, the sun comes to her as an overwhelming force similar to that of both Mrs. Greenleaf and the bull: "the
sun was directly on top of her head, like a silver bullet ready to
drop into her brain." This force stalks her while she continues to
fixate on the scrub bull and its removal from her property.[65]

The next night her suitor the bull returns to the space below
her bedroom window, although farther off this time, "away from
the hedge." As she stares through the "slit blind," the bull "paused
as if observing her." It seems to beckon her farther out into the
night, "until the iron shadow moved away in the darkness."[66] This
scene mirrors quite precisely a passage from the Song of Songs:
"My beloved is like a roe, or a young hart. Behold he standeth behind our wall, looking through the windows, looking through the
lattices. / Behold my beloved speaketh to me: Arise, make haste,
my love, my dove, my beautiful one, and come. / For winter is now
past" (2:9–11). Mrs. May's name evokes spring, of course, the sea-
son during which the story is set.

Although the bull does not literally speak, he comes courting
for a second night with an intensity associated in a second dream
of Mrs. May's with "some large stone ... grinding a hole on the
outside wall of her brain." She is content in this dream "walking"
in a natural scene, "over a succession of beautiful rolling hills,

64. O'Connor, The Complete Stories, 323.
65. O'Connor, The Complete Stories, 325.
66. O'Connor, The Complete Stories, 329.

planting her stick in front of each step."⁶⁷ There is at first no intimation of property ownership here, just a succession of hills through which she walks in the darkness. Mrs. May's apparent unconcern about who owns these hills contrasts with her persistent anxiety about possession in her waking life, most prominently the ownership of the legally "entailed" property of her farm.⁶⁸ As she becomes aware of the setting sun in the dream, however, Mrs. May recalls that this body "had to sink the way it always did outside of her property." This dream might represent Mrs. May's version of a dark night of the senses, a time when she is challenged to become detached from the world and the things of the world. Then, something powerful associated with the sun intrudes into this imaginary space: "a swollen red ball" that narrows into a "bullet," which bursts "through the tree line" and races "down the hill toward her." When she awakens from the dream with a start, she realizes that the scrub bull is just outside the window, staring, "observing her."⁶⁹ The bull calls her to an even deeper darkness.

At this point, Mrs. May's obsession with the bull culminates, and this section of O'Connor's narrative most closely follows St. John's "On a Dark Night." She will pursue the bull, with Mr. Greenleaf's help, not in the darkness but in the light of day. St. John of the Cross describes the second, more profound dark night as follows: "The pain suffered by the soul is like that endured by weak or diseased eyes when suddenly struck by a strong light. Such suffering is intense when the yet unpurified soul finds itself invaded by this cleansing light."⁷⁰ Underhill herself elaborates: the "self is in the dark because it is blinded by a Light greater than it can bear."⁷¹

67. O'Connor, *The Complete Stories*, 329.
68. O'Connor, *The Complete Stories*, 315.
69. O'Connor, *The Complete Stories*, 329.
70. Quoted in Underhill, *Mysticism*, 399.
71. Underhill, *Mysticism*, 399. On spiritual blindness in St. John of the Cross and its relevance to reading O'Connor, see Edmondson, *Return to Good and Evil*, 68–70.

This helps explain why, when Mrs. May and Mr. Greenleaf travel in a truck to find and shoot the bull, "the grass was almost too bright to look at, the sky was an even piercing blue."[72] This light, like the spiritual light that blinds the mystic seeker in the dark night of the soul, nearly blinds one into darkness. This light, as with the light of the poem "On a Dark Night," "did lead me on, / More surely than the shining of noontide / Where well I knew that One / Did for my coming bide; Where He abode might none but He abide."[73] Although Mrs. May remarks to Mr. Greenleaf that "[t]he gentleman"—the bull—"is waiting on you," she will discover in due course that it is she whom the bull seeks.[74]

In the Spanish mystic's poem, the soul is next brought, although in the night, "[l]over to lover's sight / Lover to loved, in marriage of delight!"[75] A version of this occurs after Mr. Greenleaf has disappeared with the bull into the woods and Mrs. May waits for the return of Greenleaf to the clearing in which she has parked. She "lay [sic] her head back against the hood and closed her eyes." Despite it being only "mid-morning," she is unaccountably "tired." She opens her eyes, but "the white light forced her to close them again." As before, this light is unbearable to the point of blinding. After Mrs. May honks the truck's horn three times, she encounters the bull for the last time. The creature emerges from the tree line as "a black heavy shadow that tossed its head several times and then bounded forward." The bull, charging, seems "overjoyed." In short order, the bull buries "his head into her lap," and her expression changes from "freezing unbelief" to "the look of a person whose sight has been suddenly restored but who finds the light unbearable."[76] Mrs. May's

---

72. O'Connor, *The Complete Stories*, 330.
73. Symons trans., quoted in Underhill, *Mysticism*, 352.
74. O'Connor, *The Complete Stories*, 331.
75. Quoted in Underhill, *Mysticism*, 371.
76. O'Connor, *The Complete Stories*, 332–333. Anthony Di Renzo has pointed out the striking similarity between this scene and Gian Lorenzo Bernini's famous sculpture of St. Teresa in mystical ecstasy; see Di Renzo, *American Gargoyles: Flan-*

spiritual blindness has passed, and she now enters the realm of unbearable light.

For John of the Cross, the soul suffering in the dark night will perceive itself to be "so unclean and miserable that it seems as if God had set Himself against it," but instead, God "touches the soul not to chastise it, but to load it with His graces."[77] Understood in this way, this scene not only provides a tableau of *catanyxis*, or a "thrust or sudden sensation of anguish that embeds deep in the soul an attitude, a determination," as Richard Giannone has perceptively pointed out.[78] It is more than a shock or "moment of grace."[79] It is also a moment of union that follows a dark night of the soul, in which, in the words of St. John, "His hand, with gentle care, / Did wound me in the side, / And in my body all my senses died./ All things I then forgot,/ My cheek on Him Who for my coming came, / *All ceased, and I was not,/* Leaving my cares and shame/ Among the lilies, and forgetting them."[80] Although the bull uses its horn rather than "hand" to wound, and although this wounding is anything but "gentle," the result is the same, a cessation of the self, a "whispering" of "some last discovery." This experience leaves Mrs. May's cares among the lilies of the field, whether understood literally or as a metaphor for the Greenleafs themselves.[81]

A problem arises with this interpretation of the story and particularly of the story's end, an interpretation, that is, which perceives Mrs. May as moving through the two dark nights of the senses and of the soul to a final union with the Christlike scrub bull. Mrs. May has not done the work of—that is, has not will-

nery O'Connor and the Medieval Grotesque (Carbondale: Southern Illinois University Press, 1995), 95.

77. Quoted in Underhill, *Mysticism*, 399.

78. Richard Giannone, *Flannery O'Connor: Hermit Novelist* (Urbana: University of Illinois Press, 2000), 196.

79. Flannery O'Connor, *Mystery and Manners: Occasional Prose*, ed. Sally and Robert Fitzgerald (New York: Farrar, Straus and Giroux, 1969), 112.

80. Quoted in Walsh, *Hispanic Anthology*, 248; and Underhill, *Mysticism*, 371.

81. O'Connor, *The Complete Stories*, 334.

ingly endured—the mystic way. She has resisted any inbreaking of grace and the Divine even as she obsessively pursues the intruding bull that represents these in the story. She is pulled along unwittingly, unconsciously by her idée fixe to a largely unexpected and strangely erotic embrace. One way of accounting for this may be found in O'Connor's own explanation, in a letter to Hester written about two years following the composition of "Greenleaf," of her use of "grace" in narrative: "Part of the difficulty . . . is that you write for an audience who doesn't know what grace is and don't recognize it when they see it. All my stories are about the action of grace on a character who is not very willing to support it, but most people think of these stories as hard, hopeless, brutal, etc."[82] The stumbling block with reading this and other O'Connor stories about the insistent effects of grace on a character that brings about both "conversion" and a moment of death is that the arc of the narrative can come across as overly mechanical and in retrospect inevitable. On one level, that does seem to be the case with the structure of "Greenleaf." In this sense, it is a satiric and darkly comedic retelling of the poem "On a Dark Night," along with the biblical source texts of that poem in Song of Songs chapters two and three. If we read both of these in relation to Evelyn Underhill's mystic way, then the story seems determined to shock Mrs. May into the final state of union with the Divinity.

Nancy Bishop Dessommes has read "Greenleaf" in this fashion, in that Mrs. May is "forced, in a moment of self-realization, to recognize the divine presence in the world."[83] This is a rather tame formulation in that Mrs. May not only recognizes the divine presence, but is also impaled upon its personified horn. Others, however, have discerned something more profound at work in the text. Farrell O'Gorman, for example, has described "Green-

---

82. O'Connor, *The Habit of Being*, 275.

83. Nancy Bishop Dessommes, "O'Connor's Mrs. May and Oates's Connie: An Unlikely Pair of Religious Initiates," *Studies in Short Fiction* 31, no. 3 (Summer 1994): 433.

leaf" as "profoundly mysterious," a story that provides a sense of "contact with infinite mystery."[84] Joseph Zornado similarly notes that "O'Connor dramatizes violence as a prelude to moments of unknowing."[85] Mark S. Sexton points to a "much deeper spiritual malaise" in Mrs. May than is apparent.[86] Finally, Denise Askin, employing the language of Paul Ricoeur, speaks of the "excess of signification" in this story that serves O'Connor's larger anagogical purposes.[87] I would associate this sense of mystery, unknowing, malaise, and excess in the story not just with spiritual themes but also with the story's inherently dialogic narrative voice, a modernist third-person narrator who employs pervasive free indirect discourse.

Free indirect discourse translates the "words or thoughts of the character … into the discourse of the narrator, who imposes on them his or her diegetic past tenses and third-person pronouns," as Suzanne Fleischman describes this technique.[88] Donald E. Hardy points out that such "dialogism is by no means rare across the entirety of O'Connor's fiction."[89] O'Connor's narrators are typically double or multiply voiced. That is, the narrator speaks in the third person but reports the thoughts, moods,

84. O'Gorman, Peculiar Crossroads, 66, 127.

85. Joseph Zornado, "A Becoming Habit: Flannery O'Connor's Fiction of Unknowing," Religion and Literature 29, no. 2 (1997): 29.

86. Mark S. Sexton, "'Blessed Insurance': An Examination of Flannery O'Connor's 'Greenleaf,'" Flannery O'Connor Bulletin 19 (1990): 40.

87. Askin, "Anagogical Vision," 59.

88. Suzanne Fleischman, Tense and Narrativity: From Medieval Performance to Modern Fiction (Austin: University of Texas Press, 1990), 228. Monika Fludernick likewise posits that free indirect discourse involves a "shift from external to internal perspective, from one mind to another, from thought to speech and perception"; see also Ann Banfield, Unspeakable Sentences: Narration and Representation in the Language of Fiction (New York: Routledge, 1982), 108. For a detailed analysis of this technique in O'Connor's short story "Revelation," see Donald Hardy, "Free Indirect Discourse, Irony, and Empathy in Flannery O'Connor's 'Revelation,'" Language and Literature 16 (1991): 37–53.

89. Donald E. Hardy, The Body in Flannery O'Connor's Fiction: Computational Technique and Linguistic Voice (Columbia: University of South Carolina Press, 2007), 21.

and even metaphors of a particular character—in "Greenleaf" that of the focalizing character Mrs. May. Our experience of the world of the story is filtered through her consciousness, which is expressed both directly in her own voice and indirectly through the third-person narrative voice. Although Mrs. May's own comments and conscious thoughts tend toward the pragmatic and direct, her dreams are presented in a much more poetic fashion, and as the narrative progresses, her impressions take on an ever more lyrical quality, as in the description of the templelike milking barn on O. T. and E. T.'s farm, her growing sense of the sun as a bullet, and her last thoughts as she unwittingly waits "against the hood" of the truck for her suitor the bull.[90]

This interplay of different discourses culminates in the scene of union of bull and woman so reminiscent of the ending of St. John's "On a Dark Night." Martin Kessler has explored O'Connor's juxtaposition of "declaring prose" and "an ambiguous, obscuring poetry" in this passage.[91] Examples include the statement that the bull "was crossing the pasture," which leads to the personification "as if he were overjoyed to find her again." Then, when "the bull had buried his head in [Mrs. May's] lap," the creature becomes, via simile, "like a wild tormented lover." Also, as Mrs. May "continued to stare straight ahead," she takes on "the look of a person whose sight has suddenly been restored but who finds the light unbearable."[92] This phrase evokes St. John's spiritual blindness and its giving way to a mystical and metaphoric light.[93] The interaction of straightforward comments and poetic figuration unites the two primary voices in the text, that of the narrator and that of Mrs. May. The narrator provides not just the poetic but also the mystical consciousness of the text, then, and articulates

90. O'Connor, *The Complete Stories*, 325, 332.
91. Edward Kessler, *Flannery O'Connor and the Language of Apocalypse* (Princeton, N.J.: Princeton University Press, 1986), 120.
92. O'Connor, *The Complete Stories*, 333.
93. Kessler, *Flannery O'Connor and the Language of Apocalypse*, 120–121.

Mrs. May's experiences in relation to spiritual realities: Underhill's mystic way, the Song of Songs, and the dark nights of senses and soul in St. John of the Cross.

To borrow a term from Gilles Deleuze's study of the films of Pier Paolo Pasolini, the narrative voice in "Greenleaf" has a "sacralizing" effect on Mrs. May. According to Deleuze what "characterizes Pasolini's cinema is a poetic consciousness, which is not strictly aestheticist or technicist, but rather mystical or 'sacred'." He continues: "This allows Pasolini to bring the perception-image, or the neurosis of his characters, on to a level of vulgarity and bestiality in the lowest subject-matter, while reflecting them in a pure poetic consciousness, animated by the mystical or sacralizing element. It is this permutation of the trivial and the noble, this communication between the excremental and the beautiful, this projection into myth, which Pasolini had already diagnosed in free indirect discourse as the essential form of literature."[94] This "sacralizing element," made present also through O'Connor's employment of free indirect discourse, is an apt term to describe what allows us to interpret Mrs. May as a potential mystic who might, despite her resistance to faith, accomplish something like mystical union with the Divinity at the moment of her death. That is, Mrs. May is a mystic because O'Connor's narrator presents her in the language of the mystics, notably John of the Cross, and encourages her reader to view the story's protagonist in this way.[95] There is spiritual hope

94. Deleuze, *Cinema 1*, 75. For Deleuze an "aestheticist" consciousness is found in the films of Michelangelo Antonioni and a "technicist" version in those of Jean-Luc Godard. Pasolini, in contrast, is a "mystical" filmmaker because he "succeeds in making [free indirect discourse] into a cinematographic form, capable of grace as well as horror." O'Connor's stories provide a similar combination of horror and grace. For a very helpful summary of the influence of Pasolini's theory of free indirect discourse on Deleuze and the ways that Deleuze adapts, alters, and perhaps misreads Pasolini, see Louis Georges Schwartz, "Typewriter: Free Indirect Discourse in Deleuze's *Cinema*," *SubStance* 34, no. 3 (2005): 114–127.

95. Schwartz argues that free indirect images, and by association free indirect discourse, rely on "an object heterogeneous" to what else is in the work of

for Mrs. May because O'Connor's narrator infuses the character and her world with the language of such hope, of (secret) stairs and lilies and a Bridegroom who comes to Mrs. May as "a country suitor" in the night.

O'Connor herself acknowledged to Hester that "something more fundamental" than simple narrative mechanics was at play in the composition of "Greenleaf." She admits to her friend just one week before Hester's baptism, "Perhaps you are able to see things in these stories that I can't see because if I did see I would be too frightened to write them."[96] What frightened O'Connor about her own stories is a matter of conjecture, but she certainly sought to address the pervasive and no doubt terrifying "dark night" into which she perceived Western culture had sunk. Even a seemingly irredeemable character such as Mrs. May may be invited into a mystical dark night and eventually into spiritual union, albeit one that is potentially lethal. Perhaps O'Connor's hope for her friend Elizabeth Hester on the eve of her baptism can best be summed up by St. John of the Cross in "The Flame of Love": God's "soft hand" and "touch most delicate," although "slaying" reveals "new life" and abounds in "grace," and "dost from death to life translate."[97] It is possible, then, that the message for Hester and for all those who worry that God might be dead is that God's grace can seize even *you*, whether you are ready or not, despite the world's dark night.

---

art, "a different source of enunciation and a different reading position"; Schwartz, "Typewriter," 116. In pop art this heterogeneous material is often a found object. In O'Connor's "Greenleaf," the poem "On a Dark Night" and its mystical voice function similarly.

96. O'Connor, *The Habit of Being*, 149.

97. Quoted in Underhill, *Mysticism*, 236.

Appendix: Arthur Symons's 1920 Translation of *En una Noche Escura*

Upon an obscure night
Fevered with Love's anxiety
(O hapless, happy plight!),
I went, none seeing me,
Forth from my house, where all things quiet be.

By night, secure from sight,
And by the secret stair, disguisedly,
(O hapless, happy plight!)
By night, and privily,
Forth from my house, where all things quiet be.

Blest night of wandering
In secret, when by none might I be spied
Nor I see anything;
Without a light to guide,
Save that which in my heart burnt in my side.

That light did lead me on,
More surely than the shining of noontide
Where well I knew that One
Did for my coming bide;
Where He abode might none but He abide.

O night that didst lead thus,
O night more lovely than the dawn of light,
O night that broughtest us,
Lover to lover's sight,
Lover to loved, in marriage of delight!

Upon my flowery breast
Wholly for Him and save Himself for none,
There did I give sweet rest
To my beloved one:
The fanning of the cedars breathed thereon.

When the first moving air
Blew from the tower and waved His locks aside,
His hand, with gentle care,
Did wound me in the side,
And in my body all my senses died.

All things I then forgot,
My cheek on Him Who for my coming
All ceased, and I was not,
Leaving my cares and shame
Among the lilies, and forgetting them.[98]

98. First six stanzas are in Underhill, *Mysticism*, 352; seven in Walsh, *Hispanic Anthology* 248; eight in Underhill, *Mysticism*, 371.

CHAPTER 8

O'Connor's Unfinished Novel

The Beginning of a Modern Saint's Life

Jessica Hooten Wilson

Flannery O'Connor never finished her third novel—*Why Do the Heathen Rage?* Her *Collected Works* includes a teaser from the incomplete manuscript, an excerpt that *Esquire* published in 1963. A decade later, Stuart Burns visited O'Connor's archives at Georgia College and State University, hoping to discover a treasure like James Agee's *A Death in the Family* or F. Scott Fitzgerald's *The Last Tycoon* waiting for the right editor to sift through and compile the pieces. However, Burns was disappointed by what he found: "All in all, there are about a half-dozen episodes, each extensively revised, most of them connected, in one way or another, with a porch scene—of which there are no fewer than seventeen versions. There is, in short, no novel there at all."[1] There are 378 pages of the *Why Do the Heathen Rage?* manuscript, and although Burns is right to point out that the novel lacks a cohesive plot, he too quickly dismisses what O'Connor accomplishes in these episodes. According to Burns, "O'Connor was not embarked in any new direction in her unfinished novel—if, indeed she had a direction clearly in mind at all."[2] However, I contend that O'Connor proposed and accomplished a new direction in the surviving episodes of her unfinished novel, most significantly an attempt to exhibit a postconversion narrative, one that investigates how a contemplative saint may participate in the active life, against all the modern ills.

The manuscript in its incomplete form reads like a composite novel, somewhat akin to the loose structure of William Faulkner's *Go Down, Moses*, in which the characters overlap and run into each other in various ways. In O'Connor's manuscript, the current axis is the protagonist, Walter Tilman, and his conversion. There are approximately fifteen episodes, depending on how one reads the various pieces, which include a handful of characters: Walter who is sometimes referred to as Julian or Asbury, his mother and father, Roosevelt his father's black valet, Gunnels a field hand, and his cousin Sarah and his aunt, who will later morph into a distant correspondent named Oona Gibbs. The relationship between Walter and Oona comprises the heart of the novel. Like a twenty-first-century social networker who creates false personas, Walter writes letters to satirize and mock those he does not know in person, which includes Oona, a recent convert to a fellowship group called Friendship, Inc., a "cooperative community interdenominational, interracial, whose aim was to answer any call for friendship or for help anywhere in the United

1. Stuart L. Burns, "How Wide Did 'The Heathen Range?'" *Flannery O'Connor Bulletin* 4 (1975): 26.
2. Burns, "How Wide Did 'The Heathen Range?'" 26.

States."[3] The two have never met, although Oona's encroaching visit would have begun the action of the novel.

O'Connor carved up much of the prospective novel into short stories, which were posthumously published in the collection *Everything Rises Must Converge*. She indicates her method in an August 22, 1963, letter to J. L. Mazzaro: "I am working on the long piece now and not writing any stories but I might be able to drain off another fragment of WHY DO THE HEATHEN RAGE? Sometime."[4] Nearly every work that composes her final collection can be traced back to her *Why Do the Heathen Rage?* manuscript. In one of the earliest episodes in the manuscript, Walter's father suffers a stroke, not unlike Julian's mother at the climax of "Everything that Rises Must Converge." Walter's mother in the novel resembles "Mrs. May" from "Greenleaf," and she shares a fear with Mary Fortune from "A View of the Woods" that, like Mary's grandfather, Mrs. Tilman's husband will sell their oaks for lumber. Like Asbury in "The Enduring Chill," Walter suffers an alleged sickness and sends for a priest to debate—though Marian Burns, who has written two articles on the manuscripts, makes a compelling case that "The Enduring Chill" inspired the third novel, rather than the other way around. From "Comforts of Home" Sarah Ham/Star Drake seems closely related to Walter's New York correspondent, Sarah/Oona Gibbs. In an undeveloped episode, the future O. E. Parker appears as the Tilman's fieldhand Mr. Gunnels, who is covered with tattoos, including "a large head of Christ" on his back.[5] Finally, the manuscript possesses a handful of similarities with "Judgment Day": Mr. Tilman has made eyeglasses for his servant Roosevelt, which parallels

3. Flannery O'Connor, "Why Do the Heathen Rage?" (unpublished manuscript), Georgia College and State University, Special Collections, Folder 216.5. Accessed December 14–16, 2009, and July 18–21, 2011.

4. Flannery O'Connor, "Letter to J. L. Mazzaro" (August 22, 1963), Flannery O'Connor Papers, Emory University Archives, Manuscript, Archives, and Rare Book Library, Folder 38. Accessed December 16, 2009, and July 17, 2011.

5. O'Connor, "Why Do the Heathen Rage?" 228.32.

the Tanner and Coleman relationship, and Sarah's mother repeats Tanner's desire to be buried at home in the South after she dies. In these complete stories, we can see how O'Connor accomplished her intentions. However, in the unpublished versions where these stories first germinated, we observe O'Connor working out problems that she had not yet solved.

After removing from consideration all the elements in the manuscript that overlap with the published short stories, the remaining passages of the manuscript reveal a struggle over how to respond to modern problems. O'Connor usually considered contemporary issues marginally, if at all, and always in relationship to a character's spiritual state. For instance, in her final story "Revelation," Ruby Turpin's racism is not the primary dilemma; it is symptomatic of her sinful nature, namely her pride. In his chapter on race and religion in *Flannery O'Connor and the Christ-Haunted South*, Ralph Wood illuminates O'Connor and the race issue from several sides. He contrasts O'Connor's fiction, especially her most race-conscious short story "Everything That Rises Must Converge," with a short story of Eudora Welty's "Where is the Voice Coming From?" in which "the racists were made to seem the sole evildoers."[6] For O'Connor, not only does this story descend from art to propaganda because of its social heavy-handedness but also the author, by making herself judge and jury of others' sinfulness, succumbs—as much as a racist does—to pride. Because O'Connor recognized that her art stemmed from and was dedicated to her faith, she never *used* it for a social cause.

However, O'Connor shows in these unpublished papers a growing concern with modern problems. In their letters, Walter and Oona argue contrasting responses to current issues, such as race relations. In her 1994 article, Virginia Wray establishes a dichotomy between the contemplative Walter and his socially active correspondent Sara/Oona Gibbs. Wray argues that the character

---

6. Ralph Wood, *Flannery O'Connor and the Christ-Haunted South* (Grand Rapids, Mich.: William B. Eerdmans, 2004), 97.

of Oona is based on O'Connor's real-life pen pal, the liberal social activist Maryat Lee, and Walter's autobiographical counterpart is O'Connor herself. To support her interpretation, Wray quotes O'Connor's May 4, 1963, letter to Sister Mariella Gable, in which O'Connor confesses her need for prayers for "the larger things" that she desires to do in her writing. Wray argues that these "larger things" are "issues of social justice and fairness, and love between human beings." Wray continues, "O'Connor was unable to reconcile her intellectual understanding of the need for social activism in the 1950s and 1960s with her own frequent retreat to the perspective of *sub specie aeternitatis*."[7] For Wray, the novel remains unfinished because O'Connor could not forego her transcendent concerns for the immediate problems of the day, such as the civil rights agenda. Although Wray accurately describes the split between Walter and Oona, she misplaces O'Connor's allegiance.

The "larger things" that O'Connor wanted to accomplish in her final novel were to address twentieth-century concerns but not with narratives subjugated to a contemporary agenda. First, O'Connor believed that all earthly spheres of action were subordinated to divine ends. Before Wray assigns these "larger things" to worldly issues, she addresses readers' assumptions: "For O'Connor we would generally and quite naturally think the 'larger things' to be *sub specie aeternitatis*."[8] Wray's language downplays eternal concerns as a "retreat," and she calls the two sides, social justice issues versus *sub specie aeternitatitis*, "polarized perspectives." However, readers *should* assume that O'Connor intended to remain faithful to a worldview that dominated the previous eighteen years of her writing life. For O'Connor, a concern for eternal things should not be polarized against social concerns. O'Connor draws on a tradition from which the focus on eternal things leads

7. Virginia Wray, "Flannery O'Connor's *Why Do the Heathen Rage?* and the Quotidian 'larger things,'" *Flannery O'Connor Bulletin* 23 (1994–1995): 3
8. Wray, "Flannery O'Connor's *Why Do the Heathen Rage?*" 3.

to action in social justice causes: think of the American Great Awakenings or William Wilberforce's triumphant abolition of the slave trade in Britain, for example. However, O'Connor would be untrue to her vocation if she prioritized the latter over the former. In the same letter that Wray quotes, O'Connor confesses, "If I set myself to write about a socially desirable Christianity, all the life would go out of what I do."[9] No matter how much O'Connor may have approved of socially active Christianity, she did not see her vocation as a Christian social activist.

Wray's article exemplifies the divided world that O'Connor considered her audience, one in which empirical reality is separated from the transcendent, the physical from the spiritual, and thus earthly concerns are divested of heavenly importance or vice versa. To redress this divide, O'Connor returns to the world prior to the Reformation, the patristic and medieval theologians who saw *sub specie aeternitatis* as intimately connected with the happenings of this world. O'Connor worked on *Why Do the Heathen Rage?* between 1960 and 1964. During this time, Vatican II, the council in which the Catholic Church tried to reinvigorate their relationship with twentieth-century culture, began convening. They called on the guidance of theologians, many of whom promoted *ressourcement*, or a return to the sources, including a reconsideration of the church fathers. Like these theologians, O'Connor believed that the contemporary world she lived in needed to revisit these sources.

During the years in which O'Connor wrote *Why Do the Heathen Rage?*, she reviewed books on saints, which evidence a desire to understand these sources and to proselytize them to her contemporary Catholics. For instance, in a review of three books on St. Vincent de Paul, O'Connor exalts the "shrewd peasant saint" for grappling "with the social ills of his day."[10] In an effort to see

9. Flannery O'Connor, *The Habit of Being: Letters of Flannery O'Connor*, ed. Sally Fitzgerald (New York: Farrar, Straus and Giroux, 1979), 517.

10. Flannery O'Connor, *The Presence of Grace and Other Book Reviews by Flannery O'Connor*, comp. by Leo J. Zuber (Athens: University of Georgia Press, 2008), 162.

these saints as contemporarily relevant, she repeatedly applauds the writers who make the saints more real.[11] O'Connor read and underlined all four volumes of Rev. Alban Butler's 1866 *Lives of the Saints*. She read not only writings by the saints but many biographies on them, including works on or by St. Catherine of Genoa, St. Catherine of Siena, St. Jerome, St. Teresa of Avila, St. Teresa of Jesus, St. Bonaventure, and especially Sts. Augustine and Aquinas.

Moreover, O'Connor desired that her character, who was to become a contemplative saint, would also be active in the affairs of the modern world. As models for this project, O'Connor read twentieth-century novels that attempted to accomplish a similar feat: from Georges Bernanos *The Diary of a Country Priest* to less literary works from the best-seller lists, such as Morris L. West's *The Devil's Advocate*. Of one such mass-market novel, *Light in Silence*, O'Connor praises the author Claude Koch for portraying a "saint" that is "both believable and appealing," a task that she declares the "most difficult [on which] a novelist can set himself."[12] Perhaps O'Connor's reviews of these works indicate the goal that she had undertaken for herself, to create a credible and likable saint who could act in his contemporary time and place. Unlike the distasteful atheist antiheroes of her two previous novels, *Wise Blood* and *The Violent Bear It Away*, who begrudgingly become, respectively, an ascetic and a Fundamentalist preacher, the protagonist of this unpublished manuscript, Walter Tilman is agreeable and, more significantly, Catholic.

Although Walter initially appears as a modern hero, he is destined to be, in the words of Marian Burns, "a closet medieval

---

11. In her review of *Two Portraits of St. Terese of Lisieux*, O'Connor writes, "The author shows that the life of the saint, as it has appeared in various books, has been manipulated in order to make it more edifying ... to uncover the real saint in her very human and terrible greatness, and in this process surely to widen devotion to her"; O'Connor, *Presence of Grace*, 18. And, in her review of the St. Vincent de Paul books, she finds the one by von Matt and Cognet the "most satisfying" because it "contains a short but very realistic life of the saint" (162).

12. O'Connor, *The Presence of Grace*, 73.

Catholic monk."[13] An intellectual wanderer, Walter never committed to a major in college. Then at twenty-five, he returns to
his parents' farm, where he studies religious texts during the
day and manages a liquor store in the evening. Similar to earlier characters, Walter exhibits a heightened opinion of his self,
a strained relationship with his mother, and, like Asbury Fox
from "The Enduring Chill," a fascination with religion. Although
Stuart Burns assumes that "Asbury Fox, Julian Chestny, Thomas
. . . and Calhoun are all the grandchildren . . . of Walter Tilman,"
Marian Burns asserts there is a marked difference between the
"peevish and pretentious Asbury" and the "ironical and profound
Walter."[14] Wray agrees with Marian Burn's reading; she writes,
"[Walter's] taste in reading, his contemplative posture, and his
epistolary activity set him apart."[15] In his book on O'Connor and
Walker Percy, *Peculiar Crossroads*, Farrell O'Gorman compares
Walter to Binx Bolling: "Both are fundamentally 'new men,' each
of whom is not haunted by his family and regional past but radically severed from it; not merely rejecting but in fact failing even
to consider seriously the codes of their ancestors, they are essentially valueless and trivial lives devoid of direction in a seemingly empty present."[16] Superficially, Walter first appears like the
Protestant pseudo-intellectual sons who preceded him; however,
he is more homeless, more lost, more alienated than any of his
precursors. More like Percy's hero, Walter is an existentialist
wayfarer, destined to convert to Catholicism.

Also, varying from her previous methods, O'Connor situates
the conversion not at the conclusion but at the start of the narra-

13. Marian Burns, "O'Connor's Unfinished Novel," in *Critical Essays on Flannery O'Connor*, ed. Beverly Lyon Clark and Melvin J. Friedman (Boston: G. K. Hall,
1985), 170.

14. Burns, "How Wide Did 'The Heathen Range?'" 31; and Burns, "The Chronology of Flannery O'Connor's 'Why Do the Heathen Rage?'" 63.

15. Wray, "Flannery O'Connor's *Why Do the Heathen Rage?*" 7–8.

16. Farrell O'Gorman, *Peculiar Crossroads: Flannery O'Connor, Walker Percy, and
Catholic Vision in Postwar Southern Fiction* (Baton Rouge: Louisiana State University
Press, 2004), 154.

tive. Marian Burns indicates that this structure causes problems for O'Connor, whom she believes decided not to adhere to this organization: "[O]nce having converted the main character to Christianity, what could O'Connor, within the limits of her sensibility and fictional imagination, do with him?"[17] While in O'Connor's previous work, conversion provided the climax of the story, in this piece, she wanted to explore the life of a Christian in action. Whereas Burns makes O'Connor's dilemma technical, Wray diagnoses it as a content challenge, a problem with how to write a postconversion character. The two assessments are tied together: O'Connor needed an early conversion to show a Christian life in action, but she had never before accomplished such a feat.

Although we do not know the outcome for Walter, we see the problem that O'Connor places before him in the character of Oona. The two characters are positioned in diametric opposition regarding their ways of living in the world. Whereas Walter is a contemplative not yet centered in a love of God, Oona undertakes an active life isolated from transcendent concerns. The conflict of *Why Do the Heathen Rage?* concentrates around the upcoming visit of Oona, in which these two clashing perspectives will collide. Stuart Burns notes, "Clearly the confrontation between [contemplative, aloof] Walter and [enthusiastic, socially oriented] Sara [alternately Oona] was to have been a highly important, if not critical, element in the projected novel."[18] Wray adds the descriptors "contemplative, aloof" and "enthusiastic, socially oriented" to Burns's thesis. For Wray, Sarah/Oona "is the embodiment of a love threatening to descend upon Walter."[19] True, Sarah/Oona is such an embodiment: her approaching physical presence would be a catalyst for further transformation in Walter—as it also would for Oona. Wray asserts that through his relationship with Oona, Walter would discover the good of communities such as Friend-

17. Burns, "O'Connor's Unfinished Novel," 173.
18. Burns, "How Wide Did 'The Heathen Range?'" 29.
19. Wray, "Flannery O'Connor's *Why Do the Heathen Rage?*" 4.

ship, Inc., and perhaps be converted to social activism. However, the encounter would cause so much more: both correspondents would be forced to love concretely rather than in the abstract. Their theories of love would be tested in practice: the rationalist and the humanist would have a chance to become saints.

Based on the problem that O'Connor lays out between Walter's and Oona's characters, O'Connor seems to have been designing a saint who would discover the relationship between this world and the next along the same lines as Augustine does in *City of God*. O'Connor did not own a copy of *City of God*, but she was familiar with its concepts. She had read a handful of works by Augustine, his sermons on the Psalms, his *Confessions*, a biography about him, and reviewed a critical work *The Modernity of Saint Augustine* by Jean Guitton, which stresses the contemporary relevance of Augustine's thought.[20] The theme of Augustine's rather lengthy theological treatise can be briefly summarized for our purposes: there are two cities existing simultaneously in the same space but in different times. The City of Man is temporal whereas the City of God is eternal. Thus, the obligation of the Christian is to the City of God, although his actions may have bearing and consequences on the City of Man. If O'Connor does concern herself in this novel with contemporary issues of social justice, she does so with the conviction that her character should first attend to the City of God.

The question, for O'Connor, is not whether to pledge allegiance to either the City of God or the City of Man but, rather, how does one who is a citizen of the former participate in the latter? Considering the City of God as the end or *telos* of one's life, Augustine defines

20. In *Flannery O'Connor's Library: Resources of Being* (Athens: University of Georgia Press, 2008), Arthur Kinney shows Guitton's book; a 1952 edition of *Confessions*, trans. Edward Pusey (New York: Pocket Books), *Nine Sermons of St. Augustine on the Psalms*, trans. Edmund Hill (New York: P. J. Kennedy and Sons, 1959), *The Mind and Heart of Augustine: A Biographical Sketch*, ed. J. M. Flood (Fresno, Calif.: Academy Guild Press, 1960); and Romano Guardini's *The Conversion of Augustine*, trans. Elinor Briefs (Westminster, Md.: Newman Press, 1960).

three kinds of life: "the life of studious leisure and search after truth, the life of easy engagement in affairs, and the life in which both of these are mingled."[21] Augustine draws the categorization from a Roman philosopher Marcus Varro, but he baptizes the pagan ideas for his purposes. He labels these three modes of life: "the active, the contemplative, and the mixed." Because the best kind of life is the one that mixes the active and contemplative, Augustine cautions: "No man has a right to lead such a life of contemplation as to forget in his own ease the service due to his neighbor; nor has any man a right to be so immersed in active life as to neglect the contemplation of God."[22] The two cities may be separate, but the modes should not be. For Augustine, one's contemplation of God leads to one's participation in earthly affairs.

In addition to Augustine, O'Connor draws her understanding of the contemplative and active life from the writings of St. Thomas Aquinas, whom she claims to have read for ten minutes before bed each evening. O'Connor searches through the works of her beloved saints to unlock the secret of how the contemplative life develops from an active life and also directs the active life. In Aquinas, she finds the best answers. Aquinas praises the contemplative life above the active life because it "becomes man according to that which is best in him, namely, the intellect," however one cannot merely begin and end in the life of the mind. He quotes Gregory who writes in the Morals, "Those who wish to hold the fortress of contemplation, must first of all train in the camp of action."[23] The active life concerns itself with the external world, human things, and the love of neighbor. In a 1963 review of Denis de Rougemont's *The Christian Opportunity*, O'Connor

21. Augustine, *City of God*, XIX:2, trans. Marcus Dods, from *Nicene and Post-Nicene Fathers*, ed. Philip Schaff, first series, vol. 2. (Buffalo, N.Y.: Christian Literature Publishing Co., 1887); rev. and ed. for New Advent by Kevin Knight, July 11, 2016, http://www.newadvent.org/fathers/1201.htm.

22. Augustine, *City of God*, XIX.2.

23. Quoted in Thomas Aquinas, *Summa Theologica*, 182. vi. 37, www.newadvent.org/summa/3182.htm.

writes, "[N]othing will serve the Christian purpose but an uncompromising belief in transcendence and thus a transcendence
involved in action."[24] One must excel first at the active life to
progress to the contemplative life. In other words, one must first
love her neighbor to love God. Paradoxically, the contemplative
life also directs the active life: when one loves God, she will more
consistently love her neighbor.

Wray situates this conflict in O'Connor's historical reality.
She draws the connection between O'Connor's literary creation,
Friendship, Inc. and the historically real communal society called
Koinonia, located outside of Americus, Georgia, founded in the
1930s. Wray argues that Walter's criticism of Oona coincides with
O'Connor's "disdain for Koinonia, Dorothy Day, and the liberal
causes of her day,"[25] although *disdain* may be too strong of a word.
When O'Connor writes of Dorothy Day's visit to Koinonia, she admits to "uncharitable thoughts" as well as admiration. O'Connor
worries, "I hope that to be of two minds about some things is not
to be neutral."[26] Although O'Connor is divided between her appreciation for the charitable actions of such organizations and her
repulsion at their sentimentality and idealism, her struggle with
these local events shows her desire to engage contemporary issues
despite her concerns.

As the exemplary modern humanitarian, Oona is an easy target
for Walter's ridicule. She writes with sentimental clichés, numerous exclamation points, and horrific spelling errors. Walter has
inquired about the practical application of the motto of Friendship, Inc., and she has answered him with her own testimony.
She became a member of Friendship, Inc., after she encountered
a homeless boy in an alley. She writes, "I looked at that child every
day for three months before I saw him. Then one day I saw him. . . .
I mean I SAW him, SAW him. . . . I saw him and then I saw myself

24. O'Connor, *The Presence of Grace*, 168.
25. Wray, "Flannery O'Connor's *Why Do the Heathen Rage?*" 24.
26. O'Connor, *The Habit of Being*, 218.

and that was it."[27] She never explains what this transformative vision accomplished in her or what she saw in herself, but this brief encounter induces her to join Friendship, Inc. In her letter, she explains to Walter that she lives with six other people in a New York flat, suffering alongside the oppressed. The group does not give money, food, or shelter to the poor; they act as witnesses to the injustice by sharing in it.

When Walter imagines Oona's commune, he envisions them as a "pack of lean, hungry-eyed young people, moving from place to place on the scent of injustice." Such "naivete and self-righteousness, their yearning for martyrdom" enrages him."[28] Wray connects Walter's anger with O'Connor's criticism of the 1950s social activists, admitting "Walter's harsh judgments of [Oona] have partial validity. [Oona] is guilty here in her sentimental, naïve enthusiasm of ... a false equating of Love ... with kindness."[29] She substitutes her love for the oppressed for actual kindness to them, and though Wray does not mention it, she conflates love with charitable aid. She dedicates herself to an active life apart from its source or completion in the contemplative life.

For Oona, love means to act within the world but without a transcendent purpose. She does not approve of the word *love* because it sounds "fishy," nor "charity" because of its religious connotations.[30] Despite her poor theology, her actions resemble those of the early church. She has gathered together a group of people who share all their worldly possessions and give to those who have need. Even Walter defends her group to his father, claiming they are "living like the gospels say live."[31] In Acts 4 of the Christian gospels, the verse "Why do the heathen rage?" is repeated by a group of converts. After the apostles Peter and John miraculously

27. O'Connor, "Why Do the Heathen Rage?" 222.26–27.
28. O'Connor, "Why Do the Heathen Rage?" 222.27.
29. Wray, "Flannery O'Connor's *Why Do the Heathen Rage?*" 17.
30. O'Connor, "Why Do the Heathen Rage?" 222.27.
31. O'Connor, "Why Do the Heathen Rage?" 222.22.

heal a lame beggar, they are called before the Sanhedrin to explain, and "although they are unlearned and ignorant men," both apostles speak effectively and astonish the educated leaders who subsequently release them. When Peter and John join a congregation of new believers, all sing Psalm 2 and then begin sharing their possessions. According to Augustine, Peter signifies the active life, as his actions here reveal.[32] However, Peter's active life stems from and leads to his contemplative life whereas Oona's does not.

Although Wray intuits O'Connor's sympathy with Oona, she overlooks the importance of the end for such an active life in the love of God. In O'Connor's 1963 presentation at Sweetbriar College, she worries about the reader who "has the mistaken notion that a concern with grace is a concern with exalted human behavior."[33] O'Connor foresees readers will separate grace or love from its *telos* in God, as Oona has, and locate it primarily among human concerns. She argues instead that "[i]t is a concern with a realization that breeds charity and with the charity that breeds action."[34] The contemplative life leads to love that should play out in the active life.

O'Connor fears that the all-encompassing concern that Oona expresses for the victim makes the victim an object to be loved, but an object nonetheless. Although Oona *sees* the homeless child, she offers him abstract "friendship" rather than the concrete necessity of food. When she justifies the mission of Friendship, Inc. her words echo Walter's sentiment about letter writing. She writes, "Our work is between heart and heart. The heart can move like the wind in letters where it is not tied down by the body."[35] Their love is abstract and theoretical. While the group appears to

32. St. Augustine, *Tractates on the Gospel of John*, trans. John W. Rettig (Washington, D.C.: The Catholic University of America Press, 1995), 91.

33. Flannery O'Connor, *Mystery and Manners: Occasional Prose*, ed. Sally and Robert Fitzgerald (New York: Farrar, Straus and Giroux, 1969), 204.

34. O'Connor, *Mystery and Manners*, 204.

35. O'Connor, "Why Do the Heathen Rage?" 218d.6.

be loving in action, their love is little more than what O'Connor would call "tenderness." In her "Introduction to *A Memoir for Mary Ann*," O'Connor warns, "It is a tenderness which, long since cut off from the person of Christ, is wrapped in theory. When tenderness is detached from the source of tenderness, its logical outcome is terror. It ends in forced-labor camps and in the fumes of the gas chamber."[36] Without the contemplation of the Incarnational Christ as its source, this kind of tenderness may easily become violence. Although O'Connor's conclusion may sound drastic, she does not want to allow for any middle ground between the citizens of God's City and those of the City of Man. For O'Connor, the world is divided between the crucified and the crucifiers so extremely that even those who pretend to be sufferers, to act as crucified, are only crucifiers in disguise. If someone like Oona rejects the former, then her actions in the latter are not only trifling but ultimately destructive.

In the episodes between Oona, alternatively called Sarah here, O'Connor illustrates this prospective dark side of her character. Oona's mother suffers from a bad leg or could be dying—the author seems undecided—and, in her potentially final days, to her daughter's dismay, is recanting her Sartrean existentialist worldview. Like Oona, the mother is an activist who encourages her daughter to follow suit: "Do something even if it's wrong. When I was your age I'd been in jail three times. I had a lover. I'd published a poem. I cared about humanity."[37] The emphasis is on *doing*. "Humanity" in these sections is abstract. For instance, when the two debate whether to write a will, the mother insists that the money be left to "half the world [who are] starving" to which her daughter protests, "I don't know half the world."[38] The mother wants to give to the faceless starving humanity, although her daughter recognizes the abstractness of this love.

36. O'Connor, *Mystery and Manners*, 227.
37. O'Connor, "Why Do the Heathen Rage?" 229a.2.
38. O'Connor, "Why Do the Heathen Rage?" 230b.9.

What the daughter decides to "do," as her mother has encouraged, is commit murder followed by suicide. She is frustrated that her mother, who once praised suicide as noble, now dismisses it.[39] In one of the finale episodes of the section, Sarah holds a butcher knife above her tied-up mother and says, "I'm capable of doing something great."[40] With chilling detail, O'Connor adds that she wears a good dress, a white one that has never been worn. The act is never rendered, and the next scenes in which Sarah appears, she is headed toward Walter's home repeating an existential manifesto: "I exist. Nothing matters but absolute honesty. I will look for the absolute core of truth in every human being I meet."[41] These installments complicate the interpretation of Sarah/Oona as a model for engagement in contemporary issues. Cloaked in abstract theory or Sartrean existentialism, Sarah/Oona's love for humanity may as easily lead to murder and suicide as charitable aid.

Similarly, Walter does not locate himself in his body; he lives abstractly and apart from any belief in the God that he studies. He imagines that he writes letters to bodiless others with whom he may interact on a solely mental plane. He proposes, "The soul travels rapidly through the mail, unemcumbered [sic] with real flesh."[42] He regards flesh as "the greatest interference to love" and believes that the "soul moves quickly without the body."[43] He tries not to imagine the recipients of his letters, but "whenever one of his mocked correspondents, from being a caricature, began to take on human lines—pathetic, undemanding, full of ridiculous encroaching love—Walter wrote DECEASED across the next letter he received."[44] As long as Walter can pretend that his addressee lacks physical reality, then he can mock said corre-

39. O'Connor, "Why Do the Heathen Rage?" 229a.3.
40. O'Connor, "Why Do the Heathen Rage?" 229a.11.
41. O'Connor, "Why Do the Heathen Rage?" 229a.4.
42. O'Connor, "Why Do the Heathen Rage?" 226b.29.
43. O'Connor, "Why Do the Heathen Rage?" 222.24.
44. O'Connor, "Why Do the Heathen Rage?" 222.24.

spondent. Yet once the interlocutor becomes embodied for him, he can no longer continue the pretense. One wonders whether O'Connor could not decide to whom such philosophy was better suited—the fanatical convert to a new religion or the elitist intellectual who considers himself above earthly concerns.

Walter's correspondence with Oona begins to reveal his self to his self; she reflects for him his own misconceptions about reality. Through indirect discourse, O'Connor hints that Walter recognizes this connection: "Writing to Oona was like looking into a mirror which also exposed the heart or the place where it should have been."[45] O'Connor elaborates the reflective nature of their relationship in response to race. Although both Walter and Oona profess to live apart from physical concerns, their approach to race tests these assertions. Oona avows to care little for racial distinctions because she has seceded such physical notions. She confesses her dream to move to the South and live with a Negro family, for her "heart bleeds for the poor black people of the South."[46] Attempting to unveil her prejudice, Walter claims that he is black. He even takes a picture of his field hand Roosevelt to send her as a picture of himself. He indicates the difference between her abstract love for him from a distance and the demands of love between persons in close proximity: "He pointed out that it was possible to love almost anyone who was 2,000 miles away. On closer inspection, however, she would find him very black."[47] When Walter attempts to expose what he believes is Oona's false love for the oppressed with his own charade, he emphasizes the reality of the concrete world more than he desires to admit.

When Walter reads Oona's treatise about "charity," he worries that "what the woman had done was to abrogate the place of God and set herself up where it had been."[48] By not placing the active life in relation to the contemplative life, Oona then becomes a

45. O'Connor, "Why Do the Heathen Rage?" 216.6.
46. O'Connor, "Why Do the Heathen Rage?" 218a.6.
47. O'Connor, "Why Do the Heathen Rage?" 218e.11.
48. O'Connor, "Why Do the Heathen Rage?" 222.29.

"ruler of the earth," as it says in Psalm 2, more concerned with the things of this world than the eternal or greater things. However, Walter is guilty of the same heresy that he attributes to Oona: he has set himself up in the place of God. Although he studied "the Fathers of the Church ... never for the slightest moment, had it occurred to him, even remotely, to believe any of it."[49] He disassociates the intellectual enterprise from the object of contemplation. Like those philosophers who occupy the first ring of Dante's inferno, Walter misses the "good of the intellect" (*Inferno* I.iii.18). Prior to his revelation of God's existence, Walter refers to himself as a "secular contemplative."[50] However, once Walter realizes the reality of God, he must reexamine his attempt to live a contemplative life.

In the longest continuous sections of the manuscript, approximately thirty pages in one folder, Walter's conversion occurs near the end of those sections. It was probably intended to occur within the opening chapter of the novel. O'Connor has rewritten this episode four different times but always with a subtlety that contrasts with the violent depictions of grace in her earlier work. Instead of being gored by a bull or choked by an acne-faced teenager, the truth occurs to Walter "without startling him": "the answer came, fully formed, fully rational, not wholly [*sic*] unexpected ... he believed in God."[51] With Walter's conversion to belief, O'Connor attempts to recall the biblical passage, 1 Kings 19, in which Elijah hears the voice of God. In a 1960 letter, O'Connor writes to Andrew Lytle: "I keep seeing Elias in that cave waiting to hear the voice of the Lord in the thunder and lightning and wind, and only hearing it finally in the gentle breeze, and I feel I'll have to be able to do that sooner or later, or anyway keep trying."[52] Walter undergoes a revelation before the action of the

49. O'Connor, "Why Do the Heathen Rage?" 226a.18.
50. O'Connor, "Why Do the Heathen Rage?" 226c.26.
51. O'Connor, "Why Do the Heathen Rage?" 226a.19.
52. O'Connor, *The Habit of Being*, 373.

novel has begun, and although O'Connor uses the word *deadly* to describe Walter's newfound belief, he seems destined to become a believer.

Marian Burns compares Walter to his novelistic predecessors and asserts that he too "will find Christ just like the other two heroes [Hazel Motes and Francis Marion Tarwater], but in this case his belief is that of a distinctly pre-Reformation Christianity."[53] Walter's belief will differ in being more Catholic, more medieval, more of a product of the *ressourcement* to which O'Connor prescribed. Burns delineates the numerous references to monks and conjectures that the name "Walter" itself may allude to three different medieval monks, including eleventh-century Walter the Penniless, twelfth-century archbishop of Canterbury Hubert Walter, or thirteenth-century Walter of Coventry. O'Connor drew inspiration from the early church, especially the lives of saints and mystics. In his book *Flannery O'Connor: A Hermit Novelist*, Richard Giannone asserts, "If O'Connor went to Augustine, Thomas Aquinas, and Pierre Teilhard for ideas, she looked to hermits for ways of living wisely."[54] For Walter's character, the hermit prototype is St. Jerome.

In Paul Carroll's introduction to Jerome's letters, he offers a portrait of the saint that resembles Walter's character: "Conspicuous for his scholarly achievements, and for being an astute and seminal moralist, the vain, crabby, vituperative side to his temperament also makes him one of the most fascinating saints for those who appreciate contradictory, yet somehow profound, irreconcilable traits in our greatest men."[55] Jerome's scandalous side seemed incongruent with his piety, a combination that would have intrigued O'Connor, so known for her grotesque

53. Burns, "O'Connor's Unfinished Novel," 169.

54. Richard Giannone, *Flannery O'Connor, Hermit Novelist* (Urbana: University of Illinois Press, 2000), 28.

55. Paul Carroll, introduction to *The Satiric Letters of St. Jerome*, ed. and trans. Paul Carroll (Chicago: Henry Regnery Co., 1956), vii.

amalgamations of the saintly with the offensive. Burns also acknowledges the significance of Jerome for the story: "The letters of St. Jerome in fact become a sort of ironic framework for the projected novel: [O'Connor] sustains a tacit parallel between the epistles of the early Christian saint writing in the fourth and fifth centuries, and the humorously perverse correspondence which Walter engages in with total strangers in the twentieth century."[56] Although the most modern of her heroes, Walter is also the most medieval. To counteract his Cartesian dualism and Oona's Sartrean existentialism, O'Connor returns to the models of the past, such as Jerome, who prioritized the contemplative life without neglecting the active life.

In the 1963 published excerpt, Mrs. Tilman discovers that Walter has underlined a passage from a letter from St. Jerome to Heliodorus, in which the saint advises the soldier to return to the contemplative life. Perhaps the longest passage that O'Connor has cited in full, the quote furnishes at least ten percent of the published excerpt and intimates the meaning of the story. Walter's mother is concerned about the antiquated and religious nature of the quote: "This was the kind of thing he read—something that made no sense for now."[57] Although the letter dates back to 374 AD, the translator, referring to 1956, describes the fourth century as "a time, in fact, much like our own" in its meaninglessness and restlessness.[58] O'Connor would have agreed. In her letters and lectures, she often diagnosed the modern world as "an unbelieving age": "At its best our age is an age of searchers and discoverers, and at its worst, an age that has domesticated despair and learned to live with it happily."[59] This conclusion sounds reminiscent of her fellow southern writer Walker Percy, but both of them gained

56. Burns, "O'Connor's Unfinished Novel," 170.

57. Flannery O'Connor, *Collected Works*, ed. Sally Fitzgerald (New York: Library of America, 1988), 800.

58. Carroll, introduction to *The Satiric Letters of St. Jerome*, xi.

59. O'Connor, *Mystery and Manners*, 159.

such vision of the current culture only by stepping back and looking through the lens of history, especially that of the church.

The book that Walter's mother has picked up is described in the manuscript as a "bright" "orange" "paperback" of the "Letters of St. Jerome," a description that fits O'Connor's personal edition of *The Satirical Letters of St. Jerome*.[60] Both O'Connor and Walter have underlined the same passage:

Love should be full of anger. Since you have already spurned my request, perhaps you will listen to my admonishment. What business have you in your father's house, O you effeminate soldier? Where are your ramparts and trenches, where is the winter spent at the front lines? Listen! the battle trumpet blares from heaven and see how our General marches fully armed, coming amid the clouds to conquer the whole world. Out of the mouth of our King emerges a double-edged sword that cuts down everything in the way. Arising finally from your nap, do you come to the battlefield! Abandon the shade and seek the sun.[61]

For those inundated with 1 Corinthians 13 as the summation of Christian scripture, the passage is unnerving. How can a love that is patient and kind be "full of anger"? And, how can a God who is love be a General swinging a sword? When Walter's mother realizes the General is Jesus, she experiences "an unpleasant jolt."[62] Yet Jerome defines love in a way that is consistent with the scriptures that he translated and knew so well. Moreover, by designating the contemplative life as a place of action, he overturns modern assumptions about the contemplative and active life.

Walter first attempts to live in accordance with his new belief by writing Oona a letter in which he will reveal his hoax and correct her theological errors. Oona enrages him because she offends "the order of the universe, some good perverted, gone to waste," a diagnosis seemingly pulled from the writings of Augus-

---

60. O'Connor, "Why Do the Heathen Rage?" 227a.7.
61. St. Jerome in a letter to Heliodorus, qtd in O'Connor, *Collected Works*, 800.
62. O'Connor, *Collected Works*, 800.

tine.[63] When concluding his letter, Walter hesitates over whether to add the word "love" as Oona does. Rather than imply his love for her by using the word itself, "[i]t occurred to him that he might better end it with a quotation *about* love."[64] His decision to use a quote signifies his need to maintain the distance between them. As Walter seeks the appropriate book on his shelf, they appear "like booby traps," a metaphor that recalls C. S. Lewis's account of his own conversion in *Surprised by Joy*: "A young man who wishes to remain a sound Atheist cannot be too careful of his reading. There are traps everywhere."[65] Walter picks up Jerome's letters and the underlined quote leaps out at him: "Love should be full of anger." By desiring to admonish Oona, Walter unintentionally mimics Jerome's love for Heliodorus.

Because Heliodorus is a soldier, Jerome uses military language in his letter compelling him to return to the life of an ascetic. The battlefield metaphor for the contemplative life invokes Aquinas's objection, in which he reverses his twelfth-century readers' assumptions about "the military art being the more important." Here the "military" represents the active life, which is superseded by the contemplative. When Giannone describes O'Connor as a "hermit novelist"—her own phrase—"in the tradition of fourth century spirituality," he uses words such as *weapons*, *battle*, *war*, and *warrior* to describe her fiction.[66] The soldier metaphor clarifies that the contemplative life is not a life without action but a fight in an eternal arena. Walter's name means "ruler of the army," a name that would cast him with those rulers of the earth to whom the psalmist refers. However, if Walter is to become a medieval monk, he must relinquish the role of "ruler" and submit to the General.

Although Walter acknowledges the reality of God, he does not

63. O'Connor, "Why Do the Heathen Rage?" 222.28.
64. O'Connor, "Why Do the Heathen Rage?" 227a.7.
65. C. S. Lewis, *Surprised by Joy* (New York: Houghton Mifflin Harcourt, 1995), 185.
66. Giannone, *Flannery O'Connor, Hermit Novelist*, 6.

embrace this knowledge with joy, surrender to its sovereignty, or even profess unconditional love to the said deity. Consistent with other O'Connor heroes, Walter appears unwilling to accept this knowledge and disapproving of it. In the first draft of the conversion, Walter realizes that "he was Christian, bound for hell" and calls "upon the devil, also a believer, to help him."[67] When O'Connor expounds on Walter's conversion,[68] she uses indirect discourse in which Walter calls his conversion "revolting" and an "ugly fact." Moreover, he claims "his vision [is] as clear as Satan's."[69] At this point in the narrative, O'Connor intends to connect Walter more with the demons who, as it reads in James 2:19, shudder from the knowledge that there is a God. On the final page of the manuscripts, Walter flees "the room as if from a gathering of devils," invoking the image of St. Antony fleeing demons in the desert.[70]

The manuscript ends without Walter acting in accordance with his newfound belief. Just as Walter remains with pen poised in hand, Oona is "suspended forever on the highway in her little red car speeding toward the South."[71] Stuart Burns believes that O'Connor never finished this manuscript because she lacked the ability to produce good novels; she was more of a short-story author. Wray thinks this lack of ending "indicates O'Connor's uncertainty about what to have Walter to do with the young woman."[72] In the world of O'Connor, he could marry her, seduce her, kill her, or in the best of circumstances and with a new twist for O'Connor storytelling, he could fall in love with her. Then again, he could become what O'Connor seems to have intended for him—a Christian monk.

Walter is a twentieth-century rendition of a medieval saint

---

67. O'Connor, "Why Do the Heathen Rage?" 222.29.

68. O'Connor, "Why Do the Heathen Rage?" 226a.27.

69. O'Connor, "Why Do the Heathen Rage?" 222.27.

70. O'Connor, "Why Do the Heathen Rage?" 233.65.

71. Burns, "O'Connor's Unfinished Novel," 177.

72. Wray, "Flannery O'Connor's *Why Do the Heathen Rage?*" 4.

who remains forever—because of a manuscript that will never be completed—in the liminal space between accepting or rejecting the terrifying reality of God. Rather than have the contemplative Walter forego his lifestyle for social activism, O'Connor wants to see how a Catholic contemplative participates in the active life. Through this unfinished character, O'Connor suggests that the reading of Augustine, Aquinas, and Jerome, although seemingly distant from our own culture in space and time, may have more to do with now than we know.

BIBLIOGRAPHY

Aquinas, Thomas. "Question 182. The Active Life in Comparison with the Contemplative Life." *Summa Theologica*. www.newadvent.org/summa/3182.htm.

Asals, Frederick. *Flannery O'Connor: The Imagination of Extremity*. Athens: University of Georgia Press, 1982.

———. "The Mythic Dimensions of Flannery O'Connor's 'Greenleaf.'" *Studies in Short Fiction* 5 (1968): 317–330.

Askin, Denise T. "Anagogical Vision and Comedic Form in Flannery O'Connor: The Reasonable Use of the Unreasonable." *Renascence* 57, no. 1 (2004): 47–62.

Augustine of Hippo. *The City of God*. Translated by Marcus Dods. New York: Modern Library, 1950.

———. *The Confessions*. Translated by E. B. Pusey. Mount Vernon, N.Y.: Peter Pauper, n.d.

———. *Confessions*. Translated by Henry Chadwick. New York: Oxford University Press, 1991.

———. *De Haeresibus (Heresies)*. Translated by Rev. Liguori C. Muller. Washington, D.C.: The Catholic University Press, 1956.

Bacon, Jon Lance. *Flannery O'Connor and Cold War Culture*. New York: Cambridge University Press, 1993.

Bakhtin, Mikhail. *Rabelais and His World*. Translated by Hélène Iswolsky. Bloomington: Indiana University Press, 1984.

Baldwin, Debra Romanick. "Augustinian Physicality and the Rhetoric of the Grotesque in the Art of Flannery O'Connor." *Augustine and Litera-*

ture, edited by Robert P. Kennedy, Kim Paffenroth, and John Doody, 301–325. Lanham, Md.: Lexington, 2006.

Ballinger, Philip A. *The Poem as Sacrament: The Theological Aesthetic of Gerard Manley Hopkins*. Louvain: Peeters Press, 2000.

Banfield, Ann. *Unspeakable Sentences: Narration and Representation in the Language of Fiction*. New York: Routledge, 1982.

Béguin, Albert, ed. *Cahier de poésie: Saint Jean de la Croix, Paul Claudel, Aragon, Pierre Jean Jouve, Pierre Emmanuel, Raymonde Vincent, Alain Borne, Georges Haldas, Jean Wahl, Raymond Michaud*. Les Cahiers du Rhône. Série bleu, 2. Neuchâtel: Éditions de la Baconnière, 1942.

———. *Léon Bloy: A Study in Impatience*. Translated by Edith M. Riley. New York: Sheed and Ward, 1947.

———. *Léon Bloy, l'impatient*. Fribourg: Egloff, 1944.

Béguin, Albert, and Pierre Thévenaz, eds. *Henri Bergson; essais et témoignages recueillis*. Les Cahiers du Rhône. Neuchâtel: Éditions de la Baconnière, 1943.

Benedict XVI. Homily at Cathedral of Aosta, Friday, July 24, 2009. http://www.vatican.va/holy_father/benedict_xvi/homilies/2009/documents/hf_ben-xvi_hom_20090724_vespri-aosta_en.html.

Bergson, Henri. *The Creative Mind: An Introduction to Metaphysics*. Translated by Mabelle L. Andison. Wisdom Library. New York: Philosophical Library, 1946.

———. *The Two Sources of Morality and Religion*. Translated by R. Ashley Audra and Cloudesley Brereton, with the assistance of W. Horsfall Carter. Garden City, N.Y.: Doubleday, Anchor A28, 1954.

Berkowitz, Michael, and Avinoam J. Patt. *"We are here": New Approaches to Jewish Displaced Persons in Postwar Germany*. Detroit, Mich.: Wayne State University Press, 2010.

Bernanos, Georges. *The Diary of a Country Priest*. Translated by Pamela Morris. New York: The Macmillan Company, 1937.

———. *Diary of a Country Priest*. Translated by Pamela Morris. Garden City, N.Y.: Doubleday, Image D6 (1937, 1954) 1960.

———. *The Heroic Face of Innocence: Three Stories*. New York: Eerdmans, 1998.

———. *Joy*. Translated by Louise Varèse. New York: Pantheon, 1946.

———. *The Last Essays of Georges Bernanos*. Chicago: Henry Regnery, 1955.

———. *The Star of Satan*. Translated by Pamela Morris. New York: Macmillan, 1940.

Bleikasten, Andre. "The Role of Grace in O'Connor's Fiction." *Readings on*

Flannery O'Connor, edited by Jennifer A. Hurley, 77–82. The Greenhaven Press Literary Companion to American Authors. San Diego, Calif.: Greenhaven, 2001.

Bloy, Léon. *Au seuil de l'Apocalypse, 1913–1915* [*On the Threshold of the Apocalypse, 1913–1915*]. Paris: Mercure de France, 1916.

———. *Belluaires et porchers* [*Gladiators and Swineherds*]. Paris: P. V. Stock, 1905.

———. *Celle qui pleure* [*She Who Weeps*]. Paris: Société du Mercure de France, 1908.

———. *Christophe Colomb devant les taureaux* [*Christopher Columbus before the Bulls*]. Paris: Albert Savine, 1890.

———. *Constantinople et Byzance* [*Constantinople and Byzantium*]. Paris: Georges Crès, 1917.

———. *Dans les ténèbres* [*In the Darkness*]. Paris: Mercure de France, 1918.

———. *Exégèse des lieux communs* [*Exegesis of Commonplaces*]. First series. Paris: Mercure de France, 1902.

———. *Exégèse des lieux communs: (Nouvelle série)* [*Exegesis of Commonplaces*]. Second series. Paris: Mercure de France, 1913.

———. *Henry de Groux*. Paris: La plume, 1899.

———. *Histoires désobligeantes* [*Disagreeable Tales*]. Paris: E. Dentu, 1894.

———. *Ici on assassine les grands hommes: avec un portrait et un autographe d'Ernest Hello* [*Great Men are Assassinated Here: With a Portrait and Autograph of Ernest Hello*]. Paris: Mercure de France, 1895.

———. *Illustrissime Domine: Parisiis, 4 Octobris 1890. Lettre encyclique à tous les évêques de France, les priant de plaider la cause de la béatification de Christophe Colomb auprès de la Cour de Rome* [*Illustrissime Domine: Paris, 4 October 1890. Encyclical Letter to all the Bishops of France, Asking them to Plead the Cause of the Beatification of Christopher Columbus at the Court of Rome*]. Paris: Albert Savine (?), 1890.

———. *Jeanne d'Arc et l'Allemagne* [*Joan of Arc and Germany*]. Paris: G. Crès et cie, 1915.

———. *Je m'accuse. Vignettes et culs-de-lampe de Léon Bloy* [*Vignettes and Cul-de-lampes of Léon Bloy*]. Paris: Édition de "La Maison d'art," 1900.

———. *La Chevalière de la mort (Marie Antoinette)* [*The Knight of Death (Marie Antoinette)*]. Paris: Mercure de France, 1896.

———. *La femme pauvre: Épisode contemporain* [*The Woman Who was Poor: A Contemporary Episode*]. Paris: Société du Mercure de France, 1897.

———. *L'Âme de Napoléon* [*Napoleon's Soul*]. Paris: Mercure de France, 1912.

———. *La Porte des humbles, 1915–1917* [*The Door of the Lowly, 1915–1917*]. Paris: Mercure de France, 1920.

———. *La résurrection de Villiers de L'Isle-Adam: avec une reproduction du monument de Frédéric Brou* [*The Resurrection of Villiers de L'Isle-Adam: With a Reproduction of the Monument by Frédéric Brou*]. Paris: A. Blaizot, 1906.

———. *Le Désespéré* [*The Desperate Man*]. Paris: Nouvelle Librairie A. Soirat, 1887.

———. *Le Fils de Louis XVI avec un portrait de Louis XVII en héliogravure* [*The Son of Louis XVI with a Heliographic Portrait of Louis XVII*]. Paris: Société du Mercure de France, 1900.

———. *Le Mendiant ingrat: "Journal de l'auteur: 1892–1895"* [*The Ungrateful Beggar: "Diary of the Author: 1892–1895"*]. Brussels: E[dmond] Deman, 1898.

———. *Léon Bloy. Choix de textes et introduction par Albert Béguin* [*Léon Bloy. Texts Selected and Introduced by Albert Béguin*]. Edited by Albert Béguin. Fribourg: Éditions de la Librairie de l'Université, 1943.

———. *Léon Bloy devant les cochons: suivi de Lamentation de l'épée* [*Léon Bloy before the Swine: Followed by Lamentation of the Sword*]. Paris: Chamuel, 1894.

———. *Léon Bloy. Édition du centenaire augmenté de textes inédits*. Edited by Albert Béguin. Les Cahiers du Rhône, no. 11. Neuchâtel: Éditions de la Baconnière, 1946.

———. *Le Pèlerin de l'absolu: 1910–1912* [*The Pilgrim of the Absolute: 1910–1912*]. Paris: Mercure de France, 1914.

———. *Le révélateur du globe: Christophe Colomb et sa béatification future. Préface de J. Barbey d'Aurevilly* [*The Revealer of the Globe: Christopher Columbus and his Future Beatification. Preface by Barbey d'Aurevilly*]. Paris: A. Sauton, 1884.

———. *Les funérailles du naturalisme: Conférences publiques* [*The Funeral of Naturalism. Public Lectures*]. Copenhagen: G. E. C. Gad, 1891.

———. *Le Salut par les juifs* [*Salvation from the Jews*]. Paris: A. Demay, 1892.

———. *Le Salut par les Juifs. Édition nouvelle, revue et modifiée par l'auteur* [*Salvation from the Jews. New Edition, Revised by the Author*]. Paris: J. Victorin, 1906.

———. *Le Sang du pauvre* [*The Blood of the Poor*]. Paris: Delamain et Boutelleau, 1909.

———. *Le symbolisme de l'apparition, 1879–1880* [*The Symbolism of the Apparition, 1879–1880*]. Paris: Lemercier, 1925.

———. *Letters to his fiancée.* Edited by Jeanne Léon Bloy. Translated by Barbara Wall. New York: Sheed and Ward, 1937.

———. *Lettres à sa fiancée* [*Letters to his Fiancée*]. Paris: Librairie Stock, Delamain, Boutelleau et Cie, 1922.

———, with Jules Barbey d'Aurevilly. *Lettres de J. Barbey d'Aurevilly à Léon Bloy: avec un portrait et une lettre autographe* [*Letters of J. Barbey d'Aurevilly to Léon Bloy: With a Portrait and an Autographed Letter*]. Paris: Société du Mercure de France, 1902.

———. *Le Vieux de la montagne, 1907–1910* [*The Old Man from the Mountain, 1907–1910*]. Paris: Mercure de France, 1911.

———. *L'Invendable, 1904–1907* [*The Unsaleable, 1904–1907*]. Mercure de France, 1909.

———. *Méditations d'un solitaire en 1916* [*Meditations of a Solitary in 1916*]. Paris: Mercure de France, 1917.

———. *Mon journal: 1896–1900, dix-sept mois au Danemark* [*My Diary: 1896–1900, Seventeen Months in Denmark*]. Paris: Mercure de France, 1904.

———. *Pilgrim of the Absolute.* Translated by John Coleman and Harry Lorin Binsse. Selection by Raïssa Maritain. New York: Pantheon, 1947.

———. *Quatre ans de captivité à Cochons-sur-Marne: 1900–1904* [*Four Years of Captivity in Swine-on-Marne: 1900–1904*]. Paris: Société du Mercure de France, 1905.

———. *Sueur de sang: 1870–1871* [*Sweating Blood (1870–1871)*]. Paris: E. Dentu, 1893.

———. *Sur la tombe de Huysmans* [*On the Tomb of Huysmans*]. Paris: Collection des Curiosités Littéraires, 1913.

———. *Un brelan d'excommuniés* [*Three of a Kind Excommunicated*] (*J. Barbey d'Aurevilly; Ernest Hello; Paul Verlaine*). Paris: A Savine, 1889.

———. *The Woman Who Was Poor, A Contemporary Novel of the French 'Eighties.* Translated by I. J. Collins. New York: Sheed and Ward, 1939.

Bollery, Joseph. *Léon Bloy. Essai de biographie, avec de nombreux documents inédits.* 3 vols. Paris: A. Michel, 1947–1954.

Boscanquet, Bernard. *A History of Aesthetics.* Cleveland: World Publishing, Meridian, 1957.

Bouyer, Louis. *Eucharist: Theology and Spirituality of the Eucharistic Prayer.* Translated by Charles Quinn. Notre Dame, Ind.: University of Notre Dame Press, 1968.

Brinkmeyer, Robert H., Jr. *The Art and Vision of Flannery O'Connor.* Baton Rouge: Louisiana State University Press, 1989.

Brodin, Pierre. *Présences contemporaines: écrivains américains d'aujour-d'hui.* Paris: Nouvelles éditions Debresse, 1964.

Burns, Marian. "The Chronology of Flannery O'Connor's 'Why Do the Heathen Rage?'" *Flannery O'Connor Bulletin* 11 (1982): 58–75.

———. "O'Connor's Unfinished Novel." In *Critical Essays on Flannery O'Connor,* edited by Beverly Lyon Clark and Melvin J. Friedman, 169–180. Boston, Mass.: GK Hall, 1985.

Burns, Stuart L. "How Wide Did 'The Heathen Range?'" *Flannery O'Connor Bulletin* 4 (1975): 25–41.

Carritt, E. F., ed. *Philosophies of Beauty: From Socrates to Robert Bridges, Being the Sources of Aesthetic Theory.* New York: Oxford University Press, 1931.

Carroll, Paul, ed. and trans. *The Satiric Letters of St. Jerome.* Chicago: Henry Regnery, 1956.

Carroll, Rachel. "Foreign bodies: History and Trauma in Flannery O'Connor's 'The Displaced Person.'" *Textual Practice* 14, no. 1 (2000): 97–114.

Cash, Jean. *Flannery O'Connor: A Life.* Knoxville: University of Tennessee Press, 2004.

Catherine of Genoa and Battistina Vernazza. *Treatise on Purgatory: The Dialogue.* Translated by Charlotte C. Balfour and Helen Douglas-Irvine. London: Sheed and Ward, 1946.

Chardin, Teilhard de. *Hymn of the Universe.* New York: Harper and Row, 1961.

———. *The Phenomenon of Man.* Translated by Bernard Wall. New York: Harper Perennial, 1959; 1976.

Chrétien, Jean-Louis. *Conscience et roman, I: La conscience au grand jour.* Paris: Editions de Minuit, 2009.

Cirlot, J. E. *A Dictionary of Symbols.* Translated by Jack Sage. London: Routledge and Kegan Paul, 1962.

Cohen, Gerard Daniel. *In War's Wake: Europe's Displaced Persons in the Postwar Order.* Oxford: Oxford University Press, 2012.

Copleston, Frederick, SJ. *Mediaeval Philosophy, Part I: Augustine to Bonaventure.* Vol. 2 of *A History of Philosophy.* Garden City, N.Y.: Image, 1962.

Deleuze, Gilles. *Cinema 1: The Movement-Image.* Translated by Hugh Tomlinson and Barbara Habberjan. Minneapolis: University of Minnesota Press, 1986.

Desmond, John F. *Risen Sons: Flannery O'Connor's Vision of History*. Athens: The University of Georgia Press, 1987.

Dessommes, Nancy Bishop. "O'Connor's Mrs. May and Oates's Connie: An Unlikely Pair of Religious Initiates." *Studies in Short Fiction* 31, no. 3 (Summer 1994): 433–440.

Dickinson, Emily. *The Complete Poems of Emily Dickinson*. Edited by Thomas H. Johnson. New York: Little, Brown and Co., 1961.

Driskell, Leon V., and Joan Brittain. *The Eternal Crossroads: The Art of Flannery O'Connor*. Lexington: University Press of Kentucky, 1972.

Earley Whitt, Margaret. *Understanding Flannery O'Connor*. Columbia: University of South Carolina Press, 2005.

Ebrecht, Ann. "Flannery O'Connor's Moral Vision and 'The Things of This World'." PhD diss., Tulane University, 1982.

Edmondson, Henry [Hank] T., III. "Flannery O'Connor, Gerard Manley Hopkins and Silence." *Gerard Manley Hopkins Archive*. www.gerard manleyhopkins.org/lectures_2003/flannery_oconnor.html.

———. *Return to Good and Evil: Flannery O'Connor's Response to Nihilism*. Lanham, Md.: Lexington, 2002.

Eggenschwiler, David. *The Christian Humanism of Flannery O'Connor*. Detroit, Mich.: Wayne State University Press, 1972.

Feeley, Sister Kathleen, SSND. *Flannery O'Connor: The Voice of the Peacock*. New Brunswick, N.J.: Rutgers University Press, 1972.

Feith, Michel. "The Stained-Glass Man: Word and Icon in Flannery O'Connor's 'Parker's Back.'" *Journal of the Short Story in English* 45 (Autumn 2005): 95–111. http://jsse.revues.org/index447.html.

Fleischman, Suzanne. *Tense and Narrativity: From Medieval Performance to Modern Fiction*. Austin: University of Texas Press, 1990.

Fludernick, Monika. *The Fictions of Language and the Languages of Fiction*. New York: Routledge, 1993.

Forte, Bruno. *The Portal of Beauty: Towards a Theology of Aesthetics*. Grand Rapids, Mich.: Eerdmans, 2008.

Fumet, Stanislas. *Mission de Léon Bloy. Nouvelle édition, revue et corrigée*. Bruges: Desclée de Brouwer, 1947.

Garcia-Rivera, Alejandro. *The Community of the Beautiful: A Theological Aesthetics*. Collegeville, Minn.: Liturgical Press, 1999.

Gentry, Marshall Bruce. *Flannery O'Connor's Religion of the Grotesque*. Jackon: University Press of Mississippi, 1986.

———. "O'Connor as Miscegenationist." In *Flannery O'Connor in the Age of Terrorism: Essays on Violence and Grace*, edited by Avis Hewitt and Robert Donahoo, 188–200. Knoxville: University of Tennessee Press, 2010.

Getz, Lorine. *Flannery O'Connor: Her Life, Library and Book Reviews*. New York: The Edwin Mellen Press, 1980.

———. *Flannery O'Connor, Hermit Novelist*. Urbana: University of Illinois Press, 2000.

———. "'Greenleaf': A Story of Lent." *Studies in Short Fiction* 22, no. 4 (Fall 1985): 421–429.

———. *Nature and Grace in Flannery O'Connor's Fiction*. Lewiston, N.Y.: Edwin Mellen, 1982.

———. *The Spiritual Writings of Flannery O'Connor*. New York: Fordham University Press, 1999.

Gidden, Nancy Ann. "Classical Agents of Christian Grace in Flannery O'Connor's 'Greenleaf.'" *Studies in Short Fiction* 23, no. 2 (Spring 1986): 201–202.

Gooch, Brad. *Flannery: A Life of Flannery O'Connor*. New York: Little, Brown, 2009.

Gordon, Caroline. *How to Read a Novel*. New York: The Viking Press, 1953, 1957, 1964.

Gordon, Sarah. *Flannery O'Connor: The Obedient Imagination*. Athens: University of Georgia Press, 2000.

Graybill, Mark S. "O'Connor's Deep Ecological Vision." *The Flannery O'Connor Review*, 9 (2011): 1–18.

Gretlund, Jan Nordby, and Karl-Heinz Westarp, eds. *Flannery O'Connor's Radical Reality*. Columbia: The University of South Carolina Press, 2007.

Hardy, Donald E. *The Body in Flannery O'Connor's Fiction: Computational Technique and Linguistic Voice*. Columbia: University of South Carolina Press, 2007.

———. "Free Indirect Discourse, Irony, and Empathy in Flanner O'Connor's 'Revelation.'" *Language and Literature* 16 (1991): 37–53.

———. *Narrating Knowledge in Flannery O'Connor's Fiction*. Columbia: University of South Carolina Press, 2003.

Harrison, Carol. *Beauty and Revelation in the Thought of Saint Augustine*. Oxford: Clarendon, 1992.

Hauerwas, Stanley, and Ralph C. Wood. "How the Church Became Invisible: A Christian Reading of American Literary Tradition." In *Invis-*

ible Conversations: Religion in the Literature of America, edited by Roger Lundin, 159–186. Waco, Tex.: Baylor University Press, 2009.

Havird, David. "The Saving Rape: Flannery O'Connor and Patriarchal Religion." *Mississippi Quarterly* 47, no. 1 (1993): 15–26.

Heede, Philippe van den. *Réalisme et vérité dans la littérature. Réponses catholiques: Léopold Levaux et Jacques Maritain.* Fribourg [Switzerland]: Academic Press Fribourg, 2006.

Holian, Anna Marta. *Between National Socialism and Soviet Communism: Displaced Persons in Postwar Germany.* Ann Arbor: University of Michigan Press, 2011.

House, Humphrey, ed. *The Journals and Papers of Gerard Manley Hopkins.* 2nd ed. London: Oxford University Press, 1959.

Hügel, Friedrich von. *Essays and Addresses on the Philosophy of Religion.* Vol. 1. London: J. M. Dent and Sons, Ltd., 1921.

———. *Essays and Addresses on the Philosophy of Religion.* Vol. 2. London: J. M. Dent and Sons, Ltd., 1925.

———. *The Mystical Element of Religion as Studied in Saint Catherine of Genoa and Her Friends.* London: J. M. Dent and Sons, 1908, 1923.

———. *Letters to a Niece.* Chicago: Henry Regnery, 1955.

———. *The Reality of God and Religion and Agnosticism: Being the Literary Remains of Baron Friedrich von Hügel.* London: J. M. Dent and Sons, Ltd., 1931.

Jésus-Marie, Bruno de. *Three Mystics: El Greco, St. John of the Cross, St. Teresa of Avila.* New York: Sheed and Ward, 1949.

John of the Cross. *Dark Night of the Soul.* Edited and translated by E. Allison Peers. New York: Image, 1959.

———. *The Poems of John of the Cross.* Translated by Roy Campbell. London: Harvill, 1951.

Jouve, Pierre-Jean. *Les témoins: poèmes choisis de 1930 à 1942.* Les Cahiers du Rhône. Série rouge, 10. Neuchâtel: Éditions de la Baconnière, 1943.

Kessler, Edward. *Flannery O'Connor and the Language of Apocalypse.* Princeton, N.J.: Princeton University Press, 1986.

Kilcourse, George A., Jr. *Flannery O'Connor's Religious Imagination: A World with Everything Off Balance.* New York: Paulist, 2001.

Kinney, Arthur F. *Flannery O'Connor's Library: Resources of Being.* Athens: The University of Georgia Press, 1985.

Kirkland, William. "Baron Friedrich von Hügel and Flannery O'Connor." *The Flannery O'Connor Bulletin* 18 (1989): 28–42.

————. *The Incarnational Art of Flannery O'Connor*. Macon, Ga.: Mercer University Press, 2005.

Leo XIII (Pope). *Quarto Abeunte Saeculo. Encyclical of Pope Leo XIII on the Columbus Quadricentennial*. July 16, 1892. http://www.vatican.va/holy_father/leo_xiii/encyclicals/documents/hf_l-xiii_enc_16071892_quarto-abeunte-saeculo_en.html.

Lewis, C. S. *Surprised by Joy*. New York: Houghton Mifflin Harcourt, 1995.

Lubbock, Percy. *The Craft of Fiction*. New York: Peter Smith, 1945 [1921].

Marcel, Gabriel. *Creative Fidelity*. New York: Farrar, Strauss and Giroux, 1964.

————. *Metaphysical Journal*. Translated by Bernard Joseph Wall. Chicago: Henry Regner, 1952.

————. *The Mystery of Being*. Vol. 1 of *Reflection and Mystery*. Translated by G. S. Fraser. Chicago: Henry Regnery, n.d. (London: 1950).

————. *The Mystery of Being*. Vol. 2 of *Faith and Reality*. Translated by René Hague. Chicago: Henry Regnery, n.d. (London, 1951).

————. Preface to *The World of Silence*, by Max Picard. Translated by Stanley Godman. Humanist Library. Chicago: Henry Regnery, 1952.

Marion, Jean-Luc. "*Mihi magna quaestio factus sum*: The Privilege of Unknowing." Translated by Stephen E. Lewis. *The Journal of Religion* 85, no. 1 (January 2005): 1–24.

Maritain, Jacques. *Art and Scholasticism: With Other Essays*. Translated by J. F. Scanlan. New York: Charles Scribner's Sons, 1930.

————. *Art et scolastique*. Paris: Art catholique, 1920, 1947.

————. *À travers le désastre*. Collection "Voix de France." New York: Éditions de la Maison Française, 1941.

————. *A Christian Looks at the Jewish Question*. New York: Longmans, Green, 1939.

————. *Christianisme et démocratie*. Collection "Civilisation." New York: Éditions de la Maison Française, 1943.

————. *Creative Intuition in Art and Poetry*. New York: Meridian M8, (1953) 1955.

————. *La pensée de Saint Paul: textes choisis et présentés*. New York: Éditions de la Maison Française, 1941.

————. *Les droits de l'homme et la loi naturelle*. Collection "Civilisation." New York: Éditions de la Maison Française, 1942.

————. *Les Juifs parmi les nations*. Paris: Les Éditions du Cerf, 1938.

————. "L'Impossible antisémitisme." In *Les Juifs*, by Paul Claudel et al. Paris: Plon, 1937.

———. "L'Impossible antisémitisme." In *Questions de conscience*. Paris: Desclée De Brouwer et Cie, 1938.

———. *The Living Thoughts of Saint Paul*. Translated by Harry Lorin Binsse. New York: Longmans, Green and Co., 1941.

———. *Messages (1941–1944)*. Collection "Civilisation." New York: Éditions de la Maison Française, 1945.

———. "On Anti-Semitism." *Christianity and Crisis* (October 6, 1941): 2–4.

———. *Pour la justice. Articles et discours (1940–1945)*. New York: Éditions de la Maison Française, 1943.

———. Preface to *Le Mystère des Juifs et des Gentils dans l'Église. Suivi d'un essai sur l'Apocalypse*, by Erik Petersen. Translated by Ernest Kamnitzer, Pierre Corps, and Georges Massoulard. Preface by Jacques Maritain. Paris: Desclée De Brouwer, 1935.

———. Preface to *Racisme–Antisémitisme, antichristianisme: documents et critique*, by John M. Oesterreicher. New York: Éditions de la Maison Française, 1943.

———. *Principes d'une politique humaniste*. New York: Éditions de la Maison Française, 1944.

———. *The Range of Reason*. New York: Charles Scribner's Sons, 1952.

———. *The Rights of Man and Natural Law*. Translated by Doris C. Anson. New York: Scribner, 1943.

———. *Three Reformers: Luther, Descartes, Rousseau*. [No translator indicated] London: Sheed and Ward, 1928, 1947.

———. *Trois réformateurs*. Paris: Plon-Nourrit et cie, 1925.

———. "World Trial: Its Meaning for the Future." *Contemporary Jewish Record* 6 (August 1943): 339–347.

Maritain, Jacques et Raïssa. *Oeuvres completes*. Vol. I. Fribourg [Switzerland] and Paris: Editions Universitaires Fribourg/Editions Saint-Paul, 1982.

———. *Oeuvres completes*. Vol. III. Fribourg, Switzerland, and Paris: Editions Universitaires Fribourg/Editions Saint-Paul, 1984.

Maritain, Raïssa. *Adventures in Grace, Sequel to We Have Been Friends Together*. Translated by Julie Kernan. New York: Longmans, Green and Co., 1945.

———. "Henri Bergson." *The Commonweal* 33, no. 13 (1941): 317–319.

———. *Histoire d'Abraham ou La sainteté dans l'état de nature*. Fribourg: Fragnière Frères, 1935.

———. *Les grandes amitiés: souvenirs*. Collection "Voix de France." New York: Éditions de la maison française, 1941.

———. *Les grandes amitiés. 2: les aventures de la grâce*. New York: Éditions de la Maison Française, 1944.

———. *Pilgrim of the Absolute*. Translated by John Coleman and Harry Lorin Binsse. New York: Pantheon, 1947.

———. *We Have Been Friends Together, Memoirs*. Translated by Julie Kernan. New York: Longmans, Green and Co., 1942.

Martin, Gregory, ed. and trans., et al. *Douay-Rheims Bible*. American edition. Baltimore, Md.: John Murphy, 1899.

Mauriac, François. *Flesh and Blood [La Chair et le sang]*. Translated by Gerard Hopkins. New York: Farrar, Straus, 1955.

———. *The Frontenacs [La Mystère Frontenac]*. Translated by Gerard Hopkins. New York: Farrar, Straus, 1955.

———. *God and Mammon* [No translator indicated]. London: Sheed and Ward, 1946.

———. *The Lamb [L'agneau]*. Translated by Gerard Hopkins. New York: Farrar, Straus and Cudahy, 1955.

———. *Lines of Life [Destins]*. Translated by Gerard Hopkins. New York: Farrar, Straus and Cudahy, 1957.

———. *The Loved and the Unloved*. Translated by Gerard Hopkins. Postscript by François Mauriac. New York: Pellegrini and Cudahy, 1952.

———. *Oeuvres romanesques et théâtrales complètes*. Vol. II. Edited by Jacques Petit. Paris: Gallimard, Bibliothèque de la Pléiade, 1979.

———. *Questions of Precedence [Préséances]*. Translated by Gerard Hopkins. New York: Farrar, Straus and Cudahy, 1959.

———. *The Son of Man*. Translated by Bernard Murchland. Cleveland, Ohio: World Publishing, 1960.

———. *Thérèse: A Portrait in Four Parts*. Translated by Gerard Hopkins. Foreword by François Mauriac. New York: Henry Holt, 1947.

———. *The Unknown Sea*. Translated by Gerard Hopkins. New York: Henry Holt, 1948.

———. *Vipers' Tangle*. Translated by Warre B. Wells. Garden City, N.Y.: Doubleday, Image D51, 1957.

———. *The Weakling [Le Sagouin]* and *The Enemy [Le Mal]*. Translated by Gerard Hopkins. New York: Pellegrini and Cudahy, 1952.

———. *Woman of the Pharisees [La pharisienne]*. Translated by Gerard Hopkins. New York: Henry Holt, 1946.

———. *Words of Faith [Paroles catholiques]*. Translated by Rev. Edward H. Flannery. New York: Philosophical Library, 1955.

May, John R. *The Pruning Word: The Parables of Flannery O'Connor.* Notre Dame, Ind.: University of Notre Dame Press, 1976.

McGowan, Cecilia. "The Faith of Flannery O'Connor." *Catholic Digest* (February 1983): 74–78.

Mounier, Emmanuel. *Personalism.* Translated by Philip Mairet. New York: Grove Press, 1952.

Murphy, Michael Patrick. *A Theology of Criticism: Balthasar, Postmodernism, and the Catholic Imagination.* New York: Oxford University Press, 2008.

Oates, Whitney J. Introduction to *Basic Writings of Saint Augustine.* New York: Random House, 1948.

O'Connor, Flannery. *Collected Works.* Edited by Sally Fitzgerald. New York: Library of America, 1988.

———. *The Complete Stories.* Edited by Robert Giroux. New York: Farrar, Straus and Giroux, 1971.

———. *Everything That Rises Must Converge.* New York: Farrar, Straus and Giroux, 1965.

———. *A Good Man Is Hard to Find.* New York: Harcourt, Brace and Co., 1955.

———. *The Habit of Being: Letters of Flannery O'Connor.* Edited by Sally Fitzgerald. New York: Farrar, Straus and Giroux, 1979.

———. Introduction to Our Lady of Perpetual Help Free Cancer Home (Atlanta, Ga.). *A Memoir of Mary Ann.* New York: Farrar, Straus and Cudahy, 1961.

———. Letter to J.L. Mazzaro, Aug. 22, 1963. Folder 38. Flannery O'Connor Papers. Emory University Archives, Manuscript, Archives, and Rare Book Library, Emory University. December 16, 2009 and July 17, 2011.

———. Manuscripts of *Why Do the Heathen Rage?* Folders 215–234. Special Collections. Georgia College and State University. December 14–16, 2009, and July 18–21, 2011.

———. *Mystery and Manners: Occasional Prose.* Edited by Sally and Robert Fitzgerald. New York: Farrar, Straus and Giroux, 1969.

———. *A Prayer Journal.* Edited and with an introduction by W. A. Sessions. New York: Farrar, Straus and Giroux, 2013.

———. *The Presence of Grace and Other Book Reviews by Flannery O'Connor.* Compiled by Leo Zuber. Edited by Carter Martin. Athens: University of Georgia Press, 1983.

———. *The Violent Bear It Away.* New York: Farrar, Straus and Giroux, 1960.

———. *Wise Blood.* New York: Harcourt, Brace and Co., 1952.

Oesterreicher, John M. *Racisme–Antisémitisme, antichristianisme: docu-*

ments et critique. Preface by Jacques Maritain. New York: Éditions de
la Maison Française, 1943.

O'Gorman, Farrell. *Peculiar Crossroads: Flannery O'Connor, Walker Percy,
and Catholic Vision in Postwar Southern Fiction*. Baton Rouge: Louisiana
State University Press, 2004.

Ong, Walter. *Hopkins, the Self, and God*. Toronto: University of Toronto
Press, 1986.

Orvell, Miles. *Flannery O'Connor: An Introduction*. Oxford: University
Press of Mississippi, 1991.

Petersen, Erik. *Le Mystère des Juifs et des Gentils dans l'Église. Suivi d'un essai
sur l'Apocalypse*. Translated by Ernest Kamnitzer, Pierre Corps, and
Georges Massoulard. Preface by Jacques Maritain. Paris: Desclée De
Brouwer, 1935.

Picard, Max. *The Flight from God*. Translated by Marianne Kuschnitzky
and J. M. Cameron. Note by Gabriel Marcel. Introduction by J. M.
Cameron. Chicago: Henry Regnery Co., 1951.

———. *Hitler in Our Selves*. Translated by Heinrich Hauser. Introduction by
Robert S. Hartman. Hinsdale, Ill.: Henry Regnery, 1947.

———. *The World of Silence*. Translated by Stanley Godman. Preface by Gabriel Marcel. Humanist Library. Chicago: Henry Regnery, 1952.

Prown, Katherine. *Revising Flannery O'Connor: Southern Literary Culture
and the Problem of Female Authorship*. Charlottesville: University Press
of Virginia, 2001.

Reinisch, Jessica, and Elizabeth White. *The Disentanglement of Populations: Migration, Expulsion and Displacement in Post-war Europe, 1944–
49*. Basingstoke, UK: Palgrave Macmillan, 2011.

Samway, Patrick, SJ. "Jesuit Influence in the Life and Works of Flannery
O'Connor." *Gerard Manley Hopkins Archive*. www.gerardmanley
hopkins.org/lectures_2004/jesuit_influence.html.

Schwartz, Regina Mara. *Sacramental Poetics at the Dawn of Secularism:
When God Left the World*. Stanford, Calif.: Stanford University Press,
2008.

Sexton, Mark S. "'Blessed Insurance': An Examination of Flannery
O'Connor's 'Greenleaf.'" *Flannery O'Connor Bulletin* 19 (1990): 30–37.

Shephard, Ben. *The Long Road Home: The Aftermath of the Second World War*.
New York: Alfred A. Knopf, 2011.

Shields, John C. "Flannery O'Connor's 'Greenleaf' and the Myth of Europa and the Bull." *Studies in Short Fiction* 18, no. 4 (Fall 1981): 421–431.

Shloss, Carol. *Flannery O'Connor's Dark Comedies: The Limits of Inference.* Baton Rouge: Louisiana State University Press, 1980.

Spivey, Ted. *Flannery O'Connor: The Woman, the Thinker, the Visionary.* Macon, Ga.: Mercer University Press, 1997.

Srigley, Susan. *Flannery O'Connor's Sacramental Art.* Notre Dame, Ind.: University of Notre Dame Press, 2004.

Stephens, Ralph, ed. *The Correspondence of Flannery O'Connor and the Brainard Cheneys.* Jackson: University Press of Mississippi, 1986.

Underhill, Evelyn. *Mysticism: The Nature and Development of Spiritual Consciousness* (1910). New York: Noonday/Meridian, 1955.

Walker, Alice. "Beyond the Peacock." In *In Search of Our Mother's Gardens: Womanist Prose,* 42–59. New York: Houghton Mifflin Harcourt, 1983.

———. *In Search of Our Mother's Gardens.* New York: Harcourt, 1983.

Walsh, Thomas, ed. *Hispanic Anthology: Poems Translated from the Spanish by English and North American Poets.* New York: Putnam, 1920.

Weisbrode, Kenneth. *The Year of Indecision, 1946: A Tour through the Crucible of Harry Truman's America.* New York: Viking, 2016.

Wilkes, Paul. "Through a Glass Darkly: The Worlds of Flannery O'Connor and George Bernanos." *Church* 6 (Fall 1990): 5–12.

Wood, Ralph. *Flannery O'Connor and the Christ-Haunted South.* Grand Rapids, Mich.: William B. Eerdmans, 2004.

———. "The Heterodoxy of Flannery O'Connor's Book Reviews." *Flannery O'Connor Bulletin* 5 (Autumn 1976): 3–29.

Wray, Virginia. "Flannery O'Connor's *Why Do the Heathen Rage?* and the Quotidian 'Larger Things.'" *Flannery O'Connor Bulletin* 23 (1994–95): 1–29.

Zahra, Tara. *The Lost Children: Reconstructing Europe's Families after World War II.* Cambridge, Mass.: Harvard University Press, 2011.

Zornado, Joseph. "A Becoming Habit: Flannery O'Connor's Fiction of Unknowing." *Religion and Literature* 29, no. 2 (1997): 27–59.

Zubeck, Jacqueline A. "Back to Page One in 'Parker's Back': An Orthodox Examination of O'Connor's Last Story." *Flannery O'Connor Review* 8 (2010): 92–116.

CONTRIBUTORS

MARK BOSCO, SJ, is an associate professor in the departments of English and theology at Loyola University Chicago and is the director of Loyola's Joan and Bill Hank Center for the Catholic Intellectual Heritage. He is the author of *Graham Greene's Catholic Imagination* (Oxford University Press, 2005), and editor of *Finding God in All Things: Celebrating Bernard Lonergan, John Courtney Murray, and Karl Rahner* (Fordham University Press, 2007). His main research focuses on the intersection of religion and art, especially on the twentieth-century Catholic literary revival in Britain and North America. He has published essays on Graham Greene, Flannery O'Connor, George Bernanos, Francis Poulenc, John L'Heureux, and Margaret Atwood. His current research includes a full-length documentary on the life of Flannery O'Connor, now in production.

MICHAEL BRUNER is an assistant professor of practical theology at Azusa Pacific University, an affiliate faculty member at Fuller Seminary in Pasadena, an ordained Presbyterian (USA) clergyman, and a resident scholar ("reader") at the Huntington Library in San Marino. Dr. Bruner's doctoral dissertation is on the theological aesthetics of Flannery O'Connor, particularly her understanding of the beauty of God in O'Connor's novel *The Violent Bear It Away*. Dr. Bruner's areas of interest are in theological anthropology, spiritual development, and the conversation between literature and theology, and he has taught undergraduate courses in American literature, linguistics, writing, theology, and theological anthropology, and graduate courses in Theology and the Arts and on G. K. Chesterton and C. S. Lewis. He lives in Pasadena with his wife and two children.

ANDREW J. GARAVEL, SJ, is associate professor of English at Santa Clara University, where he teaches British and Irish literature of the nineteenth and early twentieth centuries. He has published essays on Lewis Carroll, Bram Stoker, Somerville and Ross, and the Irish statesman and man of letters John Wilson Croker. He is currently at work on a book about the novelist and playwright Molly Keane.

STEPHEN E. LEWIS is professor and chair of English at the Franciscan University of Steubenville. He teaches a wide variety of periods and figures in British and American literature and writes about modern and contemporary American, British, and French literature and modern philosophy and Christianity. He is also an accomplished translator of contemporary French philosophers Jean-Louis Chrétien, Jean-Luc Marion, and Claude Romano.

BRENT LITTLE is a lecturer in the Department of Catholic Studies at Sacred Heart University. His recent research focuses on the relationship between faith and uncertainty as portrayed by twentieth-century Catholic novelists. Recent articles have appeared in the *Flannery O'Connor Review, Toronto Journal of Theology,* and *Renascence.*

MICHAEL P. MURPHY directs the Catholic Studies minor program at Loyola University Chicago and teaches in the Department of Theology. His first book, *A Theology of Criticism: Balthasar, Postmodernism, and the Catholic Imagination* (Oxford University Press, 2008), includes a chapter that explores O'Connor's contribution as a theologian. His recent publications—pieces on Cormac McCarthy, Margaret Atwood, and Robert Hugh Benson—are projects in theology and literature that seek to locate and amplify the dynamic relationship between violence and grace in the "post" age—"postmodern," "posthuman," and "post-Christian." His current research is a critical foray into the literature and poetics of late modern Catholic realism.

GEORGE PIGGFORD, CSC, is an associate professor of English at Stonehill College in Easton, Massachusetts. He has published work in *Cultural Critique*, *English Studies in Canada*, *Modern Drama*, *Mosaic*, and the *Flannery O'Connor Review*, as well as in volumes such as *American Gothic: New Interventions in a National Narrative* (University of Iowa Press, 1998) and *Through a Glass Darkly: Suffering, Sacred, and the Sublime* (Wilfrid Laurier University Press, 2010). In 2014, he was an NEH Summer Scholar at the Revisiting Flannery O'Connor institute at Georgia College, and in November of that year, he reflected on "Flannery O'Connor's Faith" at the induction of O'Connor into the American Poets Corner at the Cathedral of St. John the Divine in New York.

STEPHEN SCHLOESSER, SJ, is a professor of history at Loyola University Chicago. He is the author of *Jazz Age Catholicism: Mystic Modernism in Postwar Paris* (University of Toronto Press, 2005) and *Visions of Amen: The Early Life and Music of Olivier Messiaen* (William B. Eerdmans, 2014). He is also the editor of *Mystic Masque: Semblance and Reality in Georges Rouault, 1871–1958* (McMullen Museum of Art, 2008) and coeditor of *Mystic Modern: The Music, Thought, and Legacy of Charles Tournemire* (Church Music Association of America, 2014) and *Crossings and Dwellings: Restored Jesuits, Women Religious, American Experience* (Brill, 2017).

JESSICA HOOTEN WILSON is an associate professor of literature and creative writing, the associate director of the Honors Scholars Program, and the director of Giving Voice: A Festival of Writing and the Arts at John Brown University. She is the author of *Giving the Devil His Due: Flannery O'Connor and Fyodor Dostoevsky* (Wipf and Stock Publishers, 2016) and the upcoming *Walker Percy, Fyodor Dostoevsky and the Search for Influence* (Ohio State University Press). Her *Guide to Walker Percy's Novels* (Louisiana State University Press) should be published in 2017. In 2014, the Flannery O'Connor Estate granted her the right to produce the first edition of O'Connor's unpublished novel, which should be complete by 2020. Finally, but most significant, she is blessed to be the mother to two children.

INDEX

Absolute. See God
Adam, Karl, 127n23, 139, 140
Aesthetics: of consecration, 6, 54,
  56, 62–63, 65, 67, 69, 74, 76; of
  difference, 7, 99, 104, 107, 109–10;
  literary, 4, 6, 16, 55n7, 61, 76,
  83, 101, 106–8, 113, 115–16, 187;
  as mystery, 107, 110; objective,
  105, 117; philosophical, 58, 105;
  subjective, 105; theological, 54,
  58–61, 63, 67, 74, 102–4, 106–7,
  109; theory, 104, 110
African American, 48, 68, 89n24,
  90–91, 93–94, 207
Agee, James, 191
Agnosticism, 51–52, 75
Alighieri, Dante, 208
America, 14, 22–23, 33, 36–37, 39,
  42, 47, 81, 94, 128, 141; culture
  of, 2; Great Awakening in, 196;
  literature in, 1, 15; religion in, 2,
  18, 20, 127n22, 128, 131n33, 142;
  Rural, 22, 145
America (Jesuit magazine), 47
Analogy, 8, 108
Andalusia, 2, 46
Anti-Semitism. See Judaism

Antony, St., 213
Apocalypse: language of, 12, 186n91;
  narrative, 86, 89–90
Aquinas, St. Thomas, 106n13, 148,
  197, 201–202, 209, 212, 214;
  Thomism, 6, 55n7, 56, 124n15, 148
Aristophanes, 175
Asals, Frederick, 12n3, 60n25,
  143n80, 148, 174, 177n49,
Askin, Denise T., 44n111, 175, 177,
  185,
Atheism, 95, 96, 168, 169, 170n11,
  197, 212
Augustine, St. of Hippo, 3, 52, 85,
  106, 146–59, 161–65, 197, 200–
  201, 204, 209, 212, 214
Aurevilly, Barbey de, 27

Bacon, Jon Lance, 15, 37n91
Bakhtin, Mikhail, 177
Balthasar, Hans Urs von, 12, 23n45,
  55n6
Barth, Karl, 127n22
Beauty. See Transcendence
Beguin, Albert, 12n6, 14n12, 17,
  18n23, 27n56, 29n63, 30n67,
  34–36, 39–42, 44–46

Bergson, Henri, 16, 17, 20, 33
Bernanos, George, 5, 6, 15–18,
    20–25, 43–44, 51–53, 55, 75–76,
    127n23, 140, 197
Bible: as text, 78, 84–85, 88, 134n49,
    159, 162, 171n20, 174, 184, 208;
    References: Deut 6:4; Deut 29:3; 1
    Kings 19; Psalm 2; Ps 7:9; Ps25:2;
    Ps 44:20–21; Song 2:9–11; Song
    3:3–4; Jer 11:20; Jer 17:9–10; Is
    29:13; Ez 36:26; Mt 6:21, 28, 30;
    Mt 11:12; Ma 7:19, 21; Mt 22:37;
    Ma 12:30; Lu 8:15; Lu 10:27; John
    8:32; Acts 1:24; Acts 15:8; Rom 5:5;
    Rom 13:14; 1 Cor 13:12; 1 Cor 14:25;
    James 2:19
Bleikasten, Andre, 148
Bloy, Leon, 3, 5, 6, 10–18, 20–21,
    24–31, 34–36, 39–46, 49, 55,
    127n23
Bollery, Joseph, 36
Bonaventure, St., 197
Bosanquet, Bernard, 105
Bouyer, Fr. Louis, 6, 54, 63–67, 74,
    76
Bridges, Robert, 102, 103
Brinkmeyer, Robert, 80n6, 128–29
Brodin, Pierre, 13n8, 41n104
Buber, Martin, 169n11
Burns, Marian, 193, 198, 199,
    209–10
Burns, Stuart, 191–92, 198, 213
Bultmann, Rudolf, 127n22
Butler, Rev. Alban, 197

Campbell, Roy, 169
Carnival. See Bakhtin, Mikhail
Carr, E. H., 121n8
Carritt, E. F., 16
Carroll, Paul, 209–10
Cash, Jean, 139
Catherine, St. of Genoa, 122–23, 142,
    168, 197

Catherine, St. of Siena, 168, 197
Catholic: American, 1, 122, 128,
    131n33, 142; British, 7, 101;
    French, 3, 5–6, 13, 15–16, 18,
    20–21, 25, 27, 51, 54; intellectual
    heritage, 3–4, 7, 63, 103, 109,
    120n6, 122–27; literature, 3, 8,
    55, 57, 79, 82, 125–26, 132–33,
    140; religion, 3–6, 8, 14, 19,
    25–26, 28–34, 36–37, 39–40, 42,
    44, 47–49, 59, 75, 84, 93–94,
    102–3, 106, 122, 125, 128, 130, 148,
    167–68, 196, 198–99, 209, 214;
    theology, 3–4, 6, 9, 34, 52–53, 64,
    67, 101, 123–24, 139–140. See also
    Christianity
Celine, 167
Chapin, Anthony, 24n47
Chardin, Pierre Teilhard de, 20,
    56n10, 61, 62n27, 63n30, 120n6,
    127, 139, 140, 165, 169n11,
    174n32
Cheney, Fannie, 119, 142
Chesterton, G. K., 232
Chretien, Jean-Louis, 6, 7, 79–80,
    84–87, 90, 92, 96
Christ. See Jesus Christ
Christianity, 4, 9–10, 24–25, 33–36,
    39–40, 57–58, 61–62, 64, 69, 74,
    79–80, 84, 93n32, 94, 102, 106,
    109, 113, 115, 121n9, 126–27, 129,
    133, 138–39, 156, 161, 175–77, 196,
    199–202, 204, 209–11, 213–14. See
    also Catholicism; Jesus Christ;
    Protestantism
Christology, 53
Classicism, 49n125, 104–6, 111, 170,
    177
Columbus, Christopher, 27, 28, 41
Conversion, 8, 14, 39, 65, 136, 146–
    47, 150–52, 154, 156, 162–63, 171,
    184, 192, 199, 208, 212–13
Corn, Alfred, 60, 103

Dawkins, Cecil, 56
Day, Dorothy, 202
Deleuze, Gilles, 167, 187
Descartes, Rene, 52
Desert Fathers, 4
Desmond, John F., 4, 12, 91,
Dessommes, Nancy Bishop, 184
Devil. See Satan
Difference. See Aesthetics
Displaced Persons (historical),
    14–15, 35, 37, 38, 45–47, 48n121,
    49
Diversity, 104, 115. See also Aesthetics
Divinity. See God
Dostoevsky, Fyodor, 79, 80n5, 94
Dreyfus Affair, 13, 15, 25–26, 28–31,
    34, 36, 42, 49. See also "The Jewish Question"
Drumont, Edouard, 28

Eastern Orthodoxy, 106n13, 109,
    147n5, 163
Ecclesiology, 20, 93n32
Ebrecht, Anne, 130, 138
Edmondson, Henry T., 103, 169n10,
    173, 181n71
Eggenschwiler, David, 126, 127,
    174n32
Eighteenth-century, 22, 86, 87, 105
Eisenhower, President Dwight D., 38
Embodiment, 15, 18, 49, 51–52, 126,
    129, 136, 158, 165, 199–200, 207.
    See also Incarnation
Engle, Paul, 3
Enlightenment, 34, 64, 105
Ethics, 4, 84
Eucharist, 6, 59n20, 61, 64–67,
    73–76
Evil, 4, 19, 81, 109, 112, 134, 150, 158,
    172, 194,
Existentialism, 19, 53, 55n7, 56,
    134n48, 168–69, 199, 205–6, 210

Faith, 2–4, 9, 11–12, 14, 22, 24,
    51–52, 56–58, 61, 64–65, 70, 76,
    94, 110, 115, 126, 128, 131, 131,
    136–37, 143, 148, 153, 167–69, 178,
    187, 194, 196
Faulkner, William, 80n5, 192
Feeley, Kathleen, 149
Feith, Michel, 147–48
Fitzgerald, F. Scott, 191–92
Fitzgerald, Sally, 53n3, 61n27, 83n11
Flannery O'Connor Trust, 2
Fleischman, Suzanne, 185
Fowlie, Wallace, 16, 44n113
Franco-Prussian War, 27
French, 3, 5–7, 11n2, 13, 15–18,
    20–21, 25, 26–28, 31–36, 39–40,
    42, 51, 53–55, 61, 63, 80–82. See
    also Catholic
Freud, Sigmund, 78, 92

Gable, Sister Mariella, 103, 195
Garcia-Rivera, Alejandro, 105–6,
    109
Gaulle, Charles de, 32
Gentry, Marshall Bruce, 99–100,
    156n35, 174n32
Getz, Lorine, 138–39, 147n5
Giannone, Richard, 4, 60n25,
    127n22, 148, 176, 183, 209, 212
Gill, Eric, 140
Gilson, Etienne, 55n7, 127n23
Gnosticism, 52–53, 74, 90, 96
God, 3, 9, 25, 30, 40, 44–45, 51–52,
    54, 56–62, 64–65, 68, 70–71, 73,
    75–76, 81–85, 92, 95, 98, 102–4,
    106–9, 112–17, 125–26, 131–32,
    134–38, 142–44, 146–65, 168–70,
    206, 208, 211, 213–14
Gordon, Caroline, 6, 38–39, 81, 83
Gordon, Sarah, 16n17, 41n104,
    60n24, 103, 113, 114, 174n32
Grace, 44, 53–54, 56, 63, 71, 76,
    89n24, 100, 111–12, 129n28,

Grace (*cont.*)
131–36, 161–62, 166, 173, 183–84, 187–88, 204, 208
Graybill, Mark, 111
Great Depression, 16, 31
Greene, Graham, 15, 20, 55n7
Gregory, St. of Nyssa, 201
Griffith, Ben, 93
Grotesque, 102, 109–10, 147n5, 148, 175, 210
Guardini, Romano, 4, 120n6, 127, 139, 140, 150, 151, 167, 200n21,
Guitton, Jean, 149, 200

Hardy, Donald E., 80n6, 152n19, 185
Harris, Ruth, 26
Harrison, Carol, 153–54,
Hauerwas, Stanley, 89n24, 90n26
Hecht, Anthony, 19n28
Heliodorus, 210–12
Heppenstall, Rayner, 17n19
Heresy, 146, 160–61, 208
Hester, Betty, 3, 4, 8, 58n15, 61, 66, 93n32, 102, 110, 118–19, 131, 133n45, 140–42, 167–70, 176, 184, 188
History, 5–6, 12, 14, 27–28, 30, 34–35, 40, 45–46, 48, 52, 54, 59, 109, 123, 150, 211
Holocaust, 12n5, 14, 25, 31, 34–35, 39, 41–42, 48n122, 169n11. *See also* World War II
Holy Spirit, 7, 10, 29, 66n38, 114, 134n49, 142–43, 162
Hopkins, Gerard Manley, 5, 100–4, 106–14, 116–17
Horn, Gerd-Rainer, 25n50, 40n99
Hügel, Baron Friedrich von, 5, 7, 8, 119–33, 135, 137–45
Humanism, 127, 168, 202
Humor, 2, 6, 11, 14, 66, 73, 175, 210

Imagination: Literary, 2, 5, 12, 26, 49, 59, 76, 101, 107, 115, 130, 132, 148, 150, 174, 199; religious, 4, 6, 52, 56, 59n21, 76; sacramental, 8, 54, 60–61, 63, 147
Imago Dei, 65, 74, 75, 135, 137
Incarnation, 6, 8, 30, 44, 49, 51–55, 57–60, 66, 75, 108–10, 126, 129, 144, 147n3, 160, 205
Iowa: State, 3, 7, 13–18, 21–23, 35, 37, 39, 47; University of, 2, 25, 38, 43, 121n9; Writer's Workshop, 2, 6, 38
Israel, 11n1, 29–31, 33–34, 40, 45–47, 125

James, Henry, 80n5, 118
Jerome, St., 9, 191, 197, 209–212, 214
Jesus: Christ, 11, 23, 30, 40, 49, 53–55, 57, 59, 61–62, 64, 66–67, 70, 73, 75–76, 78, 89, 93–94, 96–98, 102, 108–12, 116, 132, 134–37, 142–43, 147, 156, 160–65, 171, 176–78, 183, 194, 205, 209, 211; Christ-haunted, 4, 59, 71. *See also* Logos
Judaism: Anti-semitism, 10, 31, 32n73, 34, 39; "The Jewish Question," 13–14, 27–28, 32, 39; religion, 26n54, 33, 134n49
John, the Apostle, 204
John, St. of the Cross, 5, 8–9, 166–73, 175, 179, 181, 183, 187–88
Jung, Carl, 3

Kant, Immanuel, 105
Kenosis, 6, 57, 177
Kessler, Martin, 186
Kilcourse, George, Fr., 4, 20n36, 174
Kinney, Arthur F., 11n1, 82n7, 91n30, 139, 170n12, 200n21
Kirkland, William, 60n25, 120, 124n15, 126n21, 130–33, 137–38

Koch, Claude, 197
Koinonia (community), 202

Lake, Christina Bieber, 4, 60n25,
    80n6, 129n28
Leo XIII, Pope, 27
Lewis, C. S., 212, 232
Lewis, Wyndham, 167
Liberalism, 60, 195, 202
Literature, 1, 19, 27, 43, 54, 57,
    59n20, 67, 187; French, 18–19;
    religious, 141
Logos (concept), 51–52, 65, 67, 69,
    75, 108, 126, 159. *See also* Jesus
    Christ
Lourdes, 26, 124–25
Lowell, Robert, 3, 94n35
Loyola, Ignatius of, 3
Loyola University Chicago, 2, 191n1,
    231–33; Joan and Bill Hank Center
    for the Catholic Intellectual Heri-
    tage, 4n1
Lubac, Henri de, 57–59, 63–64, 76
Lubbock, Percy, 91n30
Lynch, William F., 4, 57
Lytle, Andrew, 208

Manichaeism, 6, 52, 126, 148, 158,
    160
Marcel, Gabriel, 19, 20, 55n7,
    127n23, 140
Maritain, Jacques, 5–7, 14–20, 24–
    26, 28–26, 38–43, 45, 49, 54n6,
    55n7, 78–84, 86–87, 89, 92–93,
    98, 127n23, 140
Maritain, Raissa, 10, 11n1, 14, 17,
    30–33, 35–36, 39–43, 79, 82, 140
Mauriac, Francois, 6, 7, 15, 17–21, 25,
    55, 79–84, 86, 98, 127, 140
Mazzaro, J. L., 193
Merton, Thomas, 127n23
Metaphor, 102, 108, 111, 153, 169n11,
    183, 186, 212

Michelfelder, William, 130, 140
Milledgeville, 11n2, 119, 130
Modernism: Cultural, 3, 5, 10, 28n61,
    39, 55–57, 60–62, 65, 69, 71, 98,
    106, 125, 192, 194, 197, 210–11;
    literary, 6, 7, 54, 78–82, 84–85, 87,
    91–92, 94, 101–2, 185; postmoder-
    nity, 71, 76; premodernity, 52
Monica, St., 155
Moore, Brenna, 26n54, 40n100
Moran, Annette, 12,
Mounier, Emmanuel, 19, 25
Mysticism, 7, 9, 29, 43–45, 49, 63–
    64, 119, 122–26, 137n53, 140–3,
    166–68, 170, 174–79, 182–84,
    186–88, 190, 209
Myth, 111, 174n32, 177, 187

Narration, 9, 80, 83, 87–88, 90,
    92–93, 96, 175, 178, 185–88
Nature, 56, 104, 108, 110, 117, 124n15,
    129n28, 131–33, 135–39, 141, 148,
    157, 161; human, 31, 53, 130, 134,
    137, 194
Newman, John Henry, 7, 122, 128,
    140
Nietzsche, Friedrich, 48n124, 169
Nineteenth-century, 7, 8, 13, 14,
    49n125, 84, 101, 158

Oates, Whitney J., 158, 184n83
O'Connor, Flannery: archives, 9, 170,
    191, 193; as artist, 1–6, 52, 56–57,
    69, 83, 91n30, 101, 104, 110, 131,
    133, 196; her authenticity, 2, 76;
    her diaries, 2–8, 13, 17, 21–22, 25,
    39, 43, 45, 55, 109, 121n9, 124; her
    ecology, 111; as friend, 1–2, 5, 8, 46,
    52, 63, 81, 121n9, 124n17, 139, 167–
    68, 188; her humor, 2, 66, 73, 210;
    and lupus, 19, 33, 44, 102, 138; her
    politics, 5, 15, 60, 100n1; and race,
    9, 89, 100n1, 115, 193–95, 207

O"Connor, Flannery: Fiction by: "The Artificial Nigger", 83–98, 136; "A Circle in the Fire," 136; "The Comforts of Home,"136, 193; "The Displaced Person," 10–11, 14, 25, 37n93, 46–50, 136, 156; "The Enduring Chill", 136, 193, 198; "Everything That Rises Must Converge", 62n28, 73, 136, 193–94; "Good Country People," 84, 87–91, 136; "A Good Man Is Hard to Find," 69, 103n10, 111–14, 119n4, 136; "Greenleaf," 8, 72–73, 136, 166–67, 170–88, 193; "Judgment Day," 62, 136, 194; "The Lame Shall Enter First," 87, 136; " A Late Encounter with the Enemy," 136; "The Life You Save May Be Your Own," 136; "Parker's Back," 8, 73, 95, 136, 146–50; "Revelation," 48n122, 62, 69, 87, 115–16, 136, 185n88, 194; "The River," 103n10, 112–15, 136; "A Stroke of Good Fortune," 136; "A Temple of the Holy Ghost," 75, 136; "A View of the Woods," 136, 193; *The Violent Bear It Away*, 84, 94–98, 119, 134n48, 136, 142–44, 197; *Why Do the Heathen Rage?*, 9, 191–213; *Wise Blood*, 18, 21, 23, 43, 119n4, 136, 143, 197
O'Connor, Flannery: Non-Fiction by: "Catholic Novelists and Their Readers", 125, 129, 133; *The Habit of Being*, 1–4, 7, 55n7, 58n15, 61n27, 65n36, 93–94, 102, 119–20, 123–9, 138–42, 168–70, 173n31; "Introduction to *A Memoir of Mary Ann*," 11, 94n35; *Mystery and Manners*, 1, 11n1, 91n30, 94n35, 119n4, 129–33, 138–39; "On Her Own Work," 138; *A Prayer Journal*, 1–3, 17, 22–23, 43–45, 52n2, 55, 121n9,

168n4; "Some Aspects of the Grotesque in Southern Fiction," 110
O'Gorman, Farrell, 12n4, 38n96, 39n97, 60n25, 110, 184, 198
Ong, Walter, 108
Oxford, 107, 122; Gifford Lectures, 20, 122, 123n12

Paradox, 6, 8, 26, 36, 49, 54, 57, 139, 144–45, 168, 202
Pascal, Blaise, 3, 53
Pasolini, Pier Paolo, 187
Patmore, Coventry, 10n14
Paul, the Apostle, 33, 134n49, 147, 153
Paul, St. Vincent de, 197
Pearl Harbor. *See* World War II
Peguy, Charles, 17, 26, 39, 43, 44n113, 55n7, 127n23
Percy, Walker, 91n30, 198–99, 211, Peter, the Apostle, 204
Petersen, Erik, 31
Pfleger, Karl, 16–17, 43
Picard, Max, 19, 127n23
Pius IX, Pope, 27
Plato: Idealism, 104; Neoplatonism, 156, 158; philosopher, 107–8, 172
Prayer, 3–5, 8, 22, 43–45, 62, 64–65, 69, 72–73, 75, 155, 162, 164, 195
Protestantism: Anglican, 130; Lutheran, 64; Reformation, 9, 122, 196, 209; religion, 4, 30, 59–60, 64, 127–28, 131n33, 198
Proust, Marcel, 79–80, 140
Pseudo-Dionysius, 54n6, 179

Ransom, John Crowe, 167
Realism: Christian, 58, 61, 74; literary, 16n17, 27
Redemption, 9, 49, 114; and suffering, 6, 12, 29, 114
Renaissance (European), 104
Ressourcement, 57, 64, 196, 209

Resurrection (Christian), 110
Revelation, 12, 16n17, 30, 40, 44n111,
    49, 52, 68, 89n24, 100, 106, 114,
    116, 124n15, 136, 153, 208–9
Ricoeur, Paul, 185
Rougemont, Denis de, 202
Rousseau, Jean-Jacques, 78

Sale, Francis de, 3
Samway, Patrick, 103
Sartre, Jean-Paul, 168–69, 205–6,
    210
Satan, 23, 53, 134, 150, 213
Schlafer, Linda, 11, 41n104
Schmemann, Alexander, 135n50
Scott, R. Neil, 11n2, 126
Scotus, Duns, 107–8
Second Vatican Council, 20, 64, 127,
    196
Secularism, 59, 208
Sensibility, 123–25, 151, 172
Sessions, William, 2–3, 13, 21, 102,
    121n9, 122n10, 141, 173n31, 191n1
Sexton, Mark S., 185
Shloss, Carol, 147
Spivey, Ted, 52n2, 124, 126–27, 131,
    138, 140, 142
Srigley, Susan, 4, 60n25, 147n3
Starbuck, Edwin Diller, 171
Subjectivity, 84, 87, 104–8, 117
Sue, Eugene, 14n11, 49n125
Suffering, 6, 12–13, 28–30, 39–40,
    43–44, 46, 49, 74, 76, 90, 93–94,
    109, 181, 183, 203; Suffering Ser-
    vant, 29n64, 90
Supernatural, 29, 60, 89n24, 125,
    131–32
Sweetbriar College, 204
Symons, Arthur, 166, 170, 182, 189

Tate, Allen, 3, 6, 16, 38–39, 47, 52
Teresa, St. of Avila, 168, 170n12,
    182n76, 197

Teresa, St. of Jesus, 197
Therese, St., 6, 51, 73n58, 76
Theology, 2–7, 9, 15, 27–29, 33,
    52–67, 69, 73, 85, 101–9, 116, 119,
    121–23, 125–27, 138–40, 143, 147,
    149, 161, 167–68, 178, 196, 200,
    202–3, 212
Tillich, Paul, 127n22
Tilman, Walter, 192–94, 198, 210
Tragedy, 33, 104, 111, 114–15
Transcendence, 12, 40, 52–54,
    57–59, 61, 66, 104–5, 111–12, 130,
    164, 177, 195–96, 199, 202–3
Transcendentals: Beauty, 6–7, 24,
    54n6, 64, 103–9, 111–12, 114–15,
    137, 153, 187; Goodness, 54n6, 105,
    109, 115, 137, 149, 158, 160; Truth,
    6, 54n4, 68, 75, 83, 89, 95, 105,
    115–16, 137, 149, 164, 168, 201, 206
Truman, Harry S., 38, 46–47
Twentieth century, 1–4, 6–9, 13–14,
    24, 51–52, 55, 57, 59, 101, 122–24,
    127, 145, 149, 195–97, 210, 214

Underhill, Evelyn, 8–9, 122, 124,
    166–67, 170–73, 176–79, 181–84,
    187–88, 190n98
Undset, Kristen, 140

Varro, Marcus, 201
Vatican II. *See* Second Vatican Coun-
    cil
Victorian period, 101
Violence, 71–72, 130, 185, 205; Spiri-
    tual, 133–7; Rhetorical, 6, 11

Walker, Alice, 89n24
Warren, Austin, 3
Warren, Robert Penn, 3
Waugh, Evelyn, 15, 20, 55n7
Weigel, Gustave, 139
Weil, Simone, 55n7, 123n13, 140–41,
    167

Welty, Eudora, 194

West, Morris L., 197

Wilberforce, William, 196

Wood, Ralph C., 12, 89–90, 127, 147n5, 150, 176, 194

Word (of God). *See* Logos

Wordsworth, William, 122

World War II, 16, 32–35, 41, 47, 110, 168–69; postwar era, 14, 25, 28–29, 34n81, 36–37, 39–42, 46, 48–49, 61, 169

Wray, Virginia, 195–96, 198–200, 202–4, 213

Yaddo (New York), 124

Zola, Emile, 27, 29, 48

Zornado, Joseph, 185

Revelation and Convergence: Flannery O'Connor and the Catholic Intellectual Tradition was designed in Filosofia with Meta display by Kachergis Book Design of Pittsboro, North Carolina. It was printed on 55-pound Natures Recycled and bound by Sheridan Books of Chelsea, Michigan.